Economic Collapse

Prepping for Tomorrow Series

A Preparedness Guide by

Bobby Akart

&

The Staff of Freedom Preppers

First edition.

Copyright Information

DEDICATIONS

To the love of my life, thank you for making the sacrifices
necessary so I may pursue this dream.

To the Princesses of the Palace, my little marauders in training,
you have no idea how much happiness you bring
to your Mommy and me.

To my fellow preppers;
never be ashamed of adopting a preparedness lifestyle.

ACKNOWLEDGEMENTS

Writing a book that is both informative and entertaining requires a
tremendous team effort. Writing is the easy part. For their efforts in
making the Prepping for Tomorrow series a reality, I would like to
thank Hristo Argirov Kovatliev for his incredible cover art, Sabrina
Jean, my second set of eyes, with FastTrack Editing, Stef Mcdaid for
making this manuscript decipherable on so many formats, and the
Team—whose advice, friendship and attention to detail is priceless.

Thank you!

Choose Freedom!

About the Author

A two-time Amazon Top 100 Author and author of
six #1 bestsellers, in both fiction and non-fiction genres:

THE LOYAL NINE – #1 bestseller in the Financial Thriller
category

CYBER WARFARE – #1 bestseller in eight categories including
Arms Control; War & Peace; Politics, Social Sciences; Business,
Money; Engineering, Transportation; Science, Technology;
International Politics

EMP: ELECTROMAGNETIC PULSE – #1 bestseller in seven
categories including International Politics, Arms Control; Physics;
Politics, Social Sciences; War & Peace; Engineering, Transportation

ECONOMIC COLLAPSE – #1 bestseller in seven categories
including Politics, Social Sciences; Economics; World Affairs;
International Politics; Business; Money

SEEDS OF LIBERTY – #1 bestseller in three categories including
Politics, Social Sciences; Modern History; Sociology

EVIL, MEET OPPORTUNITY – #1 bestseller in two categories
including Action, Adventure; Contemporary Fiction

Bobby Akart has provided his readers a diverse range of topics that
are both informative and entertaining. His attention to detail and
impeccable research has allowed him to write bestselling books in
several fiction and nonfiction genres.

Born and raised in Tennessee, Bobby received his bachelor's degree with a dual major in economics and political science. He not only understands how the economy works, but the profound effect politics has on the economy as well. After completing his undergraduate degree at Tennessee in three years, he entered the dual-degree program, obtaining a Juris Doctor combined with an MBA—master of business administration—at the age of twenty-three.

His education perfectly suited him for his legal career in banking, trusts, and investment banking. As his career flourished, business opportunities arose, including the operation of restaurants and the development of real estate. But after meeting and marrying the love of his life, they left the corporate world and developed online businesses.

A life-changing event led them to Muddy Pond, Tennessee, where he and his wife lead a self-sustainable, preparedness lifestyle. Bobby and his wife are unabashed preppers and share their expert knowledge of prepping via their website www.FreedomPreppers.com.

Bobby lives in the backwoods of the Cumberland Plateau with his wife and fellow author, Danni Elle, and their two English bulldogs, aka the Princesses of the Palace.

SIGN UP FOR EMAIL UPDATES and receive a **FREE BOOK** from one of his bestselling series. You can contact Bobby directly by email (BobbyAkart@gmail.com) or through his website

www.BobbyAkart.com

EPIGRAPH

All empires collapse eventually. There have been no exceptions in the history of mankind. Their reign ends when they are defeated by a larger, more powerful enemy, or when their financing runs out, resulting in collapse.

~ Bobby Akart

*****

Banks have done more injury to the religion, morality, tranquility, prosperity, and even wealth of the nation than they have done, or ever will do, good.

~ John Adams

*****

Beware the greedy hand of government thrusting itself into every corner and crevice of industry.

~ Thomas Paine

*****

When the people find that they can vote themselves money, that will herald the end of the republic.

~ Benjamin Franklin

*****

History reminds us that dictators and despots arise during times of severe economic crisis.

~Robert Kiyosaki

*****

Sic transit Gloria mundi, a Latin phrase meaning *thus passes the glory of the world.*

*****

Because you never know when the day before
is the day before.
Prepare for tomorrow!

Contents

Introduction by Freedom Preppers

About Economic Collapse and the Prepping for Tomorrow Series

Because you never know when the day before —
is the day before.
Prepare for tomorrow!

Author Bobby Akart, the founder of Freedom Preppers, has been a tireless proponent of adopting a preparedness lifestyle. As he learned prepping tips and techniques, he shared them with others via his writing on the American Preppers Network website, and in his bestselling book series—The Boston Brahmin and Prepping for Tomorrow.

In The Boston Brahmin series, political suspense collides with post-apocalyptic thriller fiction. Bobby's attention to detail and real-world scenarios immerses the reader in a world of geopolitical machinations and post-apocalyptic drama. Preparedness skills and techniques are interwoven into the plot that provides the reader a real-world scenario to envision.

The Prepping for Tomorrow series is the culmination of Bobby's research and real-world experiences provided in a concise guide for new and experienced preppers alike. The goal of the Prepping for Tomorrow series is twofold. First, provide a detailed analysis of the threats we face as Americans. Second, give new and seasoned preppers alike the opportunity to enhance their preparedness plan with this knowledge.

Steven Konkoly, author of The Perseid Collapse Series, noted that Bobby has gone far above and beyond the call of duty to support and promote fellow authors. Steve added, "from the very first time I spoke with Bobby, I was impressed with his positive attitude and willingness to share. It's the kind of selflessness that makes you wonder what's the catch? Well, there is no catch! Bobby is just a stand-up guy—with many talents. Author Bobby Akart possesses the analytic capability of a supercomputer coupled with the expressiveness of an exceptional writer."

What if the preppers are right?

The media shapes public perception in all formats including news, cinema and television shows. It should come as no surprise that everyone doesn't necessarily form a point of view on every subject. Nor should you be shocked to hear that most opinions are uninformed. We can all give countless examples of this. Most Americans are *sheeple*, unable to think for themselves. They are content to follow, and many are too lazy to do the minimal research required to have an informed opinion. Their reliance on government or media sources for information makes them susceptible to manipulation. It's simply easier to be a *sheeple*.

As a student of the preparedness lifestyle, I cringe at the media's portrayal of preppers. Initially, the brunt of the ridicule was directed at survivalists. But with the success of National Geographic's Doomsday Preppers, the concept of being a prepper hit the mainstream. Now Preppers are the target of the media's derision. I have my opinion as to why that is the case, and it has its basis in politics. It is my opinion that the media is mostly left-leaning and, as a result, does not embrace the self-sufficient lifestyle that is prepping. So, if you can't join them, beat them down—repeatedly. As a recent example, consider the media's dismantling of the Tea Party movement. I see similar attacks on preppers.

From the Associated Press: "*Sandy Hook Shooter Comes from Prepper Family.*"

From CBS: "*Local 'Preppers' Stock Up For Improbable US Ebola Crisis.*"

From Washington Post: "*'Preppers' Convinced Yellowstone Volcano Spells Doom.*"

But, what if the Preppers are right?

What if?
Escalation of Global Conflict into a World War

Let's compile a list of the strongest, most dangerous *bad actors* on the world geopolitical stage:

Russia ~ China ~ North Korea ~ Iran ~ Syria ~ ISIS ~ Al Qaeda

What do these seven geopolitical foes have in common? They both hate and disrespect the United States! Think of the Seven Deadly Sins: Lust, Gluttony, Greed, Sloth, Wrath, Envy, Pride. All of these relate to the attitudes of these *bad actors* towards the United States. Is it that far-fetched that one or more of these could band together to bring the mighty United States of America to its knees? Remember the words of the great Chinese General Sun Tzu — *the enemy of my enemy is my friend.* Except ISIS and Al Qaeda, the five nations comprising this group considers each other allies.

The assassination of an Archduke precipitated World War I, but the underlying causes were geopolitical tensions in Europe. 20 million people died during the war followed by another 70 million post-war due to famine and the Spanish Flu. Are we naive to think that something like this couldn't happen again? *Geopolitical tensions* - sound familiar?

Tensions arising from invasions of other sovereign territories around the world were the principal cause of World War II. It escalated into a global conflict with the Japanese attack on Pearl Harbor. Today, Russia has invaded Ukraine. China prepares to exert more of its dominance in Asia. ISIS is taking over large parts of the Middle East to form an Islamic State. Some might say— *not our problem.* But what if one of the *bad actors* mentioned above decide to make it our problem with an attack on the heartland along the lines of Pearl Harbor? Is that so implausible? Remember 9/11?

What if?

America is Attacked

We are vulnerable to attack because of our desire to provide freedoms to all Americans, but especially because of political correctness. We are not allowed to use racial profiling to identify a potential terrorist. Our southern border is a sieve. We refuse to ban flights from Ebola-stricken countries for fear of being labeled racist. Our military has been weakened by prolonged wars and budget cuts.

Our enemies can come at us in so many ways. A day does not go by without news of a cyber-terrorism incident. What if these cyber attacks are just a series of trial runs before one large massive, coordinated attack on our banking, governmental and utility servers? An electromagnetic pulse delivered by a nuclear warhead or a series of electromagnetic pulse weapons fired at strategic locations across the country could bring down our power grid. For the first time, Russia has more deployed nuclear assets than the United States does. Can you say *outnumbered?*

What if?

Widespread Pandemic or BioTerror

In a recent survey of scientists, the majority of experts agree that a pandemic capable of infecting a billion people, resulting in one hundred and sixty-five million deaths, would occur sometime in the next two generations.

Ordinarily, any discussion surrounding being more prepared in preventing pathogens from spreading into a worldwide pandemic revolves around our first response. Most pandemic experts agree that stepping up our first response to combat outbreaks of a disease is critical. They urge our hospitals to be prepared and have vaccines stockpiled. Further, they recommend the Centers for Disease Control have several teams ready to get to the scene of the outbreak. But that's not preventing these pathogens from emerging and from causing outbreaks. This approach is akin to *after the fire has started, then we rush in with our fire extinguishers.*

Several years ago, the United States government was intent on *calming the fears* of the American people as to the likelihood of the Ebola virus hitting U.S. soil. The presence of the Ebola virus came as a result of bringing Ebola-stricken health care workers into the country. Keep in mind that these were people who are experts in treating Ebola and who were provided all of the necessary equipment to prevent contracting the disease. As the CDC was calming our fears, a Nigerian national flew into Dallas with Ebola, potentially infecting hundreds and ultimately dying while in the government's care.

The question has to be asked: *What is wrong with a little fear amongst the masses?*

Fear is a great motivator—it is designed to be compelling so that we take survival action in the form of fight, flight, or freeze. Increasing the knowledge of the public concerning the threat of a pandemic will help prevent its spread through awareness, hygiene, and limiting human contact.

Bioterror is a form of terrorism involving the intentional release or dissemination of biological agents such as viruses, bacteria, or toxins. There are examples of the use of bioweapons throughout history.

In 1763, the British fortress at Fort Pitt in Delaware was under siege. Letters were exchanged between British General Jeffrey Amherst and Colonel Henry Bouquet as to proposed defensive tactics. General Amherst suggested: "*Could it not be contrived to send the Smallpox among those disaffected tribes of Indians?*"

By the time World War I began, attempts to use anthrax were directed at animal populations. This proved to be ineffective. Shortly after the start of World War I, Germany launched a biological sabotage campaign in the United States, Russia, Romania, and France. At that time, Anton Dilger lived in Germany, but in 1915 he was sent to the United States carrying cultures of glanders, a virulent disease of horses and mules. Dilger set up a laboratory in his home in Chevy Chase, Maryland. He used stevedores working the docks in Baltimore to infect horses with glanders while they were waiting to be shipped to Britain. Dilger was under suspicion of being a German agent but was never arrested. Dilger eventually fled to Madrid, Spain, where, ironically, he died during the Spanish Flu Pandemic of 1918. In 1916, the Russians captured a German agent with similar intentions. Germany and its allies infected French cavalry horses and many of Russia's mules and horses on the Eastern Front. These actions hindered artillery and troop movements, as well as supply convoys.

In 1972, police in Chicago arrested two college students, Allen Schwander and Stephen Pera, who had planned to poison the city's water supply with typhoid and other bacteria. Schwander founded a terrorist group, "R.I.S.E.", while Pera collected and grew cultures from the hospital where he worked. Although their arrest thwarted the attack, the two men fled to Cuba after being released on bail.

Then there was the 1984 Rajneeshee bioterror attack. In Oregon, followers of the Bhagwan Shree Rajneesh attempted to control a local election by incapacitating the local population. This was done by infecting salad bars in eleven restaurants, produce in grocery stores, doorknobs, and other public domains with Salmonella typhimurium bacteria in the city of The Dalles, Oregon. The attack infected 751 people with severe food poisoning. There were no fatalities. This incident was the first known bioterrorist attack in the United States in the 20th century.

In June of 1993, the religious group Aum Shinrikyo released anthrax in Tokyo. Eyewitnesses reported a foul odor in a marketplace. Fortunately, the attack was a total failure, infecting not a single person. The reason for this, ironically, was that the group used the vaccine strain of the bacterium which was missing the genes that cause a symptomatic response. The spores recovered from the attack showed that they were identical to an anthrax vaccine strain given to animals at the time.

In the fall of 2001, several cases of anthrax broke out in the U.S., resulting in five deaths. Letters laced with infectious anthrax were concurrently delivered to news media offices and the U.S Congress, alongside an ambiguously related case in Chile.

Biological agents are relatively easy to obtain by terrorists and are becoming more threatening in the U.S. The CDC and private laboratories are working on advanced detection systems to provide early warning, identify contaminated areas and populations at risk, and to facilitate prompt treatment. Methods for predicting the use of biological agents in urban areas as well as assessing the area for the hazards associated with a biological attack are being established in major cities. Also, forensic technologies are working on identifying biological agents, their geographical origins and their initial source.

But the threat is real. Consider the proposed use of weaponized smallpox as suggested by General Amherst. Is it not plausible that our enemies could weaponize Ebola? In the name of Jihad, is it not possible that one would contract the Ebola virus and enter the United States with the intention of creating a pandemic? The news outlets that raise these possibilities are labeled fear mongers and racists. But have you noticed that Amazon is selling out of particulate masks and other bio-hazard supplies? Fear is a great motivator.

What if?

Near Earth Object - SuperVolcano Eruption - Natural Disaster

Any of the above naturally occurring events could wreak havoc on our power grid, our atmosphere, and our climate. These are not the catastrophic events known only in science fiction movies. There is a historical precedent for them all.

A major earthquake along the New Madrid Fault in the central United States could collapse bridges over the Mississippi River. An earthquake of this magnitude along the New Madrid happened before in 1811 and 1812. The New Madrid Seismic Zone (NMSZ) is comprised of eight states: Alabama, Arkansas, Illinois, Indiana, Kentucky, Mississippi, Missouri, and Tennessee.

The Wabash Valley Seismic Zone (WVSZ) in southern Illinois and southeast Indiana together with the East Tennessee Seismic Zone in eastern Tennessee and northeastern Alabama, constitute a significant risk of moderate-to-severe earthquakes throughout the central region of the USA.

Studies indicate the Tennessee will incur the highest level of economic damage and societal impact. According to the Mid-America Earthquake Center, over 300,000 buildings would be moderately or more severely damaged, over 290,000 people will be displaced and well over 70,000 casualties are expected. Total direct economic losses surpass $56 billion. These results focus on the immediate effects of the massive earthquake itself. As preppers, we consider the ancillary impact in the form of societal unrest — looting, death from sickness and murder.

The States of Missouri, Arkansas, Kentucky and Illinois would also incur significant losses. Studies indicate a potential direct economic loss reaching over $150 billion.

The indirect economic loss due to business interruption and loss of market share is at least as high if not far greater than the direct losses. Scientists and economists predict the total economic impact of a series of NMSZ earthquakes is likely to constitute the highest economic loss due to a natural disaster in U.S. history.

The financial losses and societal impact for each state should be considered separately. Since each scenario is based on a different hazard, adding results together will not reflect an accurate scenario. It's hard to gauge the potential loss of life resulting from a natural disaster of this magnitude.

Critical infrastructure and lifelines will also be heavily damaged and will be out of service after the earthquake for a considerable period. The resulting collapse of the power grid and transportation routes are likely to affect a region much larger than the eight states referenced above. Many hospitals nearest to the epicenter will not be able to care for its patients. Many of those injured during the disaster will have to be transported outside of the region for medical attention. Moreover, pre-disaster patients will be required to continue their care outside of the area to fully functioning hospitals.

It is doubtful that the transportation system will be intact. Damage to the transportation system will hinder mass evacuation efforts. First responders will be severely impaired due to police and fire stations throughout the impacted region. Public shelters will be damaged and unusable after the earthquake.

The scenario described for a New Madrid Zone earthquake can be applied to other catastrophic disaster events. Strikes by near Earth objects such as asteroids can be extinction level events. Likewise, a massive eruption of the Yellowstone Super Volcano could result in climate change that would alter the entire food production system of the Northern Hemisphere.

What if?

Cyber Warfare

We explored this concept in depth in the first book released into the Prepping for Tomorrow series titled *Cyber Warfare*. A number one bestseller in an unprecedented eight Amazon categories, Cyber Warfare is a primer on the threats we face as a nation from the bad actors mentioned above. It explores the history of cyber attacks, and discusses the nuances of the terminology. United States, and its allies, have evolved over the past decade in its policies. The problem is attribution is explored as cyber space allows hackers a convenient place to hide.

There are many bad actors on the international stage capable of cyber terror on a massive scale. The list is long, including Russia, China, North Korea, Iran, Syria and now even terrorist groups like ISIS. Each is capable of wreaking havoc in the US by shutting down our power grid and enjoying the resulting chaos.

The all-important issue is raised:

When does a cyber attack become an act of war?

After a thorough review of the threat a devastating cyber attack poses for America, in particular the critical infrastructure, Cyber Warfare provides preparedness solutions. Like Cyber Warfare, this guide will also help you answer the question:

What if the preppers are right?

Simply put, a Cyber Attack is a deliberate exploitation of computer systems. Cyber Attacks are used to gain access to information but can also be used to alter computer code, insert malware or take over the operations of a computer driven network.

Why would terrorists bother with an elaborate, dangerous physical operation—complete with all the recon and planning of a black ops mission—when they could achieve the same effect from the comfort of their home? An effective cyber attack could, if cleverly designed, produce a great deal of physical damage very quickly, and interconnections in digital operations would mean such an attack could bypass fail safes in the physical infrastructure that stop cascading failures.

One string of 1s and 0s could have a significant impact. If a computer hacker could command all the circuit breakers in a utility to open, the system will be overloaded. Power utility personnel sitting in the control room could do it. A proficient cyber-terrorist can do it as well. In fact, smart-grid technologies are more susceptible to common computer failures. New features added to make the system easily manageable might render it more vulnerable.

At least one major public official downplays the cyber attack scenario. The nation's top disaster responder, FEMA director Craig Fugate, shrugs at the threat of an power grid collapse.

"When have people panicked? Generally what you find is the birth rate goes up nine months later," he said, then turned more serious: "People are much more resilient than the professionals would give them credit for. Would it be unpleasant? Yes. Would it be uncomfortable? Have you ever seen the power go out, and traffic signals stop working? Traffic's hell but people figure it out."

Fugate's big worry in a mass outage is communication, he said. When people can get information and know how long power will be out, they handle it much better.

Don't worry, the government will take care of you. Naïve.

In poll after poll, one of the threats concerning preppers is the use of a cyber attack to cause a grid down scenario. There are many bad actors on the international stage. Each is capable of wreaking havoc in the US by shutting down our power grid and enjoying the resulting chaos.

No bombs. No bullets. No swordfights. Just a few keystrokes on the computer, and we're done.

What if?

EMP: Electromagnetic Pulse

EMP: Electromagnetic Pulse is the second book in the Prepping for Tomorrow series. A #1 bestseller in seven genres, EMP: Electromagnetic Pulse is a primer on the threats we face as a nation from an attack delivered by an electromagnetic pulse weapon. EMP:

Electromagnetic Pulse is a thorough analysis of the threats our nation faces from a devastating Electromagnetic Pulse, whether delivered by a nuclear weapon, or a powerful solar flare blast from our sun. This detailed book not only provides a historical perspective, but it discusses the present day uses of EMP weaponry and the steps you can take to be prepared.

In poll after poll, one of the threats facing our nation is the use of an electromagnetic pulse weapon to cause a grid down scenario. There are many bad actors on the international stage capable of terrorism on a massive scale. The list is long, including Russia, China, North Korea, Iran, Syria and now even terrorist groups like ISIS. Each is capable of wreaking havoc in the United States by shutting down our power grid and enjoying the resulting chaos. The constant barrage of cyber intrusions into the public and private sector have captured the news headlines in recent years, but it is time to refocus on the threat an EMP poses for our nation's critical infrastructure.

Senator Ron Johnson of Wisconsin, chair of the Senate Committee on Homeland Security and Governmental Affairs, began hearings in the summer of 2015 on the threat of an EMP detonation over the U.S. The witnesses included, among others, James Woolsey, former Director of Central Intelligence, Joseph McClelland, Director of the Office of Energy Infrastructure Security at FERC, and Christopher Currie, Director of Homeland Security and Justice with the Government Accountability Office.

The conclusion: The threat is real, and the need of the U.S. to prepare for this eventuality is critical. Chairman Johnson, in his opening remarks, stated although the issue of EMP has been on the government radar for years, it has gone largely ignored. He pointed out the fact that not one of the suggestions put forward by the congressionally mandated EMP Commission formed in 2002 has been put in place.

The science behind an electromagnetic pulse might be considered complicated, and frightening. An EMP event can occur either naturally (through solar flares, as discussed above) or artificially, as the result of a high-altitude nuclear explosion. The high-energy particles from such an explosion would cascade down to Earth, interacting with the planet's magnetic field and destroying the electronic systems below. The resulting pulse of energy can destroy millions of transformers in America's power grid as they travel along transformer lines.

The possibility of man-made EMP events has grown in tandem with the technological sophistication of America's adversaries. It is widely known that both Russia and China already have this capability, and both countries have carried out serious work relating to the generation of EMP in recent years as part of their respective military modernization programs.

Now, America's enemies like Iran and North Korea may not be that far behind. Iran, for example, is known to have simulated a nuclear EMP attack several years ago using short-range missiles launched from a freighter. Recently, the Iranians test fired a medium range missile capable of carrying a nuclear warhead. North Korea, meanwhile, has acquired the blueprints to build an EMP warhead. In July of 2013, a North Korean freighter made it all the way to the Gulf of Mexico through the Panama Canal carrying two nuclear capable missiles in the ship's hold.

In addition, all of these countries have successfully orbited a number of satellites that could evade U.S. early warning radars. The Strategic Defense Initiative, or Star Wars, as former President Ronald Reagan once called it, was widely panned as bizarre by political opponents and the mainstream media. Today, satellites carrying nuclear warheads are at the ideal altitude to generate an EMP across the entire continental US. Perhaps, President Reagan was right.

Scientists concur that such an attack, if it occurs, would have devastating consequences. A nuclear warhead detonated three hundred miles above St. Louis, Missouri could collapse the entire nations power grid. According to the EMP Commission, the recovery time from a nationwide EMP event might be anywhere from one to 10 years. In the meantime, ninety percent of Americans would likely die from starvation, disease, or societal collapse.

There are solutions, and the clarion bell has been rung. Our nation's leaders have a duty to protect the homeland. This book is intended to raise awareness of the threat and provide the reader preparedness solutions. *EMP: Electromagnetic Pulse* will also help you answer the question:

EMP: A threat from above to America's soft underbelly below.

The clock is ticking. One second after. One year after.

What if?

The Deadly Threat of a Coronal Mass Ejection – Solar Flare

A powerful electromagnetic pulse, whether resulting from a nuclear delivered EMP or a massive solar storm, could collapse the power grid and the critical infrastructure of our nation.

What are solar storms?

Every minute, huge eruptions of magnetically charged plasma are emitted from the sun's roiling interior, exploding outward into space. Known as coronal mass ejections, or CME, these moderate solar storms occur fairly regularly and harmlessly, sometimes causing spectacular auroras that illuminate the sky over the North and South poles. But even typically benign solar storms generate energy many times more powerful than our planet's combined nuclear arsenals.

Is the threat real? Renowned American astronomer Phil Plait, who is a self-proclaimed skeptic, is known as The Bad Astronomer because of his work in debunking common misunderstandings about space events. "People sometimes ask me if anything in astronomy actually worries me," says Plait, when asked about the threat of a deadly CME. "Something like this is near the top of the list."

There is good reason to be concerned. A National Academy of Sciences study found there is a 12 percent chance that a monster solar storm will strike Earth within the next decade, concluding a solar event of that magnitude could cause $2 trillion of damage in the first year of recovery alone—twenty times the cost of Hurricane Katrina.

But, what about the human cost? Studies frequently cite economic loss. How would the destruction of the power grid and other critical infrastructure like the internet, banking, and government be effected? Has such a storm ever hit Earth?

Yes, several times. Imagine our way of life without power for weeks on end as a result of a massive solar flare striking the Earth. It happened in 1859 in what is commonly referred to as the Carrington Event.

On Sept. 1, 1859, British astronomer Richard Carrington noticed a brilliant solar flare over England. In the days that followed, a succession of coronal mass ejections struck Earth head-on. Auroras illuminated night skies from Africa to Hawaii. "The light appeared to cover the whole firmament," one Baltimore newspaper reported. "It had an indescribable softness and delicacy." The effects were more than aesthetic. EMPs from the storm caused telegraph systems — known as the *Victorian internet* — to fail throughout North America and Europe; in some cases, lines sparked and offices caught fire. Otherwise, the damage was minimal.

Nonetheless, for telegraph operators in the Americas and Europe, however, the experience caused chaos. Many found that their lines were just unusable—they could neither send nor receive messages. Others were able to operate even with their power supplies turned off, using only the current in the air from the solar storm.

From historical reports, one telegraph operator said "The line was in perfect order, and skilled operators worked incessantly from eight o'clock last evening until one o'clock this morning to transmit, in an intelligible form, four hundred words of the report per steamer Indian for the Associated Press."

Other operators experienced physical danger. Washington, D.C., operator Frank Royce said "I received a very severe electric shock, which stunned me for an instant. An old man who was sitting facing me, and but a few feet distant, said that he saw a spark of fire jump from my forehead to the sounder."

At the time, the telegraph was a new technology and never experienced technical difficulties of this type. But the story offers an important warning for modern society. The Carrington Event provides evidence of the fragility of electrical infrastructure. Scientific American reported in October of 1859: "The electromagnetic basis of the various phenomena was identified relatively quickly. A connection between the northern lights and forces of electricity and magnetism is now fully established."

This event was long before humanity became utterly reliant on electronics — as it was when history repeated itself 153 years later.

In 1989, a far smaller solar flare sent a pulse of radiation that left 6 million people in Quebec without power for up to nine hours. Much more alarming was a solar super storm that barely missed Earth in July 2012. Astronomers say the sun spewed out a huge magnetic cloud that tracked straight through our planet's orbit. Fortunately for civilization, Earth was elsewhere in its path around the sun at the time, but had the storm roared through nine days earlier, a worst-case scenario would have occurred. Satellites involved in crucial global communications (including GPS) would have been ruined, large electrical transformers would have been destroyed, and ATMs would have stopped functioning. The internet would have been disabled on a massive scale. Most people wouldn't even have been able to flush toilets, which rely on electric pumps.

Three years later, "we would still be picking up the pieces," says astronomer Daniel Baker. "The July 2012 storm was in all respects at least as strong as the Carrington Event. The only difference is, *it missed.*"

In a word—TEOTWAWKI—**T**he **E**nd **O**f **T**he **W**orld **A**s **W**e **K**now **I**t.

Over the last one hundred and fifty years, the world's critical infrastructure has become a more integral part of daily life. In the nineteenth century, telegraphs composed a comparatively small and relatively non-essential part of everyday life. Their successors today—including the electrical grid and much of the telecommunications network—are essential to modern life.

Is the current system any more protected from catastrophic interference than the telegraph of the nineteenth century? Can the power grid handle a terrorist attack, or severe weather events, or a solar storm?

There's never been a real test to prove it, but there is a robust debate about the vulnerability of the power grid. The most dangerous and costly possibilities for major catastrophes, the collapse of the nation's critical infrastructure, might visit the United States from any number of methods.

One scenario is a repeat of the solar storm as big as the 1859 Carrington Event. A solar event of this magnitude hasn't struck the earth since, although there have been smaller ones. In 1989, a coronal mass ejection caused a blackout across parts of Canada, especially in Quebec. As a result of complications across the interconnected grid, a large transformer in New Jersey permanently failed.

In 2003, residents of the northeastern United States experienced a grid down scenario. It doesn't take an unprecedented solar flare to knock out power. The combination of a few trees touching power lines, and a few power companies asleep at the wheel, plunged a section of the nation into darkness. The darkness can spread. As the difficulties at Ohio-based FirstEnergy grew and eventually cascaded over the grid, electrical service from Detroit to New York City was lost. The 2003 event was a comparatively minor episode compared to what might have happened. Most customers had their power back within a couple of days, and the transformers were relatively unaffected.

Compare this event with the incident in Auckland, New Zealand. Cables supplying power to the downtown business district failed in 1998. The center of the city went dark. Companies were forced to shutter or relocate their operations outside the affected area. The local Auckland utility had to adopt drastic measures to move in temporary generators. They even enlisted the assistance of the world's largest cargo plane—owned by rock band *U2*, to transport massive generators into the area. It took five weeks for the power grid to be fully restored.

There are contrarians. Jeff Dagle, an electrical engineer at the Pacific Northwest National Laboratory who served on the Northeast Blackout Investigation Task Force, argues "one lesson of the 2003 blackout is that the power grid is more resilient than you might think."

The task force investigators pinpointed four separate root causes for the collapse, and human error played a significant role. "It took an hour for it to collapse with no one managing it," Dagle said. "They would have been just as effective if they had just gone home for the day. That to me just underscores how remarkably stable things are."

As Congress raised awareness, the National Academies of Science produced a report detailing the risk of a major solar event. The 2008 NAS report paints a dire picture based on a study conducted for FEMA and Electromagnetic Pulse Commission created by Congress.

While severe solar storms do not occur that often, they have the potential for long-term catastrophic impacts to the nation's power grid. Impacts would be felt on interdependent infrastructures. For example, the potable water distribution will be affected immediately. Pumps and purification facilities rely on electricity. The nation's food supply will be disrupted, and most perishable foods will spoil and lost within twenty-four hours. There will be immediate or eventual loss of heating/air conditioning, sewage disposal, phone service, transportation, fuel resupply, and many of the necessities we take for granted.

According to the EMP Commission, the effects will be felt for years, and its economic costs could add up to trillions of dollars— dwarfing the cost of Hurricane Katrina. More importantly, the commission's findings state a potential loss of life that is staggering. Within one year, according to their conclusions, ninety percent of Americans would die.

But skeptics say it's the opposite. Jon Wellinghoff, who served as chairman of the Federal Energy Regulatory Commission—commonly known as FERC, from 2009 to 2013, has sounded the alarm about the danger of an attack on the system. The heightened awareness came as a result of an April 2013 incident in Silicon Valley, California in which a group of attackers conducted a coordinated assault on an electrical substation, knocking out 27 transformers. FERC points to the fact that the U.S. power grid is divided into three big sections known as *interconnections*. There is one each for the Eastern United States, the West, and—out on its own—Texas. In fact, the East and

West interconnections also include much of Canada and parts of Mexico.

In a 2013 report, FERC concluded that if a limited number of substations in each of those interconnects were disabled, utilities cannot bring the interconnect back up again for an indeterminate amount of time. FERC's conclusion isn't classified information. This information has been in government reports and widely disseminated on the internet for years.

FERC also notes it could take far longer to return the electrical grid to full functionality than it did in 2003. Wellinghoff said, "If you destroy the transformers—all it takes is one high-caliber bullet through a transformer case, and it's gone, you have to replace it," he said. "If there aren't spares on hand—and in the event of a coordinated attack on multiple substations, any inventory could be exhausted—it takes months to build new ones."

"Once your electricity is out, your gasoline is out, because you can't pump the gas anymore. All your transportation's out, all of your financial transactions are out, of course because there are no electronics," Wellinghoff said.

FERC's proposed solution is to break the system into a series of *microgrids*. In the event of a cascading failure, smaller portions of the countries can isolate themselves from the collapse of the grid. There is a precedent for this. Princeton University has an independent power grid. When a large part of the critical infrastructure collapsed during Superstorm Sandy, the Princeton campus became a place of refuge for residents, and a command center for first responders.

These doomsday scenarios may be beside the point because the electrical grid is already subject to a series of dangerous stresses from natural disasters. Sandy showed that the assumptions used to build many parts of the power grid were wrong. The storm surge overwhelmed the infrastructure, flooding substations and causing them to fail. Significant portions of the grid might need to be moved to higher ground.

Even away from the coasts, extreme weather can threaten the system in unexpected ways. Some systems use gas insulation, but if the temperature drops low enough, the gas composition changes and the insulation fails. Power plants in warmer places like Texas aren't well-prepared for extreme cold, meaning plants could fail when the population most needs them to provide power for heat. As utilities rely more heavily on natural gas to generate power, there's a danger of demand exceeding supply. A likely scenario is a blizzard in which everyone cranks up their propane or natural gas-powered heating systems. As the system becomes overwhelmed, the gas company can't provide to everyone. Power providers don't necessarily have the first right of refusal from their sources, so they could lose supplies and be forced to power down in the middle of a winter storm.

Summer doesn't offer any respite. Even prolonged droughts play a role. As consumers turn up their air conditioners, requests for more power increased. There can be a ratcheting effect. If there are several days of consistently high temperatures, buildings never cool completely. The demand from local utilities will peak higher and higher each day. Power plants rely upon groundwater to cool their systems. They will struggle to maintain cooling as the water itself heats up. Droughts can diminish the power from hydroelectric plants, especially in the western United States.

If extreme weather continues to be the norm, the chaos unleashed on the grid by Sandy may be just a preview of the sorts of disruptions to the grid that might become commonplace. Or as the New York Herald posited in 1859 when referring to the Carrington event, "Phenomena are not supposed to have any reference to things past—only to things to come. Therefore, the aurora borealis must be connected with something in the future—war, or pestilence, or famine." Although the impact of solar storms was not fully understood at the time, the prediction of catastrophe remains valid.

What protective measures are possible?

The Obama administration has taken steps to replace some aging satellites that monitor space weather and extra-high-voltage transformers that are vulnerable to solar storms. Its new plan also calls for scientists to establish benchmarks for weather events in space, incorporating something like the Richter scale. The strategy also includes assessing the vulnerability of the power grid, increasing international cooperation, and improving solar-flare forecast technology — a crucial step.

But Dr. Peter Pry, chairman of the EMP Commission, says neither the White House nor Congress is taking the threat seriously enough or acting with appropriate urgency. It would cost about $2 billion — the amount of foreign aid we give to Pakistan — to harden the nation's power grid to minimize the damage from either a nuclear EMP or a solar flare, he says. "If we suspended that [aid] for one year and put it toward hardening the electrical grid," Pry says, "we could protect the American people from this threat."

What if?

Economic Collapse

ECONOMIC COLLAPSE is a primer on the reality that our nation will ultimately perish at the hands of economic and societal collapse.

The United States economy can collapse as a result of our own government's mismanagement of our national debt or external factors such as a global financial meltdown, an attack on the US Dollar, and other *predictable* events. Why do you think the Federal Reserve is so frightened of raising interest rates despite apparent underlying inflation data? Our economy is a house of cards. We are just a few steps away from a collapse of the dollar and hyperinflation.

History is replete with the rise and fall of empires. Are Americans so arrogant, or oblivious, to not realize that we are in a stage of decline and collapse? Some of the signs of a decline include a downward cultural spiral, an over-reliance on government and the inability to protect the integrity of a nation's borders. Sound familiar?

All empires collapse eventually. There have been no exceptions in the history of mankind. Their reign ends when they are defeated by a larger, more powerful enemy, or when their financing runs out, resulting in collapse.

What is the natural consequence of the aforementioned collapse events?

Societal Collapse

Societal collapse is typically the gradual disintegration of human civilization and culture. Although there have been examples of an abrupt cessation of a society's existence, as in the case of the Mayan Civilization, most sociological studies of societal collapse point to a slow decline in institutions, cultures, and civilizations over many years.

Many factors can cause the collapse of society. Often, a general decline in economic, cultural, and social norms can cause a cascading effect which results in breakdown. Natural disasters such as earthquakes, tsunamis, or volcanic activity may precipitate a collapse of a particular society. Some argue that the overpopulation of a region, or the planet as a whole, results in resource depletion such as food and water, leading to collapse.

There are any number of trigger events which can result in societal collapse. Regardless of the precipitating cause, a population's response can be broken down into three prior models.

First, there is the *Dinosaur* response. This response occurs when a large scale society collapses rapidly due to the inability of their leaders to adapt to the changes in their economic resources or social values. When an empire's ruling elite insists upon maintaining the status quo, or provides for those favorable to their power base, the masses of their empire will rise, demanding equality.

Second, there is the *Runaway Train* society. In history, there have been empires which must maintain their power through continuing and constant growth. The ability to function under this type of strain is unsustainable, and once the growth stops, the society collapses. Examples of the unsustainability of the Runaway Train Empire include the Romans, Assyrians, and the Mongols. Some argue that capitalist societies fall under this category as well. The argument is that a capitalist society measures its success on an ever-expanding balance sheet and employs the effective manipulation of supply and demand. As this author has written in prevous works, *our nation may be one bad news story away from economic and societal collapse.*

Third, there is the *House of Cards*. The House of Cards society is an empire that has grown so vast and complex, with ever-expanding social institutions, that it becomes unstable under the weight of itself. The *House of Cards* scenario is typically found in communist and socialist nations where the government controls most aspects of society. In these cases, the government must either stifle dissent or exercise less authority over the population. If they choose the latter, their authority and power is undermined. If they choose the former, inherently free-thinking humans will revolt.

Societal collapse is usually identified historically, after much study and debate. Only on rare occasions have societies broken down or ceased to exist due to a catastrophic collapse event. But history is full of examples. It has happened before, and it will happen again. It always does. We have maintained that it is society's reaction to a collapse event that is the biggest threat, not the event itself.

Civilization is like a thin layer of ice upon a deep ocean of chaos and darkness. It won't take much to fall through.

Is this Science Fiction or Reality?

All of the events described above are plausible and have their roots in history. What could happen? Global Panic. Martial Law. Travel Restrictions. Food and Water Shortages. An Overload of the Medical System. Societal Collapse.

This is why we prep. Prepping is insurance against both natural and man-made catastrophic collapse events. The government now requires you to carry medical insurance. Your homeowner's insurance may include damage from tornadoes. Even though you may never incur damage from a tornado, you pay for that coverage monthly nonetheless.

As Preppers, we allocate time and resources to protect our families in the event of seemingly unlikely crises, but potential collapse events that are occurring daily or have historical precedent.

At Freedom Preppers, we hope none of these catastrophic events occur, but *what if?*

Author's Note

President Theodore Roosevelt once quipped, "The more you know about the past, the better prepared you are for the future."

Our three-million-year-old human ancestor Lucy led the way, followed by cave-dwellers, mummies, monuments, Cleopatra, and the birth of modern human civilization. As humans formed into groups and learned social interaction, the earth experienced the birth of major religions like Judaism, Christianity, Islam, Hinduism, and Buddhism.

Increased human interaction was accompanied by the creation of organized societies, mighty empires, the first Olympics, Julius Caesar, Samurai warrior armies, and the birth of democracy.

As man became more aware, and knowledgeable, great minds discovered the inventions of writing, paper, and the wheel. They conceived and built kingdoms of stone in Africa, the Great Wall of China, the Pyramids, the Sphinx, and palaces of gold.

Their minds raced in all directions, introducing such concepts as zero, time, gravity, and space.

It's amazing what man has accomplished in such a short period, relatively speaking. It's a heady subject that most people don't bother to contemplate.

The study of ancient civilizations and human interaction raises some profound questions. Who are humans? Where did we come from? Where are we going?

History has the answers. The famous author and Nobel Prize winner William Faulkner once wrote, "The past is never dead. It's not even past." But history will help you see where you are going.

The knowledge of history is empowering. A major news-worthy event today is only a small wrinkle of an ever-expanding, billowing sheets of information blowing in the wind of events. One who learns from history, and recognizes the lessons taught, is able to harness its power.

The United States and our world today represent the most recent chapter in the history of humanity. This book focuses on the history of empires, and the economics factors that both created, and burdened them. Here is much of the historical back-story that helps us all understand where we are, and what we face in the years ahead.

Thanks for reading.

To learn more about the Prepping for Tomorrow series **SIGN UP FOR EMAIL UPDATES** and receive a **FREE eBOOK** from one of his bestselling series.

You can contact Bobby directly by email

(BobbyAkart@gmail.com) or through his website

www.BobbyAkart.com

PART ONE

THE RISE AND FALL OF EMPIRES

Chapter One
The Course of Empire

In 1836, artist Thomas Cole completed The Course of Empire. American Poet and long-time editor of the New York Evening Post, William Cullen Bryant, called the five painting set *remarkable*, and echoed James Fenimore Cooper's words characterizing the paintings as one of the *noblest works of art that has ever been wrought*. What was it about these paintings that garnered such high praise from two masters of literature?

Over a period of three years, Cole employed his substantial talents as a writer, coupled with his artistic prowess, to depict a history of the rise and fall of civilization. The five paintings are set at the same location during later times of the day, including different moods and weather conditions.

In each of the paintings, a valley is viewed from a different vantage point, and as the valley progresses through time from its Savage State, to its Arcadian Phase, through the Consummation of Empire, the empire's Destruction, and then its ultimate Desolation.

There has never been an artistic work that better symbolizes the rise and fall of empires. As you read the description and analysis of each, ask yourself, *At what stage is the United States in The Course of Empire?*

THE SAVAGE STATE by Thomas Cole

The Savage State depicts a peaceful valley viewed from the shore with a mountain in the background, surrounded by a tempest at dawn. Early man, dressed in animal skins, stalks his prey and forages through the wilderness. He is a hunter-gatherer, banding together with others like him, for the mutual necessities of protection, sustenance, and perhaps worship.

Other inhabitants travel up the river in primitive canoes. The primitive vessels represent the beginning of transportation and exploration.

On the far shore, Cole provides a vision of a clearing with a grouping of teepees surrounding fire. The Savage State is Cole's interpretation of an early society being formed. It is an ideal and healthy world, unchanged by humanity.

The first painting in the series represents the beginning of an empire—primitive and serene, wild and fresh.

It's been said that great empires are rarely formed by willful and conscious thought, but more often out of necessity and mutual benefit. Groups are created by like-minded individuals, who then seek out other groups with which to associate, and trade. Mighty empires were formed when a group of people was large enough and powerful enough, to impose its will on others.

THE ARCADIAN STATE by Thomas Cole

In the second painting of The Course of Empire series—The Arcadian State, the morning storm clouds have cleared, and the new settlers find themselves in the fresh morning of a day in spring. The point of view has shifted, as the mountain is now on the left-hand side of the painting.

Much of the wilderness and its hunter-gatherers have advanced, creating lands with furrowed fields and grazed pasture visible. Various activities typical of the pre-modern world are being carried on in the background—plowing, boat-building, herding, and social interaction.

In the background, a large structure has been constructed signifying the beginning of monumental architecture and the advancement of man's technical knowledge.

In the foreground, an old man sketches in the dirt with a stick. This activity symbolizes the beginning of advanced scientific and mathematical thought. A young boy draws a primitive stick figure of a woman posing with her staff. These activities herald the start of the society's culture through drawings and paintings.

But there is also a harbinger of problems to come for this newly formed, agrarian community. A tree stump, apparently cut by man, stands prominently in the painting. Analysts of Cole's work believed he inserted cut tree stumps into his paintings to comment on the negative effects of an over-expanding civilization. In addition, two mounted horseman, together with a soldier in armor, alludes not only to human control over animals but the need for policing and possible military deployment.

The civilization is growing. It is creating crops and tending to its flock. Each member has a job, a duty that contributes to the new society. An economy is forming as the inhabitants perform a function, get paid in the currency of the day, and use that money to purchase itmes for their basic needs.

THE CONSUMMATION OF EMPIRE by Thomas Cole

The Consummation of Empire, the third painting in Coles' series, depicts this newly formed society in the height of its prominence. A bright summer day fills a city in all of its advanced glory, setting the tone for an empire at its peak.

Both sides of the river valley are now surrounded in gold-adorned, marble structures, constructed from elaborate columns and ornate architecture. Contrary to the prominent mountain and the natural setting shown in the first two paintings, the painting's entire landscape is subject to man and his expansive domination of nature.

The large structure in the background, possible a place of worship, now seems to have been transformed into an enormous domed structure overlooking the river-bank. The mouth of the river is guarded, and ships filled with goods go out to sea to meet with their trading partners. The population is joyous as it celebrates the opulence of the time, raising glasses high and cheering one another on the massive balconies and terraces, overlooking elaborate fountains. Consumption is the norm, not the exception.

The economy is flourishing with an ample combination of production, consumption, and services.

A giant statue of the goddess Athena presides over the scene, symbolizing past wars and significant victories for this empire. But a society built upon war pays a price within its culture. Two boys are playing in the shallow water with their boats. One of the boys is sinking his friend's toy ship, indicating his comfort with war and dominance.

Finally, Cole provides a glimpse of a scarlet-robed ruler or victorious military leader as he crosses a bridge spanning the two sides of the river in a celebratory procession. Empires are hungry creatures, always needing to be fed with the spoils of victory. To sustain an ever-expanding economy, one that requires more and more sustenance from outside the boundaries of their existence, the Empire must continue to conquer, or perish under its own weight.

THE DESTRUCTION OF EMPIRE by Thomas Cole

It bears repeating. All empires collapse eventually. There have been no exceptions in the history of mankind. Their reign ends when they are defeated by a larger, more powerful enemy, or when their financing runs out, resulting in collapse.

The fourth in the series, The Destruction of Empire provides the observer a wider view of the condition of Cole's imaginary empire. The painting, of course, portrays the downfall and destruction of the city, in the midst of a threatening storm which is seen in the distance.

An army of enemy warriors sailed up the river, has overrun the empire's defenses, and is pillaging the city while killing and raping its inhabitants. A woman, who once celebrated with wine, is now fleeing a soldier and throws herself into the harbor, indicating a society which has devolved into sexual violence.

The statues of the city's mighty warriors have been beheaded. Lifeless bodies covered with blood are strewn about the promenade.

The bridge which supported the procession led by their ruler in the previous painting, has been destroyed. A temporary crossing strains under the weight of soldiers and refugees. Columns are broken, the ornate buildings have crumbled, and flames fan out from the palace situated on the river bank. A palace which once presided gloriously over the city, is now on the verge of ruin.

The front porch of the once magnificent temple has now become the base of an enormous catapult, indicating that the violence of civilization replaced the virtues of religion. The ships which once promoted trade with other civilizations are sinking, or on fire. The once thriving economy has collapsed.

This fourth painting depicts the results of an empire which has lost its way. Through difficult trials and tribulations, it rose to prominence and greatness. But its continued desire to grow and consume was unsustainable. It lost its moral fabric. It became susceptible to collapse both socially and economically, which made it vulnerable to overthrow by a more powerful conqueror.

DESOLATION by Thomas Cole

Sic transit Gloria mundi, a Latin phrase meaning *thus passes the glory of the world*. The fifth painting, Desolation, shows the results of the collapse of the empire, many years later. Now that the civilization has collapsed, the mountain has returned to its natural state and prominence in the center of the scene.

The remains are viewed in the closing light of the day, completing the dawn to dusk cycle of Cole's works. Whereas the sunrise is prominent in the first painting, the pale light of the moon is reflected in the river while a solitary column reflects the final light of day.

Nature is slowly reclaiming the ruins of the once mighty empire. The landscape has begun to return to wilderness, and no person, living or dead, are to be seen—only the remnants of their architecture emerge from beneath a mantle of trees, ivy, and overgrowth. As in The Savage State, the deer once again roam freely across the landscape.

The broken statue of their warrior hero stands desolate in the background. The supports of the destroyed bridge, and the columns of the former house of worship are still visible— but only a single column stands in the foreground, its only use as a home for birds.

The infrastructure has crumbled, the economy has collapsed, and the society has ceased to exist—its human inhabitants vanquished.

CHAPTER TWO
WHAT IS ECONOMIC COLLAPSE?

To understand economic collapse, you have to understand economics. This book will delve into economics first, to give you the most prevalent warning signs of a looming economic collapse. Simply put, economics is the study of how people choose to marshal resources. Resources include the time and talent people have at their disposal—the land, buildings, equipment, and other assets on hand, and the comprehension of how to incorporate them into useful products and services.

Economic collapse occurs when the system breaks down entirely. There are stages of economic downturns ranging from recession, to depression, to collapse. The case studies provided will reveal the characteristics of each, so that you can identify the signs and prepare accordingly. But the complete collapse of a national or global economy is characterized by economic depression, social unrest and widespread poverty. During an economic collapse, financial markets will be in total disarray and government attempts to intercede will fail. Other indicia include high bankruptcy rates, unemployment, a breakdown in free markets due to hyperinflation, and a sharp decline in population.

The Great Depression in the United States, which will be explored in depth, is an example of a national economic collapse. As a result of the 1929 stock market crash, America suffered an economic collapse which lasted many years. The collapse of Weimar Germany in the 1920s and Russia near the turn of the twenty-first century, are further examples.

As in any catastrophic event, fingers of blame are quickly pointed. Some are of the opinion that a lack of government control and intervention leaves the free market unable to sustain itself. Others believe government over-regulation and manipulation is the problem. Even more believe the economy is capable of correcting itself unless a catastrophic event occurs—a trigger event, which forces an already unsteady economic climate over the edge.

CHAPTER THREE
WHAT IS SOCIETAL COLLAPSE?

The End is Near, read the sign of a man wearing a loin cloth as he walked down New York's Fifth Avenue one day. In the Bible, Joel warned that the end of the world is nearing and after seeing the last warning message from God, he wrote, "Multitudes, multitudes in the valley of decision, for the day of the Lord is near in the valley of decision."

Modern sociologists have studied the mindset predicting the end of the world and reached varying conclusions. From the Mayan Apocalypse of 2012, to the movies like *The Day After Tomorrow,* humans have been predicting the end of days since the beginning of time. The former was a real world example of societal collapse, the latter, pure fiction.

As laymen, we can identify those events and changes in society which are a harbinger of the end of an empire. Societal Collapse is one such indicator.

The phrase, *going to hell in a handbasket,* has been uttered about as many times as *the end is near.* Originally popularized in the mid-nineteenth century, *going to hell in a handbasket,* and its variants were often used to describe a state of affairs headed for disaster—at least in the mind of the person using the phrase. In recent pop culture, Kathleen Turner played a character named *Helena Handbasket* in the hit comedy series *Friends.*

For example, many adults lamented the arrival of the *Beatles* onto the American music scene in the early 1960s. They are widely known as the foremost influential act of the rock and roll era. As their popularity grew, *Beatlemania* began to signify the ideals embodied in the 1960s counterculture movement which focused on the free expression of human sexuality, experimentation with drugs, and the open defying of authority. To be sure, more than one parent uttered the phrase, *the world is going to hell in a handbasket*, during that tumultuous decade.

The popularity of the Beatles and the counterculture of the 1960s did not result in societal collapse, although history may prove that this was the beginning of the decline in American values and morals. True societal collapse is much more dramatic and has been recurrent throughout history. In fact, it has been so worldwide in scope, that it's more the rule than the exception.

The failures of cultural, social, and economic institutions are the primary features of collapse. Simply put, a society finally loses it, and anarchy reigns supreme.

PART TWO

ECONOMIC THEORY: BASIC ECONOMICS IN MODERN TIMES

"Economics is the study of people
in the ordinary business of life."

~ Alfred Marshall, Author, 1890

CHAPTER FOUR
WHAT IS ECONOMICS, AND WHY SHOULD YOU CARE?

Using a working definition of economics as the interaction between people and their resources, economists study the relationship of labor, land, and investments, of money, income, and production, and of taxes and government expenditures. Economists seek to measure well-being, to learn how well-being may increase over time, and to evaluate the relative prosperity of the rich and the poor.

The behavior of people is important, but the study of economics also considers the collective interaction of businesses, countries, and governments, at all levels. Microeconomics starts by examining how individuals make decisions. Macroeconomics examines aggregate outcomes. The two points of view are essential in understanding most economic phenomena.

The most prominent book on the study of economics is the *Inquiry into the Nature and Causes of The Wealth of Nations* written by Adam Smith, published in 1776 in Scotland. The *Wealth of Nations*, a synopsis of which can be found in Appendix C, is a massive treatise written about what builds a nations' wealth, and how it affects the individual. From an individual standpoint, Smith wrote *it is not from the benevolence of the butcher, the brewer, or the baker, that we expect our dinner, but from their regard to their own interest.*

Smith's statement is economics in a nutshell. Each of us has a duty to sustain ourselves, and our families. We do this by contributing to society through work and deeds. In return, we receive sufficient payment to acquire our sustenance. This cycle of work, receipt of payment, and purchase of goods constitutes economics.

What about currency—money?

A key element of the study of economics is the theory of currency or money. At first glance, the concept of money is straightforward. You get paid twenty dollars for an hour's work, and then you take that twenty dollars and purchase an article of clothing. The business that sells you the article of clothing takes half, and uses the other half to pay for another article of clothing to sell to a future customer. And so on.

Without money, you could have approached the business and offered to work for an hour in exchange for the article of clothing, but the business owner may not have needed another employee. Throughout history, a medium of exchange has been established by society which was used to intermediate the exchange of goods and services. A community might be prolific growers of corn. They use their extra harvest to trade for something they can't produce, like sugar. In the free marketplace, values are established based upon supply and demand—a bushel of corn might be worth a pound of sugar, for example.

As the world's population grew, items of value were agreed upon as a method of payment—gold being the most common. Gold was considered fungible, which meant one ounce of gold was readily interchangeable with another ounce of gold. It was durable, allowing it to be repeatedly used. Gold was portable, allowing individuals to carry this form of currency easily. This portability allowed for the exchange to others for goods and services. In addition to being divisible and acceptable, it was also limited in supply. A finite supply of a given currency in circulation ensures that values remain relatively constant.

Understanding these characteristics of currency enables us to discover the truths surrounding the problems of money.

If money is the center of the economic universe upon which all transactions are conducted, what happens to money if it no longer holds its value? In Zimbabwe, as the value of their currency collapsed during a period of extreme hyperinflation, a loaf of bread cost thirty-five million Zimbabwean dollars. The infamous hyperinflationary period in Zimbabwe from 2006 through 2008 is the perfect illustration of what happens when money no longer holds its value.

Likewise, similar results can occur when the supply of money is no longer limited. If all nations traded goods and services using gold, which is limited in supply, the price of those goods and services would remain stable. For example, in the United States, the monetary base—defined as the portion of monetary reserves in a commercial bank's vault plus the amount of US dollars in circulation, remained constant at $800 billion for many years. However, in 2009 through 2016, the nation's monetary base rose exponentially to $4,200 billion—a five-time increase. The Federal Reserve called this *Quantitative Easing*. Others simply referred to it as firing up the printing presses.

What happens if a government is tempted to print too much money over a short period, thus reducing its value? Prices for goods and services will rise artificially, resulting in hyperinflation. The society will soon lose faith in their currency, and seek out another, more stable form of money. The result is the economic collapse of the formerly stable currency.

Governments have always been tempted to issue more money because it allows them to finance their expansion and increase their popularity with their constituents. But without money, the world would be reduced to a barter economy, which is not plausible in this hugely populated, interconnected planet. There has to be a happy medium between these two extremes.

CHAPTER FIVE
GOLD, AND ITS ROLE IN ECONOMIC THEORY

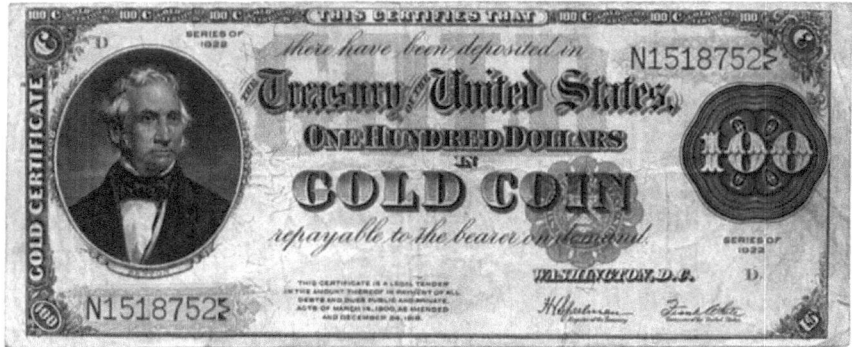

Precious metals like gold and silver seem to serve all the needs of society for establishing a stable medium of exchange. It is a solid unit of account, a durable store of value, and a convenient medium of exchange. They are hard to obtain. There is a finite supply of precious metals in the world. They stand up to time well. They are easily divisible into standardized coins and do not lose value when made into smaller units. In short, their durability, limited supply, high replacement cost, and portability makes all precious metals more attractive as money than other goods.

Until relatively recently, gold and silver were the main currency people used. However, gold and silver are heavy, and over time, instead of carrying the actual metal around and exchanging it for goods, people found it more convenient to deposit precious metals at banks, which would issue a note evidencing ownership of the gold or silver deposits. The holder of the note could go to the bank and exchange the note for the precious metal it represented.

Eventually, the paper claim on the precious metal was delinked from the metal. When that link was broken, fiat money was born. Fiat money is materially worthless but has value only because a nation collectively agrees to ascribe a value to it. In short, money works because people believe that it will. As the means of exchange evolved, so did its source—from individuals in barter, to some collective acceptance based upon the promise of governments in more recent times.

What is the gold standard?

The gold standard has been recognized as the ultimate backer of a nation's currency. It is a monetary system where a country's currency or paper money has a value directly into a fixed amount of gold using gold certificates like the one in the illustration. With the gold standard, countries agreed to convert paper money into a fixed amount of gold. A nation that uses the gold standard sets a fixed price for gold and buys and sells gold at that price. That fixed price is used to determine the value of the currency. For example, if the U.S. sets the price of gold at $500 an ounce, the value of the dollar would be 1/500th of an ounce of gold.

The gold standard is not currently used by any government. Britain stopped using this system by which currency was valued in 1931 and the United States abandoned the system in 1971. Fiat money completely replaced the gold standard. The term fiat money is used to describe a currency that is used because of a government's order, or fiat, that the currency must be accepted as a means of payment.

There are many advocates for the return to the gold standard in the United States. Other economists claim it would result in an economic disaster that would rival the Great Depression. The biggest positive associated with the return to the gold standard is it would force fiscal discipline upon governments, business, and individuals.

Considering the nearly $20 trillion debt that has been amassed by the U.S. government, fiscal discipline sounds enticing. The negative side of the coin (pardon the pun), argue some economists, is that the economy will grow at a much slower rate because the money supply will be drastically reduced. As an economy grows, they argue, more wealth is generated. By cutting off the supply of money, a nation would choke off the growth because the money supply could never grow faster than, or greater than, the limited supply of gold. Under our present system, for every dollar a commercial bank has, it can lend out $10 to $15. If these dollars are convertible to gold, the ability to generate wealth and economic growth through borrowing ceases, causing the economy to retract, or collapse.

What are the odds of a return to the gold standard?

Not likely, although the rhetoric will ramp up after the 2016 election if a Republican is elected president. Other than the possibility of a commission being established to study the concept, or entertain an open audit of the Federal Reserve, politicians are likely to stay the course because of the potential economic downturn caused by such a change. In the opinion of one economist, the only circumstances under which the U.S. would return to a gold standard is in the event of a major world war, or some other cataclysmic event.

Must we destroy our society in order to create a new one or start over? Will it take a reset of epic proportions to get it right the next time?

Chapter Six
The Great Economists

The economy has a huge impact on the quality of our lives. An economist is a person who has studied and is well versed in the policies and practices of the field of economics. Not only are these people knowledgeable about the intricacies of economics but they are also the people who create, propose and even implement monetary policies. The sectors where they are generally found include the private and the public sector.

When it comes to economics and economic theory, a few thinkers dominate the landscape. Coming up with a list of influential economists from the past is easy enough. Here is a list of those we consider the most influential economists of all time, followed by a detailed discussion of three who represent the liberal, conservative, and libertarian point of view politically.

Karl Marx

From each according to his abilities, to each according to his needs.

The philosopher, social scientist, historian and revolutionary, Karl Marx, is without a doubt the most influential socialist thinker to emerge since the nineteenth century. Although he was largely ignored by scholars in his lifetime, his social, economic and political ideas gained rapid acceptance in the socialist movement after his death in 1883. Until quite recently, almost half the population of the world lived under regimes that claim to be Marxist.

More commonly remembered as a revolutionary advocate of

communism, Marx was in fact also a classical economist. His theories essentially predicted that capitalism would lead to fluctuations and economic crises. Marx went on to publish *The Communist Manifesto*, having a huge influence on the communist movement of the twentieth century, and profoundly shaping the political landscape. Had communism not been brushed aside by capitalism, Marx' contribution to economic development may be more widely acknowledged today.

Milton Friedman

Underlying most arguments against the free market is a lack of belief in freedom itself.

If you put the federal government in charge of the Sahara Desert, in five years there'd be a shortage of sand.

Milton Friedman, an avid supporter, and proponent of free markets, was educated at Rutgers University, the University of Chicago and Columbia University. Awarded the 1976 Nobel Prize in Economics, he is most notable for his work on consumption analysis, monetary history and theory, and stabilization policy.

Friedman is associated principally with two big ideas which have inspired economists in the modern era. One is an uncompromising restatement and development of Adam Smith's views on the merits of free markets. He made the case for floating exchange rates - a process where a country's currency value is set by the foreign exchange market (FOREX) through the supply and demand for that particular currency in relation to other nations' currencies.

His other significant contribution, the quantity theory of money which linked the money supply to inflation, was embraced in the 1980s by Western governments. It has moved back to center stage in the recent economic crisis as central banks have fought recession and the risks of deflation using aggressive monetary policy, minimal interest rates, and expanding money supply via quantitative easing.

John Maynard Keynes

Capitalism is the astounding belief that the most wickedest of men will do the most wickedest of things for the greatest good of everyone.

British economist and author, John Maynard Keynes argued against the long-held view that free markets would automatically provide full employment, spearheading a revolution in economic thinking. He proposed that state intervention is required during boom and bust cycles of the economy, a policy adopted by most western economies during the 1930s.

Keynes was one of the most groundbreaking economists of his day. He created many of the new ideas that went on to become accepted after the Great Depression. Many national governments began to follow certain macroeconomic statistics more closely, including interest rates and employment because of Keynes' academic efforts.

Although this went out of fashion by the 1980s, the world has seen a return to Keynesian policy during the recent global economic crisis following the bank failures of 2008, notably in the US where the administration, in conjunction with the Federal Reserve, increased fiscal stimulus in an attempt to combat the recession.

The liberal economic theory known as Keynesian economics was set forth by Keynes in his Treatise—*General Theory of Employment, Interest and Money* which intended to provide a theoretical basis for government full-employment policies.

While some economists argue that full employment can be restored if wages are allowed to fall to lower levels, Keynesians maintain that employers will not employ workers to produce goods that cannot be sold. Because they believe unemployment results from an insufficient demand for goods and services, Keynesianism is considered a *demand-side theory* that focuses on short-run economic fluctuations.

Keynes argued that investment, which responds to variations in the interest rate and expectations about the future, is the dynamic factor determining the level of economic activity. He also maintained that deliberate government action could foster full employment. Keynesian economists claim that the government can directly influence the demand for goods and services by altering tax policies and public expenditures.

One more quote from Keynes, as it relates directly to the topic of economic collapse:

There is no subtler, no surer means of overturning the existing basis of society than to debauch the currency. The process engages all the hidden forces of economic law on the side of destruction, and does it in a manner which not one man in a million is able to diagnose.

Friedrich Hayek

'Emergencies' have always been the pretext on which the safeguards of individual liberty have been eroded.

Born in Austria in 1899, Friedrich Hayek was a noted social theorist and political philosopher of the twentieth century. According to the official Nobel Prize website, Hayek won the Nobel Prize in Economics in 1974 *for his pioneering work in the theory of money and economic fluctuations and his penetrating analysis of the interdependence of economic, social and institutional phenomena.*

His major work was titled The Road to Serfdom, in which he warns of the danger of tyranny that inevitably results from government control of economic decision-making through central planning. He further argues that the abandonment of individualism inevitably leads to a loss of freedom, the creation of an oppressive society, the tyranny of a dictator, and the serfdom of the individual. Significantly, Hayek challenged the general view among western academics that fascism and National Socialism, which prevailed in Germany under Hitler, was a capitalist reaction against socialism. He argued that fascism, National Socialism and socialism had common roots in central economic planning and empowering the state over the individual.

Hayek is considered the leading libertarian oriented economist. Those that have followed his theories include Milton Friedman,

Walter E. Williams, Thomas Sowell, and Art Laffer.

Adam Smith

It is not from the benevolence of the butcher, the brewer, or the baker, that we expect our dinner, but from their regard to their own interest.

People who intend only to seek their own benefit are led by an invisible hand to serve the public interest which was no part of their intention.

Adam Smith was an economist and philosopher who wrote what is considered the bible of capitalism, *The Wealth of Nations*, in which he provides the first detailed analysis of a free market economy. This extensive treatise has formed the basis for the free market, capitalist economic systems employed around the globe.

While his exact date of birth isn't known, Adam Smith's baptism was recorded on June 5, 1723, in Kirkcaldy, Scotland. He attended the Burgh School, where he studied Latin, mathematics, history and writing. Smith entered the University of Glasgow when he was 14 and in 1740 went to Oxford.

In 1748, Adam Smith began giving a series of public lectures at the University of Edinburgh. Through these lectures, in 1750, he met and became lifelong friends with Scottish philosopher and economist David Hume. This relationship led to Smith's appointment to the Glasgow University faculty in 1751.

In 1759 Smith published *The Theory of Moral Sentiments*, a book whose main contention is that human morality depends on sympathy between the individual and other members of society. On the heels of the book, he became the tutor of the future Duke of Buccleuch (1763–1766) and traveled with him to France, where Smith met with other eminent thinkers of his day, such as Benjamin Franklin and French economist Turgot.

Adam Smith's The Wealth of Nations

In 1776, after toiling for nine years, Smith published *An Inquiry into the Nature and Causes of the Wealth of Nations* (usually shortened to *The Wealth of Nations*), which is considered the first work dedicated to the study of politically-driven economies. Economics of the time were dominated by the idea that a country's wealth was best measured by its store of gold and silver. Smith proposed that a nation's wealth should be judged not only by this metric but by the total of its production and commerce—today known as gross domestic product (GDP). He also explored theories of the division of labor, an idea dating back to Plato, through which specialization would lead to a qualitative increase in productivity.

Smith's ideas are a reflection on economics in light of the beginning of the Industrial Revolution, and he states that free-market economies (i.e., capitalist ones) are the most productive and beneficial to their societies. He goes on to argue for an economic system based on individual self-interest led by an *invisible hand*, which would achieve the greatest good for all.

Smith argued for free trade, market competition, and the morality of private enterprise. He saw government's role in a society as to establish laws and instill justice, as well as provide for a nation's security, education and basic infrastructure.

In time, The Wealth of Nations won Smith a far-reaching reputation, and the treatise, considered a foundational work of classical economics, is one of the most influential books ever written. We have provided a synopsis of this important thesis in Appendix C, *A Condensed Version of The Wealth of Nations*.

The theory of Supply-Side Economics

In essence, supply-side economics proposes that production or supply is the key to economic prosperity and that consumption or demand is merely a secondary consequence.

Supply-side economics found its roots in the economic theories of

Adam Smith and one of our Founding Fathers, Alexander Hamilton. But it is better known to some as *Reaganomics* or the *trickle-down policy* espoused by 40th U.S. President Ronald Reagan. He popularized the controversial idea that greater tax cuts for investors and entrepreneurs provide incentives to save and invest, and produce economic benefits that trickle down into the overall economy.

Like most economic theories, supply-side economics tries to explain both economic phenomena and offer policy suggestions for stable economic growth. In general, the supply-side theory has three pillars: tax policy, regulatory policy and monetary policy.

However, the single idea behind all three pillars is that production (i.e. the "supply" of goods and services) is most important in determining economic growth. The supply-side theory is typically held in stark contrast to Keynesian theory which, among other things, includes the idea that demand can falter, If a lagging consumer demand drags the economy into recession, the government should intervene with fiscal and monetary stimuli.

The supply-demand dichotomy is the single biggest distinction. A pure Keynesian economist believes that consumers and their demand for goods and services are key economic drivers while a supply-sider believes that producers and their willingness to create products and services set the pace of economic growth.

The Argument That Supply Creates Its Own Demand

Economists continually study the supply and demand curves. Smith would argue that aggregate demand and aggregate supply intersect to determine overall output and price levels. Thus, Reagan and others adopt the supply-side premise that an increase in supply (i.e. production of goods and services) will increase production and lower prices.

Supply-side economists go further and claim that demand is largely irrelevant. The theory holds that over-production and under-production are not sustainable phenomena. Supply-siders argue that when companies temporarily over-produce, excess inventory will be created, prices will subsequently fall, and consumers will increase their purchases to offset the excess supply.

This essentially amounts to the belief in a mainly vertical supply curve. With an increase in demand, prices rise, but output doesn't change much. Under such a dynamic where the supply curve remains vertical, the only thing that increases production and therefore economic growth is increased production in the delivery of goods and services.

The Three Pillars of Supply-Side Economics

The three supply-side pillars follow from this premise. On the question of tax policy, supply-siders argue for lower marginal tax rates. By instituting a lower marginal income tax, supply-siders believe that lower rates will induce workers to prefer work over leisure. Regarding lower capital-gains tax rates, they believe that lower rates cause investors to deploy capital productively. At certain rates, a supply-sider would even argue that the government would not lose total tax revenue because lower rates would be more than offset by a higher tax revenue base—due to greater employment and productivity.

On the question of regulatory policy, supply-siders tend to ally with traditional political conservatives—those who would prefer a smaller government and less intervention in the free market. The conservative approach is logical because supply-siders, although they might acknowledge that government can temporarily help by making purchases, do not think this induced demand can either rescue a recession or have a sustainable impact on growth. A political conservative would warn that this stimulus comes with a hefty price—higher debts and deficits.

The third pillar, monetary policy, is especially controversial. By monetary policy, we are referring to the Federal Reserve's ability to increase or decrease the quantity of dollars in circulation (i.e. where more dollars mean more purchases by consumers, thus creating liquidity). A Keynesian economist tends to think that monetary policy is an important tool for tweaking the economy and dealing with business cycles, whereas a supply-sider does not believe that monetary policy can create economic value.

While both supply-siders and Keynesian theorists acknowledge that the government has a printing press, the Keynesian believes this printing press can help solve economic problems. But the supply-sider thinks that the government, or its central bank, is likely to create problems with its printing press by either creating too much inflationary liquidity with expansionary monetary policy or not sufficiently *greasing the wheels* of commerce with enough liquidity due to a tight monetary policy. A strict supply-sider is, therefore, concerned that a powerful central bank may inadvertently stifle growth—the law of unintended consequences.

What's Gold Got to Do with It?

Since supply-siders view monetary policy, not as a tool that can create economic value, but rather a variable to be controlled, they advocate a stable monetary policy or a policy of gentle inflation tied to economic growth - for example, three to four percent growth in the money supply per year. This principle is the key to understanding why supply-siders often advocate a return to the gold standard. The idea is not that gold is particularly special, but rather that gold is the most obvious candidate as a stable *store of value*. Supply-siders argue that if the U.S. were to tie the dollar to gold, the currency would become more stable, and fewer disruptive outcomes would result from currency fluctuations. Linking our currency to gold would also reduce the effect of currency manipulation by our trading partners.

As an investment tool, supply-side theorists say that the price of gold, since it is a relatively stable store of value, provides investors with a leading indicator or signal for the dollar's direction. Indeed, gold is typically viewed as an inflation hedge. And, although the historical record is hardly perfect, gold prices have often given early signals about the upcoming fluctuations in the dollar.

The Bottom Line of Adam Smith's Economic Theories and Supply-Side Economics

Supply-side economics has a colorful history. Some economists view supply-side as a useful theory. Other economists so utterly disagree with the argument that they dismiss it as offering nothing particularly new or controversial as an updated view of classical economics. Based on the three pillars discussed above, you can see how the supply side approach cannot be separated from the political arena since it implies a reduced role for government and a less-progressive tax policy.

CHAPTER SEVEN
INFLATION

How does the government define inflation? From *Investopedia*, "Inflation is defined as a sustained increase in the general prices for goods and services. It is measured as an annual percentage increase. As inflation rises, every dollar you own buys a smaller percentage of a good or service. The value of the US Dollar does not stay constant when there is inflation."

The Bureau of Labor Statistics is the agency of the Department of Labor responsible for calculating data for dissemination to the public. Over time, the definition has changed and now the widely accepted number is known as the Consumer Price Index. The CPI is often cited in the mainstream media.

Inflation is typically associated with the growth of an economy, but wide swings can actually be an indication of problems.

For example, to purchase an item of clothing in 2009 for $100 would require $110 today. Historically, over a seven-year period, an average inflation rate of just above one percent is considered very low. This is an example of an economy experiencing little or no growth.

On the opposite end of the spectrum, consider the four-year period of 1977 through 1981. An item costing you $100 in 1977 would command $150 just four years later. This is an example of an economy experiencing rapid economic acceleration driven by artificially higher prices. It does not quite give rise to hyperinflation, as in Zimbabwe, but it was accelerating too fast.

Inflation is often referred to as a hidden tax upon your money. As your money sits in the bank, it's losing value because its purchasing power is constantly dwindling.

Moderate inflation, once generally accepted as three percent, is a sign of a healthy economy, as long as wages follow suit. An economy which produces a higher inflation rate than wage rate increases is subject to collapse. Inflation is caused by two economic phenomena—*demand pull and cost push.*

If the economy is at or close to full employment, then an increase in demand leads to an increase in the price level. As a business reaches full capacity in production, they respond by increasing prices, leading to inflation. Also, near full employment, workers command higher wages which increase their spending power. This is how *demand pull inflation* works. The economy is *heating up*, as the media terms it.

Rising house prices - Rising home prices not only cause inflation, but they can create a positive wealth effect and encourage consumer-led economic growth. This can indirectly cause demand-pull inflation.

Cost push inflation results when there is an increased cost to manufacturers to produce their goods or services. Many factors can cause Cost-push inflation.

Rising wages – The collective bargaining laws of the United States allow unions if they can present a united front, to bargain for higher wages. Rising wages are a key cause of cost-push inflation because wages are the most significant variable cost for many firms.

Import prices – The US trade gap is currently $47 billion. There are many reasons for this, but for purposes of the inflation discussion, a massive trade deficit allows for higher import prices leading to an increase in inflation.

Raw Material Prices - The best example is the price of oil. If oil prices rise by twenty percent, then this will have a significant impact on most goods in the economy, leading to cost-push inflation. For example, when the price of oil skyrockets, the costs of certain oil-based products rise accordingly. If the cost of asphalt-based shingles increases due to the higher price of oil, the cost of installing a new roof goes up. Consequently, the building contractor raises the price of the new home he is selling, which is factored into the CPI.

Profit Push Inflation - When a firm pushes up prices to get higher rates of profit, inflation is the result. Profit-push inflation is more likely to occur during periods of strong economic growth.

Declining productivity - If firms become less productive and allow costs to rise artificially by reducing the supply of goods, this invariably leads to higher prices.

Higher taxes - If the government raises taxes, this will result in higher prices, and therefore the CPI will increase. A common misconception is that the government can *sock-it-to-the-rich* corporations with higher taxes and it won't affect consumers. The business simply increases its prices to pass the new tax onto the backs of all of us.

Printing more money - If a central bank prints more money, you would expect to see a rise in inflation because the money supply plays an important role in determining prices. If there is more money chasing the same amount of goods, then prices will rise. Hyperinflation is usually caused by an extreme increase in the money supply. However, in exceptional circumstances – such as recession, it is possible to increase the money supply without causing inflation. During a recessionary period, an increase in the money supply may be saved, e.g. banks don't increase lending but enhance their bank reserves.

Inflation expectations - Once inflation sets in it's hard to reduce. For example, higher prices will cause workers to demand higher wages causing a wage-price spiral. Therefore, expectations of inflation are important. If people expect high inflation, it tends to be self-serving.

CHAPTER EIGHT
RECESSION

A recession is commonly defined as two consecutive quarters of negative economic growth. It is often referred to as an *economic slowdown* during which trade and industrial activity are reduced, resulting in a fall in GDP. During a recessionary period, real incomes, employment, industrial production and retail sales all suffer. As the economy and the business cycle contracts, household income, business profits, and spending falls. Bankruptcy filings tend to rise.

Many factors contribute to an economy's fall into a recession, but the primary cause is inflation. As a reminder, inflation refers to a general rise in the prices of goods and services over time. The higher the rate of inflation, the smaller the percentage of goods and services that can be purchased with the same amount of money. Inflation can happen for reasons as varied as increased production expenses, higher energy costs and the national debt.

In an inflationary environment, consumers tend to cut out leisure spending, reduce overall expenditures, and begin to save more. But as individuals and businesses curtail expenditures in an effort to trim costs, this causes GDP to decline. Unemployment rates rise because companies lay off workers to cut capital outlays. It is these combined factors that cause the economy to fall into a recession.

Recessions have psychological and confidence aspects. For example, if companies expect economic activity to slow, they may reduce employment levels and save money rather than invest. Such expectations can create a self-reinforcing downward cycle, bringing about or worsening a recession.

What to Watch For

Consumer confidence is one measure used to evaluate economic sentiment. The term *animal spirits* has been used to describe the psychological factors underlying economic activity. Economist Robert J. Shiller wrote that the term "...refers also to the sense of trust we have in each other, our sense of fairness in economic dealings, and our sense of the extent of corruption and bad faith. When animal spirits are on ebb, consumers do not want to spend and businesses do not want to make capital expenditures or hire people." Shiller's expertise in the field resulted in the creation of the Case-Shiller Home Price Index which is a leading indicator of a future recession caused by a slowdown in the real estate market.

Economists have searched for the perfect recession indicator. Many media sources will dwell upon unemployment numbers. But, by the time an economy is suffering from high unemployment, a recession has already begun. For that reason, economists refer to the unemployment rate as a lagging indicator of recession–an indicator that reveals where an economy has been, rather than where an economy is going.

The Federal Reserve is well aware of the recession forecasting power established by the trend in the unemployment rate. In early 2016, New York Fed President William Dudley discussed the matter explicitly in a speech.

"Looking at the post-war period, whenever the unemployment rate has increased by more than 0.3 to 0.4 percentage points, the economy has always ended up in a full-blown recession with the unemployment rate rising by at least 1.9 percentage points. This is an outcome to avoid, especially given that in an economic downturn the last to be hired are often the first to be fired. The goal is the maximum sustainable level of employment—in other words, the most job opportunities for the most people over the long run."

Other indicators to watch as a predictor of a recessionary period are slowing industrial production and reduced growth in earnings per share of major US corporations. One of the barometers we watch most often is the Conference Board of Leading Economic Indicators.

The Conference Board is a non-profit research group organization located in New York comprised of over twelve hundred public and private corporations and other organizations from around the world. Founded in 1916, the Conference Board publishes a series of indicators for the United States and international economies that are the most widely tracked by investors and policy makers.

Their research reports produce the U.S. Consumer Confidence Index, the Employment Trends Index, and the CEO Confidence Survey. Together with other leading economic indexes which they compile, the Conference Board is considered the world's leader in producing regular global and regional economic outlooks. If economic collapse concerns you, visit the Conference Board organization website regularly.

CHAPTER NINE
DEFLATION

Deflation is one of the least-understood economic environments for investors, yet one of the most potentially devastating to the unprepared. When the overall price level decreases so that the inflation rate becomes negative, it is called deflation. It is considered the opposite of inflation.

On the surface, deflation sounds like a good thing. In fact, it is the grim reaper stalking the world's weakest economies in recent years, a threat many nation's central banks have learned to fear. The monster threatening the present world economy isn't inflation and a period of rising prices, but its opposite—falling prices.

Its name is deflation, and it appears friendly. Why should those who dictate monetary policy be concerned when the cash in people's wallets buys more fuel and televisions, not less? Because when deflation grabs hold of a nation's economy, companies and consumers stop spending. It strangles borrowers because their debts get harder to repay—a menace for countries still struggling to recover from the recent 2009 global recession, the worst in a generation. Under these circumstances, inflation comes dressed as a knight in shining armor as policymakers debate how to create just enough of it to keep deflation at bay.

When prices rise at a slower pace, it can help consumers boost their purchasing power. Falling prices can also provide a lift if limited and temporary. Some economists praised the drop in oil and other commodity prices in 2014 as *good deflation* that would open up room for companies and consumers to spend.

But when prices drop across a wide range of products and for a long time, economic activity can screech to a halt. Companies postpone investment and hiring as they are forced to cut prices. Sliding prices eat into sales and tax receipts, limiting pay raises and profit margins. They add to corporate and government debt burdens that would otherwise be eroded by inflation. Following the 2009 global recession, state and local tax revenues dropped dramatically, but the corresponding governmental operations didn't contract. The result was major municipalities filing bankruptcy and the near-collapse of the State of California.

Deflation fueled two of the worst economic disasters in modern times — the Great Depression of the 1930s, and the less catastrophic but more recent experience of Japan's lost decades with almost no economic growth. Deflation took hold in Japan in the 1990s when banks, wounded by a burst real estate bubble, stopped lending. Wages stagnated and consumers reined in spending.

The International Monetary Fund studied which economies are vulnerable to deflation, and has raised concern that even a period of ultra-low inflation could do damage. "If inflation is the genie," IMF Managing Director Christine Lagarde warned in January 2014, "then deflation is the ogre that must be fought decisively."

A reduction in money supply or credit availability is the usual reason for deflation. Reduced spending by government or individuals may also lead to this situation. Deflation generally leads to a period of increased unemployment due to slack in demand.

Central banks aim to keep the overall price level stable by avoiding situations of severe deflation or inflation. They may infuse a higher money supply into the economy to counter-balance the deflationary impact. In most cases, deflation gives rise to a period of depression, which occurs when the supply of goods is more than that of money.

Central bankers find it easier to beat inflation than deflation. When prices rise too fast, policymakers raise interest rates, then pull back when the economy slows. It's harder to calibrate the right dose of medicine to ward off deflation. Interest rates in most large countries were held near zero for years, and the European Central Bank even cut a key rate into negative territory in June 2014.

In Greece, deflation may be a price worth paying to make the country competitive again after years of living beyond its means. Bond-buying programs like those that helped revive the U.S. and Japan have also had dangerous side effects. They've sent money flowing into stocks and property, boosting the prices of assets rather than products, raising concern that too much easing was creating bubbles. Even so, when the threat of deflation seems small, history tells us that it's a huge risk.

There are fears that Japan's anti-inflation strategy is unraveling as we enter 2016. There have been several sharp rises in the value of the yen (12% in three months) against the dollar in the first quarter of 2016. This signals a trend toward *selfishness* by the Japanese in combatting their deflationary period. Excess volatility and disorder in the foreign exchange markets create instability in world market's overall. This protection sentiment by the Japanese—boosting its own economy in the hope of higher levels of growth—signals a potential world-wide currency war which harms the largest importers of goods, like the United States.

Further, as the value of the Japanese yen is manipulated, the Bank of Japan increased its production of Y10,000 bills exponentially in early 2016. As interest rates have remained at zero worldwide, and negative interest rates came into use, the Japanese are keeping their money at home, rather than in banks. In 2015, it was estimated that the amount of yen stashed out of the banking system rose from five trillion yen to forty trillion yen. To provide historical context, similar activity was taken in Zimbabwe at the start of its hyperinflationary period.

There has been no period of deflation since the six year period from 1927 to 1933, so few living Americans have experienced this. Had the Fed not poured a massive amount of money into the economy from 2009-2013, the US would have experienced deflation. Deflation existed, but it was covered with wallpaper in the form of newly printed Federal Reserve Notes, our currency. As a result, the national debt has risen from $10 trillion to nearly $19 trillion since 2009.

Deflation is the Fed's worst nightmare for many reasons.

Deflation increases the real value of government debt, making it harder to repay. Deflation also increases the value of private debt, creating a wave of defaults and bankruptcies. A period of deflation in the United States at this time could be catastrophic.

CHAPTER TEN
STAGFLATION

Stagflation, a hybrid of *stagnant inflation*, is a condition of slow economic growth and relatively high unemployment—economic stagnation—accompanied by rising prices, or inflation together with a decline in Gross Domestic Product (GDP). Stagflation is an economic problem defined in equal parts by its rarity and by the lack of consensus among academics on a precise definition.

Under most circumstances, when unemployment is high, spending declines, as do prices of goods. Stagflation occurs during a period of rising prices while unemployment increases and spending reductions. Stagflation can prove to be a particularly severe problem for governments to deal with due to the fact that most policies designed to lower inflation tend to make it more difficult for the unemployed, and policies designed to ease unemployment necessarily results in increased inflation.

In the 1970s, world oil prices rose dramatically, increasing the costs of goods and contributing to an increase in unemployment. The following period of stagnation increased the inflationary effects on the economy. Since the OPEC oil embargo created a crisis in the 1970s, there has been little consensus on what else contributed to the resulting stagflation. Each school of economics offers their understanding of what exactly went wrong and why. But the numbers speak for themselves. Inflation rose from a low of 5.2% in 1977 to a high of 14.8% in 1980. During the same period, unemployment fluctuated from a low of 5.9% to a high of 10.4%.

Theories on the Causes of Stagflation

There are two main theories on what causes stagflation. Using the price of oil as an example, one theory states that this economic phenomenon is caused when a sudden increase in the cost of oil reduces an economy's productive capacity. When transportation costs rise, producing products and getting them to shelves gets more expensive, and prices rise even as people get laid off.

Another theory is that the confluence of stagnation and inflation are results of poorly made economic policy. Allowing inflation to run rampant, and then suddenly snapping the reigns on inflation is one example of a poor policy that some have argued can contribute to stagflation. While others cite harsh regulation of markets, goods, and labor combined with allowing central banks to print excessive amounts of money, as another possible cause of stagflation.

Contemporary economists like Oliver Blanchard cite both supply shocks on the prices of goods and worker output, as well as incorrect predictions made by Keynesian economists as the cause of stagflation and the inability to understand it.

Since 2009, following the Federal Reserve's policy of quantitative easing which substantially increased the money supply, some economists argue the Fed is out of options to combat any number of things, including a plummeting dollar, rising inflation, and consumer prices.

"The biggest bubble of them all, the one in U.S. Treasuries, may finally be pricked," warns economist Peter Schiff. "That is when the Fed's nightmare scenario finally becomes everyone's reality."

What to Watch For

The website *Market Watch* recently issued a warning to its online visitors concerning the risk of a period of stagflation. The article provided the following:

"It has been a long time since the U.S. economy experienced stagflation— which Bank of America defines narrowly as any period when growth breaks

below the 25th percentile of its historical average while inflation trends above its 75th percentile.

When making these determinations, BoA uses growth data dating back to 1960, but only factors in core inflation dating back to 1990. It does this to eliminate the exorbitantly high inflation from the 70s and 80s from calculations of the historical average.

For stagflation to recur, according to Bank of America's standards, GDP growth would need to slip below 1.4% while the quarterly growth rate for core PCE (Personal Consumption Expenditures are measures of price changes in consumer goods and services) rises above 2.3%. Bank of America calculates quarterly changes in core PCE at an annualized rate.

That's not such an outlandish idea: growth during the fourth quarter of 2015 was just 1%, according to the most recent reading.

Meanwhile, core inflation nearly doubled in the 12 months leading up to January, according to the PCE.

Bank of America's big data leading indicator suggests this might already be happening. It's forecasting below-trend growth for both the first and second quarters. The indicator is compiled "from a large panel of economic and financial variables," the analysts said.

So how should investors prepare for this eventuality? According to Bank of America's historical analysis of market trends, gold, oil and U.S. Treasurys tend to outperform during periods of stagflation, while equities tend to underperform.

The U.S. dollar also tends to weaken, but the impact is more muted."

Stagflation, while rare, has historic precedent during our lifetimes. The tools available to central banks cannot adequately control all three variables which embody periods of stagflation. It is yet another reminder to keep an eye on inflation, unemployment, and GDP numbers.

CHAPTER ELEVEN
HYPERINFLATION

Hyperinflation is an extremely rapid period of inflation, usually caused by a rapid increase in the money supply. The most common cause of hyperinflation is the unrestrained printing of fiat currency.

Unfortunately, there is no exact percentage where inflation turns from *ordinary inflation to hyperinflation*. One can't argue that 9.9% inflation is normal while 10% inflation is hyperinflation. Typically, a period of hyperinflation gets progressively worse. Every month the inflation rate increases until the curve goes hyperbolic.

When associated with depressions, hyperinflation coincides with a sharp increase in the money supply not supported by gross domestic product growth, resulting in an imbalance in the supply and demand for the money. Left unchecked this causes prices to increase, as the currency loses its value.

Unlike low inflation, where the process of rising prices is gradual and not noticeable except by studying past market prices, hyperinflation sees a rapid and continuing increase in nominal prices and the supply of money. Because people try to get rid of the devaluing money as quickly as possible, the price levels rise even more rapidly than the money supply. The real stock of money—the amount of circulating money divided by the price level, decreases.

A hyperinflationary period is usually caused by large persistent government deficits financed primarily by money creation rather than taxation or borrowing. Hyperinflation is often associated with wars, their aftermath, sociopolitical upheavals, or other crises that make it difficult for the government to tax the population. A sharp decrease in real tax revenue coupled with a strong need to maintain the status quo, together with an inability or unwillingness to borrow, can lead a country into an economic condition wrought with hyperinflation.

When associated with wars, hyperinflation often occurs when there is a loss of confidence in a currency's ability to maintain its value in the aftermath. Because of this, sellers demand a risk premium to accept the currency, and they do this by raising their prices.

Hyperinflation effectively destroys the purchasing power of private and public savings, distorts the economy in favor of the hoarding of real assets, causes the monetary base to flee the country, and makes the afflicted country unfavorable to investment. But one of the most important characteristics of hyperinflation is the accelerating substitution of the inflating money for that of more stable foreign currencies, gold, and silver.

Causes of Hyperinflation

There are several theories on the causes of hyperinflation. But nearly all hyperinflationary periods have been caused by government budget deficits financed by money creation by its central bank. After an analysis of twenty-nine recent examples, economists conclude that runaway deficits have caused at least twenty-five of them.

Moreover, a necessary condition for hyperinflation has been the existence of fiat money not convertible at a fixed parity into gold or silver. This theory is suggested by the fact that most known hyperinflations in history with some exceptions, such as the French hyperinflation of 1789-1796, occurred after the breakdown of the gold standard during the time of World War I.

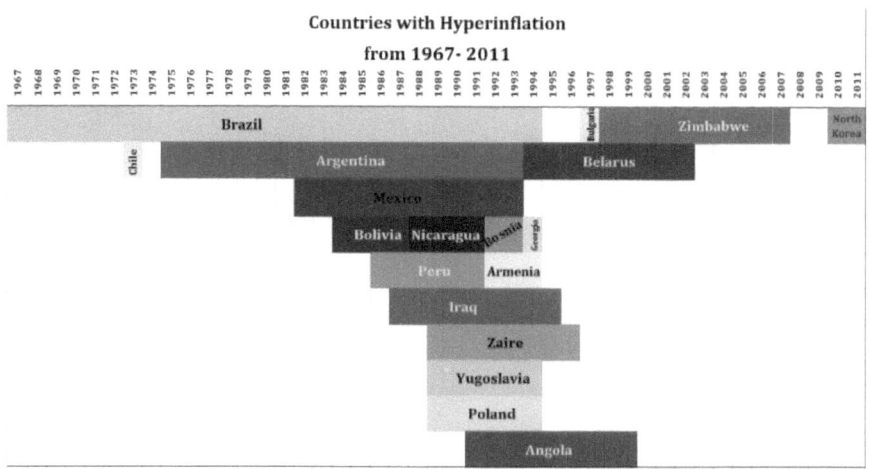

Countries with Hyperinflation
from 1967- 2011

Hyperinflationary Episodes

Hyperinflation is not as uncommon as you think. The above chart provides a list of twenty nations that have experienced a hyperinflationary period in the last fifty years. Two of the best-known examples include the hyperinflation of Weimar Germany and the more recent Zimbabwean hyperinflation period which reached 2.2 Million Percent.

Weimar Germany, 1914 – 1923

In Germany, prices doubled in only five years between 1914 and 1919, but then the economy fell into a death spiral of hyperinflation at the rate of one trillion to one.

During this five year period, and as time passed, economic conditions worsened, retailers and service providers stopped asking for currency, seeking payment in barter exchange instead. Prices rose not just by the day, but by the hour. If you had your morning coffee in a café, and you preferred drinking two cups rather than one, it was less expensive to order both cups at the same time.

The flight from currency that had begun with the buying of diamonds, gold, country houses, and antiques now extended to minor and common household items. During times of hyperinflation, people realize their money will be worth less tomorrow, so they exchange any cash they have for any physical goods they can get their hands on—whether needed or not. After all, a bar of soap will still be a bar of soap tomorrow, but it may take twice as many dollars to buy it. Excessive consumer spending has the effect of further stoking the fires of inflation by increasing the velocity of money.

Hyperinflation leads to lawlessness and societal collapse. In most cases of hyperinflation, the lack of a reliable system of exchange leads to a breakdown in society and a *wild-west* sort of atmosphere.

In Germany, the law-abiding country crumbled into petty thievery. Copper pipes and brass fixtures weren't safe. Gasoline was siphoned from cars. People bought things they didn't need and used them to barter. Prostitutes of both sexes roamed the streets, exchanging *services* for goods.

By 1922, the gold value of money in circulation fell from three hundred million marks before World War I to twenty million marks. The Reichsbank, Germany's central bank at the time, attempted to stem the currency collapse by printing more marks, which only caused a more rapid devaluation. 1923 was the height of the hyperinflationary period. The rate of inflation hit 3.2 million percent per month—the equivalent of prices doubling every two days.

Zimbabwe, 1998 – 2008

At the time of the nation's independence in 1980, the exchange rate of the Zimbabwe dollar to the US dollar was about 1.25. In 1998, President Robert Mugabe had consolidated his power over the entire socialist government. As part of his social reforms, he forcibly took real estate from white settlers throughout the country and returned it to native Zimbabweans. The government taking of income-producing private lands effectively halted the production of food in the country, which was their leading export. The political and social unrest discouraged foreign investment in the country. Mugabe and the Zimbabwe central bank responded by printing more money with higher face values.

By 2008 the hyperinflation rate in Zimbabwe had reached 2.2 million percent. Eggs sold for a million Zimbabwe dollars each. There was no stable medium of exchange. The overall impact of hyperinflation was 1 = 1025. Inflation was making it impossible for families to afford basic commodities they needed to live day by day. The media interviewed one Chivhu resident who asked to be identified only as *Innocent*. She said inflation is obliging many Zimbabweans to make a living by means that are sometimes *less than reputable*.

The final result was a total elimination of the Zimbabwean dollar and only foreign currencies were traded thereafter.

Examples of Hyperinflation Throughout History

United States 1779

47% inflation per month. During the Revolutionary War, the Continental Congress created a paper currency called Continental Currency. Until then, the colonies had issued their own fiat currencies, each less valuable than the British pound. Each colonial government got to devalue it as they saw fit, hoping and praying that they could tax the citizenry enough to get the fiat money back and retire it. Adam Smith called this a *fraudulent scheme*.

At the same time, the Spanish dollar – perhaps the first modern-day world currency – had been circulating in the U.S. as well. Somehow, this hodge-podge system of using precious metals, various fiat currencies, international currencies, and even beaver pelts as currency hummed along for some time. But the newly convened Continental Congress, leaders of a forthcoming nation during it's revolution, saw fit to step in and issue its own currency. Only it issued way too much.

Within a few years, the newly created currency wasn't worth but pennies on the dollar. It's not that the people lost confidence in them—it's that the government screwed up. By November 1779,

Continental Currency had a monthly inflation rate of 47%. Quite simply, it put the ancient Roman drachma to shame.

United States 1861-1865

Total hyperinflation of 1,200 to 1. The civil war exhibited one of the classic hyperinflations of history with confederate notes becoming worthless by the end of the war. But interestingly inflation was not a straight line to infinity. Confederate notes provided an excellent lesson in how money supply affects currency value.

From October of 1861 to March of 1864 the commodity price index rose an average rate of 10 percent per month. When the Civil War ended in April 1865 the cost of living in the South was 92 times what it was before the war started. This inflation was obviously caused by the expansion of the money supply. The role of the money supply in establishing the price level is confirmed even more strongly by the results of an attempt to curb the growth of the money supply in 1864.

This is an explicit example of how currency creation results in inflation.

Austria 1914- 1923

Inflation in one year (1922) reached 1426% and overall the consumer price index rose by a factor of 11,836. Political ineptitude ruled the day in post-World War I Austria. All state agencies ran at a loss resulting in massive deficits for their time. The result, like in other cases, was a period of hyperinflation fueled by the printing of the Austrian krone.

Hungary 1945-1946

Total hyperinflation 400,000,000,000,000,000,000,000,000,000 to 1. Political instability caused by a rift with the former Soviet Union resulted in a crashing economy. To solve the problem, the Hungarian government levied a twenty percent tax on all private bank deposits. The actions caused mistrust in the banks by the public, who pulled their deposits out of the depository institutions. Unable to tax the citizenry, the government resorted to printing money. Some historians believe this hyperinflation was actually an act of war as

Russian Marxists tried to destroy the Hungarian middle and upper classes.

China 1947-1949

Total hyperinflation 15,000,000,000,000,000,000 to 1. China had an early history of troubles caused by hyperinflation. As one of the first users of fiat currency, they funded their wars with the printing of money. The economic collapse led to the demise of the Yuan Dynasty via a revolution.

France 1789-1803

The Assignats were created as notes by the French government based on the value of confiscated church property. But they were printed with no relation to the underlying value and eventually became totally worthless.

Egypt 276 AD – 334 AD

One million percent inflation in fifty-eight years. A measure of wheat which sold for 200 drachmae in 276 AD increased to more than 2,000,000 drachmae in 334 AD

Hungary 1919-1924

Inflation reached 98% per month in 1922

Poland 1918-1924

Hyperinflation reached 800,000 to 1

Philippines 1942-1944

Conquering Japanese army issued fiat currency which rapidly became worthless.

Greece 1942-1953

Total hyperinflation 50,000,000,000,000 to 1

Brazil 1967-1994

Total hyperinflation of 2,750,000,000,000,000,000 to 1.

Mexico 1982-1993

Total hyperinflation of 10,000%

Bolivia 1984-1987

New currency replaced the old currency at a rate of 1 Million to one.

Iraq 1987-1995

Total hyperinflation of 10,000 to 1.

Nicaragua 1988-1991

Total hyperinflation of 50,000,000,000 to 1.

Argentina 1975-1993

By the end the hyperinflation currency exchanged at 100 Billion to one.

Peru 1986-1991

Total hyperinflation of 1,000,000,000 to 1.

Yugoslavia 1989-1994

By the end the hyperinflation currency exchanged at 1027 to one.

Poland 1989-1994

By the end the hyperinflation currency exchanged at 10,000 to one.

Zaire 1989-1996

By the end the hyperinflation currency exchanged at 300,000,000,000 to one.

Angola 1991-1999

By the end the hyperinflation currency exchanged at 1 Billion to one.

Bosnia and Herzegovina 1992-1993

Hyperinflation at the rate of 100,000 to 1.

Belarus 1994-2002

By the end the hyperinflation currency exchanged at 1 Million to one.

CHAPTER TWELVE
DEPRESSION

An economic depression is a severe and sustained downturn in economic activity in multiple economies. In economic theory, a depression is commonly defined as an extreme recession that lasts two or more years—longer than a normal business cycle. A depression is characterized by economic factors such as substantial increases in unemployment, a drop in available credit, diminished manufacturing and production, business bankruptcies, sovereign debt defaults, reduced trade and commerce, and sustained volatility in currency values. In times of depression, consumer confidence and investments decrease, causing the economy to shut down.

Economists agree that for a severe recession to give rise to the level of an economic depression, the downturn cannot be a normal part of the business cycle, lasting for months. A depression is an extreme fall in economic activity lasting for a number of years. However, economists disagree on the duration of depressions; some economists believe a depression encompasses only the period plagued by declining economic activity. Other economists, however, argue that the depression continues up until the point that most economic activity has returned to normal levels.

Some of the common elements of a depression that don't occur during a recessionary period include price devaluation, financial market closures, and bank failures. Periods labeled depressions are marked by a substantial and sustained shortfall of the ability to purchase goods relative to the amount that could be produced using current resources and technology. Another accepted criteria of an economic depression include a decline in real GDP exceeding ten percent, and a recession lasting two or more years.

Notable Economic Depressions

There have been several significant depressions throughout history—The Great Depression being the most studied. We will discuss it in depth in a later chapter.

The Panic of 1837 was a financial crisis in the United States that touched off a major recession that lasted until the mid-1840s. Profits, prices, and wages went down while unemployment went up. Pessimism abounded during the time. The panic had both domestic and foreign origins. Speculative lending practices in western states, a sharp decline in cotton prices, a collapsing land bubble, and restrictive lending policies in Great Britain were all to blame.

On May 10, 1837, banks in New York City suspended payments to depositors in coinage, meaning that they would no longer redeem commercial paper at full face value in coins rather than notes. The decision was a reaction to the growing concerns about excessive speculations of land after the Indian removal, which was mostly done with soft currency. The sale of public lands increased five times between 1834 and 1836. Speculators paid for these purchases with depreciating paper money. While government law already demanded that land purchases be completed with coin or paper notes from authorized banks, a large portion of buyers used paper money from state banks not backed by hard money. Despite a brief recovery in 1838, the recession persisted for approximately seven years. Banks collapsed, businesses failed, prices declined, and thousands of workers lost their jobs. Unemployment may have been as high as twenty-five percent in some parts of the country. The period from 1837 to 1844 were, generally speaking, years of deflation in wages and prices.

The Long Depression was a worldwide price recession, beginning in 1873 and running through the spring of 1879. It was the most severe in Europe and the United States, which had been experiencing strong economic growth fueled by the Second Industrial Revolution in the decade following the American Civil War. The episode was labeled the Great Depression at the time, and it held that designation until the more commonly designated Great Depression of the 1930s. Though a period of general deflation and contraction, The Long Depression did not have the severe economic retrogression of the Great Depression.

It was most notable in Western Europe and North America, at least in part because reliable data from the period are most readily available in those parts of the world. The United Kingdom is often considered to have been the hardest hit—during this period it lost some of its large industrial lead over the economies of Continental Europe. While it was occurring, the economy of the United Kingdom had been in continuous depression from 1873 to as late as 1896.

In the United States, the Long Depression was kicked off by the Panic of 1873, and followed by the Panic of 1893. The National Bureau of Economic Research dates the contraction following the panic as lasting from October 1873 to March 1879. At five-and-a-half years, it is the longest-lasting contraction identified by the NBER, eclipsing the Great Depression's forty-three months of contraction.

In the US, from 1873–1879, eighteen thousand businesses went bankrupt, including eighty-nine railroads. Ten states and hundreds of banks failed. Unemployment peaked in 1878, long after the panic ended. Different sources peg the peak unemployment rate anywhere from nine to fourteen percent.

The Greek Depression or the Eurozone sovereign-debt crisis began in 2009. Greece sank into a recession that, after two years, became a depression. The country saw an almost twenty percent drop in economic output, and unemployment soared to near twenty-five percent. Greece's high amounts of sovereign debt precipitated the crisis, and the poor performance of its economy since the introduction of severe austerity measures has slowed the entire Eurozone's recovery. Greece's continuing troubles have led to discussions about its departure from the Eurozone.

The European sovereign debt crisis occurred during a period in which several European countries faced the collapse of financial institutions, high government debt and rapidly rising bond yield spreads in government securities. The crisis began in 2008 with the collapse of Iceland's banking system and spread to Greece, Ireland, and Portugal during 2009. The debt crisis led to a crisis of confidence for European businesses and economies.

The European sovereign debt crisis was brought to heel by the financial guarantees of European countries who feared the collapse of the euro and financial contagion, and by the International Monetary Fund (IMF). Bond rating agencies downgraded the debt of several Eurozone countries, with Greek debt at one point being moved to junk status. As part of the loan agreements, countries receiving bailout funds were required to meet austerity measures designed to slow down the growth of public sector debt. The demand for austerity resulted in the near societal collapse of Greece.

The European sovereign debt crisis deepened by the end of 2009 when the peripheral Eurozone member states of Greece, Spain, Ireland, Portugal, and Cyprus were unable to repay or refinance their government debt or bail out their beleaguered banks. Without the assistance of third-party financial institutions such as the European Central Bank (ECB), the IMF and the newly-created European Financial Stability Facility, the Eurozone might have collapsed.

Some of the contributing causes of the sovereign debt crisis included the financial crisis of 2007-2008, the Great Recession of 2008-2012, as well as the real estate market crisis and property bubbles in several countries, and the aforementioned states' fiscal policies regarding government expenses and revenues. These factors collided in 2009 when Greece revealed its previous government had grossly underreported its budget deficit, signifying a violation of EU policy and spurring fears of a euro collapse via political and financial contagion.

A 2012 report for the United States Congress summarized the situation as follows: "The Eurozone debt crisis began in late 2009 when a new Greek government revealed that previous governments had been misreporting government budget data. Higher than expected investor levels eroded investor confidence, causing bond spreads to rise to unsustainable levels. Fears quickly spread that the fiscal positions and debt levels of a number of Eurozone countries were unsustainable."

In 2010, with increasing fear of excessive sovereign debt, lenders demanded higher interest rates from Eurozone states with high debt and deficit levels, making it harder for these countries to finance their budget deficits when faced with overall weak economic growth. Some affected countries raised taxes and slashed expenditures to combat the crisis, which contributed to social unrest within their borders, and a crisis of confidence among their leadership, particularly in Greece. During this crisis, several of these countries including Greece, Portugal and Ireland had their sovereign debt downgraded to junk status by international credit rating agencies, worsening investor fears.

In early 2010 these challenging developments reflected in rising spreads on sovereign bond yields between the affected peripheral member states of Greece, Ireland, Portugal, Spain, and most notably Germany. The Greek yield diverged in early 2010 with Greece needing Eurozone assistance by May 2010. Greece received two bailouts from the EU over the following five years during which the country adopted EU-mandated austerity measures to cut costs while experiencing a further economic recession as well as social unrest. In June 2015, Greece, with divided political and fiscal leadership and a continued downturn, was facing a sovereign default. However, on July 5, 2015, the Greek people voted against further EU austerity measures, with a possibility of Greece leaving the European Monetary Union entirely. The withdrawal of a nation from the EU would be unprecedented, and the speculated effects on Greece's economy if the currency was returned to the drachma range from total economic collapse to a surprise recovery.

Ireland followed Greece in requiring a bailout in November 2010, with Portugal next in May 2011. Italy and Spain were also vulnerable, with Spain requiring official assistance in June 2012 along with Cyprus. By 2014, Ireland, Portugal and Spain, due to various fiscal reforms, domestic austerity measures and other unique economic factors, all successfully exited their bailout programs requiring no further assistance. Cyprus, too, reported a slow but steady ongoing recovery, averting further financial crisis thus far. The road to full economic recovery is still underway.

PART THREE

CASE STUDIES IN ECONOMIC COLLAPSE

CHAPTER THIRTEEN
THE ROMAN EMPIRE

The Romans built an empire of legendary stature. At the height of its expansion, it covered the entire European continent as well as parts of the Middle East and Africa. The empire stretched from England to Egypt, from Spain to Iraq, and from southern Russia to Morocco. Incredibly, ancient Roman civilization prospered for nearly one thousand years. During its peak, the Roman Empire's population was one hundred thirty million over an empire comprising one and a half million square miles. The influence of the Romans over all of those subjects defies measure.

After adopting Christianity, the Romans systematically spread it to every corner of their empire. As they conquered more territory, they also brought their brand of law and order. Concepts of Roman justice such as being *innocent until proven guilty* have been carried forward into modern civilization.

Latin, the native language of the Romans, became the basis for several modern European languages, including Italian, French, and Spanish. Today, our alphabet, calendar, literature, and architecture have their roots in the Roman Empire.

Trade was vital to Rome. Their primary commodities included grain, beef, olive oil, glassware, wines, spices, and silk. The Roman Empire was also rich in iron, silver, lead, marble, timber, and tin. The ability to form trading alliances was critical to Rome's success as it generated vast amounts of wealth for the empire.

The Romans were adept in organization, government administration, and engineering. They had a highly trained and disciplined military, and an efficient administrative bureaucracy. Without these qualities, the Romans would never have been able to manage their sprawling empire. They built fifty thousand miles of roads, as well as many aqueducts, amphitheaters, and other elements of modern critical infrastructure.

The Romans were pioneers in creating a form of government—a republic, that was copied by countries for centuries. In fact, the government of the United States is based partly on Rome's model—a government in which citizens elect representatives to rule on their behalf. A common misconception is that the United States form of government is a democracy. A republic is quite different from a democracy, in which every citizen is expected to play an active role in governing the state.

Aristocrats, known as patricians, were the wealthiest Romans and they dominated the political landscape of the early Roman Republic. The highest positions in the government were held by two consuls who ruled the Roman Empire. A senate, composed entirely of patricians, chose these consuls via an election process. At this time, lower-class citizens, or plebeians, had no say in the republic.

Although men and women were legal citizens in the Roman Republic, only men could vote.

Roman customs dictated that patricians and plebeians should be rigorously separated and, therefore, marriage between the two classes was prohibited. Over time, the plebeians were given a greater voice and elected their representatives, called tribunes, who gained the power to veto measures passed by the Senate. Although the plebeians obtained more power, and eventually could hold the position of consul, the patricians were still able to use their wealth to buy control and influence over elected leaders.

From time to time, an emergency situation arose, such as a war, that required the decisive leadership of one individual. Under these circumstances, the Senate and the consuls could appoint a temporary dictator to rule for a limited time until the crisis was resolved. The position of the dictator was very undemocratic in nature. Indeed, a dictator had all the power, made decisions without any approval, and had full control over the military.

The best example of an *ideal dictator* was a Roman citizen named Cincinnatus. During one severe military emergency, the Roman Senate called Cincinnatus from his farm to serve as a temporary dictator and to lead the Roman army. When Cincinnatus stepped down from the dictatorship and returned to his farm only fifteen days after he successfully defeated Rome's enemies, the republican leaders resumed control over Rome. The republican form of government worked for the Romans.

For centuries, historians have tried to understand the causes of the decline of the Roman Empire, in particular the causes of the third-century crisis. The fact that opinions are so numerous reflects the complexity of the issue and the views themselves often tend to take into account the time in which they were written. For example, Enlightenment intellectuals such as Voltaire and Gibbon were obsessed with political reasons and the effect of the rise of Christianity. Machiavelli spoke of the barbarian invasions as being central, and Paulo Paruta felt that the relations between the Senate and the people were largely to blame. Other factors which have been put forward as crucial include, the decline in military spirit, disease (plague, malaria), depopulation, and immorality.

One of the essential causes of Rome's decline was structural economic weakness inherent within the empire long before the third century AD. These shortcomings include things like the inherent problems of a slave-economy, decentralization of industry and agriculture, and the unsustainable bureaucracy administering the Roman Empire.

However, this is not to suggest that there were no other important factors at play other than economic ones. Things like the increasing barbarization of the military and the political classes, intellectual and spiritual decline and the growing pressure on Rome's borders could also be cited as important. The decline of Rome should be seen as part of a complex process without a single, concise explanation. It was the result of a complicated process of interwoven weaknesses, defects, and contingencies.

In the famous work *The Decline and Fall of the Roman Empire* written by English historian Edward Gibbon in 1776, he states that the period in the history of the world when the human race was most happy and prosperous was in the first and second century AD. This period, known as *Pax Romana*, or Roman Peace, exemplified the Roman Empire in its glorious prime. A vast area of the Roman Empire around the Mediterranean was now linked economically, politically and culturally. There was prosperity, peace and security throughout the region and life was perceived to be running smoothly.

The end of this apparently *good period* was marked by the onset of civil wars lasting from 180 to 285 AD. Beginning with the death of famed Roman emperor, Marcus Aurelius in 180 AD, twenty-seven emperors or would-be emperors, met violent deaths during this intense period.

Meanwhile, the Persians raided Antioch in the East and in Europe, the barbarians broke through the frontiers. Vast areas of countryside were devastated. The middle-classes were increasingly squeezed out of existence, and many farmers and laborers were transformed into serfs. When Diocletian pulled the empire together again in 285 AD, there was little left of the prosperity of the Pax Romana. What seems clear is the causes of the decline must have been evolving during the Pax Romana period of happiness and prosperity. Many of the most serious weaknesses developing during this time were of an economic nature, and one can trace back the roots of some of these fundamental structural economic weaknesses to the Republic and before.

The early expansion of Rome in Italy was as much the product of hard work as it was of aggression and domination. Roman advances were strengthened by the settlement of farmers on confiscated territory and a prudent treatment of conquered neighbors minimized the difficulties and dangers. Occasionally, subject communities were admitted to Roman citizenship. The strength of this agriculturally based system was tested severely in wars. The wealth of the Republic was built upon the sweat of the provinces, the loot from wars and the suffering and exploitation of slaves. Like Greece, Rome had inherited a low level of technical skill and achievements were only possible because of the enormous amounts of labor and exploitation involved. The Romans seemed to lack any modern notions of returns and productivity. They appeared to lack the ability to improve methods of production, find superior sources of energy and improve transportation and communications.

A growing number of provincial taxes brought into being a large class of investors whose speculations tended to generate substantial returns. This ever-expanding and a highly influential class known as the Knights Templar had little care for the rapidly disappearing peasantry. Initially, their primary activity was to squeeze concessions from the Senate thereby meaning that for a time, popular leaders were able to engage their support against the ruling nobility. However, selfish interests gradually became the guiding force, and they joined with the senatorial nobles to form a party of property. Any attempts to reform the system were normally met with hostility. After that, an era of government corruption was born.

The slave-based economy seemingly worked well but only as long as there was an abundant supply of slaves. The slavery institution declined significantly as a result of the Augustan Peace instituted in the late second century, which led to a period of peace. Historians saw the decline in war and piracy in this so-called "golden age" as an entirely positive thing for the empire, but the Romans did not understand the unintended consequences of their good intentions which are that these two activities were the primary source of slaves. The days of the great slave markets were over, and there was now a severely diminished workforce. Growing humanitarian sentiments within the empire also facilitated this problem as many of the remaining slaves were freed. The fundamental basis of ancient economic activity was significantly undermined.

The issues of slavery and exploitation were among the root problems of Roman society. The empire was built upon the labor of the conquered subjects. This division of society ensured that the masses of the empire never tasted the fruits of their labor. The two major problems which this lead to were that people lacked the incentive to master their work, and they also had little consuming power for the goods they produced.

The need to create new trading partners and markets was one of the factors that lead to the continued drive for expansion. The lack of good communications leads to industry increasingly moving into new territories. The growing need to find fresh supplies of slaves was also a factor that contributed to the shifting of industry to the peripheral areas.

This process of decentralization was also linked to the lack of technology within the Empire. In modern industry, the efficient use of technology reduces overhead significantly, but there was not a tendency to do this in the Roman Empire. Increasing slave concentrations did not reduce overhead, and therefore, there was no incentive to maintain established trading marketplaces, as it was more profitable to move to new areas.

The lack of adequate transportation also hindered these attempts to expand their markets. Even the best forms of transportation were unsuitable for the high circulation of consumer goods. This was another factor leading to the need for industry to be close to its markets and therefore it encouraged expansion into outlying areas. The ineffectiveness of transportation lead to an inefficient distribution of goods, often creating gluts in one regiion and shortages in another. The communication challenges created market inefficiencies.

The insecurity of the credit system encouraged industry outwards towards new trading partners and markets. It was very costly to raise capital for a business venture because of the potential risks involved. There was no equivalent of the stock exchange to ensure some degree of responsibility for financial investments. Further problems were created by the primitive nature of the ancient banking system which saw little development of the system of a central bank with branch establishments and in some cases a backward movement towards a system of local independent banks.

All of the events mentioned did not operate at once or to the same extent but over a period of years. They resulted in a definite movement of industry outwards from the old marketplaces dominating the landscape in the early years of the empire. Overall, there was a slow reversion to small-scale, hand to mouth craftsmanship whose production was focused on the immediate vicinity. Progress in areas like Roman Germany and Gaul was canceled out by the decay of Italy. By the second century A.D., there were indicators that Italy was losing its once predominant position. There were increasing signs of depopulation and large shrinkages in the export of both agricultural and industrial products.

Soon, large estates became more self-sufficient, which increasingly detracted from the classical economic system, as there were fewer customers for the goods that circulated on the old markets. The constant desire to expand the empire contributed significantly to the restriction of trade and the speeding up of the process of decentralization. By the late third century, history has shown that the rise of the large estate was a real sign of Rome's severe economic decline.

Alongside this growth of the large estates was the shrinkage of the towns and a reduction in the quality and extent of ancient civilization.

The cities began to wither away and urbanization slowed down as the empire became more decentralized in structure.

Beneath the surface, problems persisted within the currency. Administrative, logistical, and military costs were adding up. The Roman Empire was beginning to feel the weight of hyperinflation, a fractured economy, burdensome taxes, and an overall financial crisis that threatened to cripple Rome. With the strain of foreign demand and the steady movement of currency outward as a result of the adverse trade balance, evasive action was taken.

The primary form of currency used during the first three centuries of the Roman Empire was the *denarius*. The coin, between the size of a modern nickel and a dime, was worth a day's wages for a skilled laborer or craftsman. During the first days of the Empire, these coins were of high purity, holding about four to five grams of pure silver. The currency was the Roman equivalent of the gold standard.

However, with a finite supply of silver and gold entering the empire, Rome's spending was limited by the amount of their minting capability. This created a challenge for the expanding bureaucracy and put limits on an emperor's ability to spend.

The infamous emperor, Nero, undertook to debase the Roman currency. The weight and quality of their coinage constantly fell until the time when inflation was reaching cataclysmic proportions. By decreasing the purity of their coinage, they were able to make more silver coins, at a significantly reduced purity level, with the same face value. With more currency in circulation, the government could spend more. During Nero's reign, the silver *denarius* sank to one-third of its former value, and wholly ceased to circulate outside the Empire. The gold *aureus* became so unreliable that by 200 A.D. it had ceased to be accepted abroad without testing for weight and quality. Over a period of two hundred years, the silver contained in the denarius dropped from nearly one hundred percent to less than five percent.

The recognizable effects of debasement took time to appear. By adding the newly minted coins with lower silver content into circulation, prosperity did not increase. It reduced the purchasing power of Roman citizens. In effect, it transferred wealth away from the people, and it meant that more coins were needed to pay for essential goods and services.

The story of the third century was one of worsening inflation and the minting of bad money. The situation became so bad that many Romans fell back on the natural economy of bartering thus further perpetuating the economic problems.

Despite the considerable contraction of the population and resources, this was not accompanied by a corresponding reduction in the price of imperial administration. The maintenance costs of the empire were huge and continued to expand all the time. With soaring administrative expenses, and a peacetime period which didn't yield any precious metals in the form of plunder, Rome sought a means by which to raise funds. They began to levy heavy taxes against the population to sustain the Empire.

Taxes had to be collected, frontiers were defended, while the empire had to be policed and maintained. The upholding of the Roman standard of culture meant huge amounts had to be spent to provide an adequate supply of the amenities that were considered essential to the full life of a Roman citizen.

There was the cost of building, repairing and maintaining the numerous temples, public baths, municipal buildings, gymnasia, town halls, market places, triumphal columns, and amphitheaters. Civic sacrifices, religious processions, feasts and the Olympic games also drained huge amounts from the financial reserves of the empire.

The cost of this critical infrastructure and entitlements weakened the empire's finances. Under Marcus Aurelius, there was a daily distribution of pork, oil and bread to the vast majority of Roman citizens. Originally, this was passed out once a month.

Another area in which Rome spent massive amounts of money was the army. An important implication of the Roman peace was that the military changed its economic role. Whereas previously it had been an important source of plunder it was now mainly used as a peaceful garrison force. The army became a financial liability, as there were thousands of mouths to feed and nothing for them to do. Of course, even in peace, the military was essential to the security of the empire, but the cost of it more than doubled between 96 and 180 AD. The empire was over-spending by epic proportions, yet the economic structure meant that nothing could be done to counter-act this.

Another crucial cause of the financial problems came during the reign of Marcus Aurelius when there was a sudden explosion of calamities afflicting the empire. For one hundred and fifty years of the Roman golden age, there had been virtually no cataclysmic events with the exception of the civil war and a few other minor revolts. During the reign of Marcus Aurelius, the Roman Empire's good fortunes suddenly changed for the worse.

Wars erupted on the outskirts of the Roman Empire and proved to be extremely expensive. To make matters worse, the returning army brought back a deadly plague with them. There were several citizen revolts during this period.

All of these problems put enormous financial pressure on the empire. The evidence supporting this is clearly shown by the fact that Marcus Aurelius and subsequent emperors reduced the gold surplus of three million in 161 A.D. to one million in 193 A.D.

One of the consequences of the financial crisis was to put a massive amount of stress on the bourgeoisie. There was a huge rise in the financial pressure imposed on wealthy. This was met with a growing reluctance to help ease the growing economic burden. There are many examples of the patrician class in this period being forced to carry out public works. Generally, the wealthy would volunteer to donate to the public, but the fact the Roman aristocracy were being increasingly forced to help shows the direness of the situation.

By the third century, the burden was so heavy that it began to consume the capital resources of the empire. However, this increase in taxation did not increase production. The increases in tax seemed to coincide with a decrease in manpower and production. The economy became paralyzed as hyperinflation, increased taxation, and worthless money crushed the Roman economy.

From the third century onwards, the question of how to fund the

Empire became fundamental due to widespread economic contraction. The problem of indebtedness was so common that it was seriously hindering economic enterprise. It got to the stage when taxpayers simply had to pay what was demanded of them. The police powers of the Empire would necessarily have to become strengthened in order to collect the taxes.

Here we see the growth of bureaucracy and a parallel development of what we today would call the *police-state*. During the Republic, the money for Rome's expansion came mostly from the plunder of foreign war. However during the Pax Romana, we see a morose state of affairs emerging whereby the only means of keeping the empire funded was through legalized extortion. By the start of the third century, the Roman bureaucracy was intertwined in every aspect of the citizen's lives, similar to modern times. This tendency sowed the seeds for the tyranny of the third century.

The relentless system of taxation, requisition, and compulsory labor was administered by an army of military bureaucrats. Soon, there was the development of a system of secret police and informers, the personal agents of the emperor, who were rewarded for reporting on the slightest hint of tax evasion.

The over-consumption and pampering of the Roman citizens during the imperial period also created other problems. It has often been suggested that the increasingly materialistic and greedy lifestyles that many Romans lead began to affect them spiritually and intellectually. A sense of futility seemed to be permeating society. The Roman spirit which had conquered the world was becoming increasingly lethargic. During the *Pax Romana* period, it seemed that peace, comfort and security took priority above political freedom and trying to solve the problems which were blighting their civilization.

Many historians mention the change in racial stock as a reason for this. Others say that plague and malaria were also possible causes. Others suspect that the real reason was the disease of materialism and the rise of the entitlement society.

We need not look solely to Rome for this tendency; it is happening in the west today. The price that western society seems to be paying for the considerable wealth and comfort of most of its inhabitants is a corresponding rise in apathy, complacency, and unreflective indulgence. Consumerism is the leading economic driver in the United States.

The modern industrialized West seems to share several of the characteristics which predominated during the *golden era* of the Roman Empire. The growing sense of negativity existed then and now, as does the obsession with violence (blood-sports in Rome versus Hollywood films and video games), sex, and indulgences.

Another interesting parallel is the growth of Oriental and Muslim religions which appeared in Rome in the third century. The increasing popularity of non-Christian religions throughout the Roman Empire was also a sign of the influence which the lower classes were increasingly having on the upper classes and therefore represented a sort of barbarization of the Roman culture. This represents a prominent feature in the Roman world which included the gradual absorption of the higher classes by the lower classes, resulting in a subsequent leveling down of standards.

As if all this wasn't enough to be concerned with, the Romans suffered a second devastating plague in 252 A.D, which proceeded to devastate the Roman world for fifteen years. Alexandria lost two-thirds of its population and at its peak, Rome lost five thousand each day. During the invasions, there is evidence to suggest that due to the exploitation and maltreatment of many of the Roman citizens, the invasions and disintegration of the empire was often met with indifference.

By the time the Persians and Barbarians invaded the Roman Empire at the end of the third century, the Roman world was in a state of disarray, and all that was required to create a total collapse was a gentle push. The empire was split into three states and was in free-fall. During the seemingly happy period of *Pax Romana* in the first and second century, Rome was sleepwalking into a catastrophe. The invasions of the third century were not so much a cause of Rome's decline as a result of its significant economic and political weakness at this stage.

The attitude of the lower classes towards the Barbarians was by no means always one of fear and hostility. They were often met with feelings of relief and the desire to co-operate especially amongst the poorer men who were unendurably burdened by taxation. Evidence shows us examples of people deserting to the barbarians or of appealing for help from them. Some of the numbers mentioned are so strikingly huge that there must have been civilian defectors as well as military defectors. The fact that so many people wished to rebel against their empire speaks volumes about the state of the empire during the third century.

Economic weaknesses and their social repercussions were largely to blame for the decline which Rome went through during the third century. The costs of running the empire continued to increase exponentially along with a corresponding decrease in productivity and the ability of many to pay. From this, we see the rising bureaucracy and therefore further pressure on the Roman citizens and the middle classes, in particular.

The increasing materialism of the Romans also seemed to contribute to a general weakening of the Roman *spirit*. The empire had dug itself into a hole from which it could not escape and went into terminal decline.

The civil wars which were the result of this along with its political, economic and social problems affected the empire to such an extent that it could no longer defend itself effectively against its enemies. By the fourth century, such damage had been inflicted that the Roman world was never the same again and eventually collapsed.

CHAPTER FOURTEEN
THE GREAT DEPRESSION

Economists crunch numbers; they apply theory, and then they hope for the best. Some believe in government intervention and manipulation. Others prefer to let the free market adjust to economic conditions. All would agree that a perfect market with no recessions or crashes is preferable, but not likely. The one factor that applies, making predicting the ebb and flow of market conditions as unpredictable as chaos theory, is the human factor. It is the collective mindset of humanity—human behavior—that can turn an ordinary financial bubble or recession into a full-blown economic depression.

The Great Depression was the most severe economic depression ever experienced in modern times. It was considered the world's most famous case of deflation. The aftermath, the depression, was so intense, that the economic policy of the last one hundred years has been designed to prevent deflation at all costs. Between 1929 and 1932, worldwide GDP fell by fifteen percent. Personal income, tax revenues, profits and prices plunged by fifty percent.

The crash of the New York Stock Exchange on October 29, 1929, signaled the start of the Great Depression, the worst economic crisis in U.S. history. This period would last until 1941 when the United States began preparations to enter World War II.

When the stock market began to spiral downward, many looked on in disbelief. However, others recognized that the plummeting prices were a confirmation of severe economic problems long in the making. The stock market crash of 1929, usually cited as the beginning of the Great Depression, was preceded by the Roaring Twenties, a period when the American public discovered the stock market and dove in head first.

For much of the 1920s, the United States seemed prosperous. Many Americans were employed, and goods such as automobiles, appliances, and furniture flowed out of factories. Economic growth picked up as new technologies like the car, household appliances, and other consumer-oriented goods led to a vibrant consumer culture.

It also began the advent of consumer debt. More than half of automobiles in America were sold on credit by the end of the twenties, during which consumer debt more than doubled. At the peak of prosperity in 1927, the United States enjoyed the highest standard of living in the history of the world.

An undercurrent of unhealthy factors ran through the American economy—including the growth of income inequality. After the decade of the roaring twenties, the income of the top one percent had increased by seventy-five percent while the incomes for the remainder of Americans had only risen by nine percent.

The Dow Jones Industrial Average (DJIA) doubled, stock values raced upward, and the future looked promising. On an everyday level, the car, radio, and motion pictures were stirring up high hopes, and Henry Ford had shaken up America by offering great pay for shorter hours, forcing other industries to follow his lead. Also, America was feeling its power. World War I provided the United States with global trading ties and almost every major European nation became a debtor to Washington.

With the value of stocks skyrocketing, reports of people making fortunes lured people into investing heavily in the market. At the same time, the Federal Reserve Bank was very accommodating with an easy-credit policy. It expanded the money supply and lowered interest rates. In this loan-friendly environment, brokers, amateur investors, and even banks were leveraging everything on margin to get more of the action. The buying glut caused prices to break away from the fundamentals and sent them soaring. By 1928, signs that such prosperity was not sustainable began to appear.

On June 12, 1928, the New York Stock Exchange (NYSE) saw five million shares trade hands during a seemingly random drop across the board. This market hiccup was fleeting, and the bull market picked up again, but with perhaps a slight sense of unease over how quickly the market could go down. The Fed noticed and set about reversing the loose monetary policies that had added momentum to the bull market by increasing interest rates and announcing a ban on loans for margin trades in February of 1929. In most runaway markets, this should have been enough to cool the economy down, but investors were leveraged to the hilt and their greed and desperation kept the market on an upward trajectory.

In the summer of '29, many banks also tried to tamp down speculative investing by raising the discount rate on loans to brokers, many of whom were trading with huge outstanding debts. This hike effectively halted the bull market. The Dow slumped for weeks before rallying briefly in early September to reach a pre-crash high of 381.17. Markets entered into a relatively quiet period until reality set in late October.

October 24 and 25, Black Thursday and Black Friday, heralded the beginning of the chaos to follow. The DJIA plunged eleven percent at the open in very heavy volume on Black Thursday. The NYSE watched as thirteen million shares traded hands in furious bouts of panic selling. Intervention by wealthy industrialists, bankers, and investors—primarily the buying up of huge blocks of plummeting shares—halted the slide briefly.

The crash resumed on Black Friday, and into the following Monday, as more investors rushed to get out of the market while Wall Street continued to artificially prop up prices. The Dow dropped thirteen percent despite Wall Street's best efforts and, the following day, the situation worsened. On Tuesday, more than sixteen million shares were traded in panic selling that lasted the whole day. The market lost $14 billion.

The crash was severe, but the aftershocks were proved more damaging. If everyone had been investing with money they could afford to lose, the crash wouldn't rank among the most severe market corrections. However, with everyone, including banks, trading on margin, the bloodletting on Wall Street meant millions of dollars in bad loans. The banks holding the bad loans could call in the collateral, but in the market slide, even that meant losing money.

Soon enough, banks began to fail. The shock to the overall banking system was so severe that the U.S. economy spiraled into a recession, which deepened into a depression. As the economy soured, the markets continued to fall. On the worst day of the crash, the DJIA lost thirteen percent, but throughout the following years of the Great Depression, it shed eighty-nine percent of its pre-crash high.

The crash wiped out many people's investments and the public was understandably shaken. When bank failures erased the savings of those who weren't even invested in the stock market, the American public was devastated. Historians argue that although the stock market crash was unavoidable, the bank failures could have been prevented with better regulation.

The Fed, politicians and investors had not learned from history. Twenty-two years earlier, the panic of 1907 offered a similar scenario, as panic selling sent the NYSE spiraling downward and led to a run on bank deposits. With no central bank in place (the Federal Reserve was founded in 1913) to inject cash into the market, it fell upon investment banker J.P. Morgan to organize Wall Street's elite. Morgan rallied people who had cash to spare and moved that capital to banks lacking funds. The panic led the government to create the Federal Reserve, in part to cut its reliance on financial figures like Morgan in the future.

Famed economist Milton Friedman studied the Great Depression and created a poignant analysis of the events leading up to the 1929 stock market crash. He lays the blame for the crash squarely on the shoulders of the Federal Reserve.

During the crash of 1929, the Fed took the course of action of cutting the money supply by nearly a third, thus choking off hopes of a recovery. Consequently, many banks suffering liquidity problems failed. The Fed's harsh reaction, puzzling to most economists, may have occurred because it wished to send Wall Street a message by refusing to bail out careless banks. In their mind, a bailout of reckless banks would only encourage more fiscal irresponsibility in the future.

Ironically, by increasing the money supply and keeping interest rates low during the twenties, the Fed instigated a rapid expansion that preceded the collapse. In some ways, it set up the market bubble leading to the crash and then kicked the economy when it was down. Although some economists, such as Friedman, have correctly suggested that the Fed's mismanagement of the economic situation significantly contributed to the Great Depression. Proper monetary policy, or even abstention, they argue, would probably have resulted in a minor recession.

Following the crash, economists claimed that the Federal Reserve was making a huge mistake by keeping money too tight. Editorials from 1930 and 1931 had headlines like *No Wampum* and *More Juice, Please*. Here is an excerpt from one impassioned plea for easier money issued on Aug. 6, 1930: "The Federal Reserve system, instead of continuing a helpful release of credit to counteract the creeping paralysis of deflation, has done nothing."

Freidman demonstrated that the expectations of deflation among well-informed observers were indeed driven by the Fed's monetary contraction, not outside factors. This appears to show that the Fed was to blame and that Friedman was correct. If this result holds up in other narrative sources, it will provide important confirmation of the monetary explanation of the Depression.

As further evidence of Friedman's analysis, business magazine editors weighed in during the height of the Depression. "The deflationists are in the saddle," Business Week editors wrote in October 1930. "Our idle gold hoard piles up without increasing the means of payment by credit expansion because of paralysis of banking policy, thus prolonging price deflation."

Unfortunately, the Fed—and other central banks—didn't listen.

And this, from Sept. 9, 1931, refers to signs of economic weakness: "They are symptoms of a sudden, mysterious, universal shrinkage and shortage of the money and credit medium by which everything is exchanged and the supply of which rests solely in the hands of the world's banking institutions."

By 1933, President Roosevelt rode into office by characterizing a *do-nothing* attitude on the part of the government and the Fed. In truth, however, his predecessor, Herbert Hoover, had done far too much to try to halt the recession following the crash. One of Hoover's main concerns was that workers' wages would be cut following the economic downturn. To ensure artificially high wages among all businesses, he reasoned, prices needed to stay high so companies would continue producing. To keep prices high, consumers with the money would need to pay more. The public had been burned badly in the crash, and most did not have the resources to overpay for products.

This bleak reality forced Hoover to use legislation, the government's trump card, to try to prop up wages. Congress tried to restrict the flow of foreign goods by passing the Smoot-Hawley Tariff Act. Because foreign nations weren't willing to buy over-priced American goods any more than Americans were, Hoover decided to choke out cheap imports. The Smoot-Hawley Act started out as a way to protect agriculture but swelled into a multi-industry tariff. Other nations retaliated with their own tariffs, essentially cutting off international trade. Not surprisingly, the economic conditions worsened worldwide and the U.S. economy sunk from a recession into a depression.

Although Roosevelt promised change when he came into office, he continued Hoover's economic intervention, only on a bigger scale. He created the New Deal with the best intentions, but like Hoover's wage controls, it backfired. With previous recession/depression cycles, the U.S. suffered one to three years of low wages and unemployment before the dropping prices led to a recovery. Responding to this historical trend of a few hard years followed by a recovery, American industrialist, and philanthropist J.D. Rockefeller remarked, "These are days when many are discouraged. In the 93 years of my life, depressions have come and gone. Prosperity has always returned and will again." By attempting to recover immediately without swallowing the bitter pill of two hard years, Hoover and Roosevelt may have prolonged the pain.

The New Deal set lofty goals to maintain public works, full employment, and healthy wages through price, wage, and even production controls. The New Deal was loosely based on Keynesian economics, specifically on the idea that government works can stimulate the economy. Occasionally these projects were ideal, but there were just as many cases of mismanagement, political back-scratching and general waste that accompanies government-run initiatives.

One of the most heartbreaking results of the New Deal was the destruction of excess crops to justify the artificially high prices, despite the need for cheap food. In fact, many of the agencies created by the New Deal broke up black markets selling cheap goods. This forced factory workers to stop working and halted the production that was needed for recovery. Even unemployment remained high because companies couldn't afford to keep large payrolls at the rates set by the government.

Eventually, the economic recovery came in the form of World War II. Some argue that the war ended the Great Depression. The global conflict did open up international trading channels and reversed price and wage controls. Suddenly, the government wanted lots of things made inexpensively and pushed wages and prices below market levels. When the war finished, the trade routes remained open and the post-war era went from recovery to a bull run in a few short years.

The Great Depression was the result of an unlucky combination of factors—a non-committal Fed, protectionist tariffs and a Keynesian, government-centered recovery plan. It could have been shortened or even avoided by a change in any one of these.

Despite some serious downturns and corrections since the crash of 1929 still reigns as the most dreadful market event in history. This is partially because of the severity of the event, but mostly because the entire economy buckled and then broke under the strain, starting America on the way to the Great Depression.

Another general factor that contributed to the Depression was the *get rich quick* mentality that developed during the 1920s. Many Americans believed their fortune was just around the corner. This belief was fueled by the mass production of consumer goods, unsubstantiated advertising in magazines and newspapers, and exotic silent movies telling tales of riches and success. With this *get rich quick* attitude, many Americans began to recklessly spend what little money they had. Hoping to look like glamorous movie stars, they bought a vast array of beauty products.

On a larger scale, many Americans purchased, sight unseen, parcels of land in Florida and southern California. When some investors went to visit the lots that had been purchased, they found swamps or desert. Realizing they had made a poor investment, many turned to the roaring stock market to overcome their losses. Focused on their own individual situations, these people did not recognize that their actions would soon combine with a number of other factors to produce the Great Depression.

Historians recognize a number of causes for the Great Depression, including the following:

(1) Chronic agricultural overproduction and low prices for farm products

(2) Excessive production of consumer goods by manufacturing industries

(3) Concentration of wealth in the hands of a few

(4) The structure of American business and industry itself, which included several large holding companies

(5) Investors' speculation, greed through orchestrated optimism

(6) The lack of action by the Federal Reserve System

(7) An unsound banking system

Here are three different perspectives on the cause of the Great Depression from three different economists.

Keynesian

Keynes saw the causes of the Great Depression as based upon over-production, and a lack of commensurate demand. In 1936, when he published The General Theory of Employment, Interest, and Money, he focused on this factor. His solutions were two-fold. First, through Federal Reserve monetary policy, reduce interest rates. Second, through US government fiscal policy, increase federal spending in the form of infrastructure investment.

Smith and Friedman

Their view would lay the blame on the Federal Reserve and the fall in the money supply. US investors were holding money and consuming less. This caused a contraction in employment and production since prices were not flexible enough to adjust. Friedman was quoted as saying, "The Great Depression, like most other periods of severe unemployment, was produced by government mismanagement rather than by any inherent instability of the private economy."

In most contexts, the term "crash" is used for market downturns that are sudden and harsh. The Great Crash of 1929, however, is used to refer to more than three years of economic misery. While the crash of 1981 almost doubled the single-day loss of Black Tuesday and several subsequent crises have shed more market value, the crash of 1929 encompasses the many crashes, slides and general misery that followed during the Depression years. With any luck, it will remain both the first and last crash to earn the title of "great."

Hayek

Libertarian economists would also lay blame at the feet of the Federal Reserve. The extraordinary rise in credit, fueled by the Fed's easy credit policies, led to an unsustainable credit-driven boom.

Could it happen again?

History repeats itself, but never in exactly the same way. To apply the lessons of the past, one must understand the differences to present circumstances. Let's use the military context by way of example.

During the American Revolution, the British came prepared to fight a successful war, but against a typical European army. Their formations, which gave them devastating firepower, and their red coats, designed to emphasize their strength in numbers, proved the exact opposite of the tactics needed to fight the guerrilla war planned by the colonists.

Before World War I, generals still saw the cavalry as the pride of their armies because of their mobility. Of course, the horse soldiers proved worse than useless in the trenches.

Following the end of World War I, in anticipation of a future German attack, the French built the impenetrable Maginot Line—a series of concrete fortifications, obstacles and weapon installations that France constructed on its borders with Switzerland, Germany and Luxembourg during the 1930s. History repeated itself and the attack came, but not in the way the French expected. Their preparations were useless because the Germans didn't attempt to penetrate it. They simply went around it, and France was defeated.

The military doesn't prepare for the last war out of perversity or stupidity, but rather because past experience guides them. The majority of military leaders don't know how to interpret that experience. They are correct in preparing for another war but wrong in relying upon what worked in the last one.

Investors, unfortunately, seem to make the same mistakes in marshaling their resources as do the generals. If the last thirty years have been prosperous, they base their actions on more prosperity. Talk of a depression isn't real to them because things are, in fact, so different from the 1930s. To most people, a depression means thirties-style conditions, and since they don't see that, they can't imagine a depression. Because most modern-day investors don't know what the last depression was like, it's hard to visualize something you don't understand.

It's impossible to predict with absolute certainty how the next depression will affect the world's economy, but you can be well-assured it won't be an instant replay of the last one. To define the likely differences between the Great Depression, and the next one, it's helpful to compare the situation today to that in the early 1930s.

CORPORATE BANKRUPTCY

1930s

Banks, insurance companies, and big corporations went under on a major scale. Institutions suffered the consequences of past mistakes, and there was no financial safety net to catch them as they fell. Mistakes were liquidated and only the prepared and efficient survived.

Today

The world's financial institutions are in even worse shape than the last time, but now business ethics have changed and everyone expects the government to initiate a bailout. Laws are already in place that not only allow, but require, government intervention in many instances. This time, mistakes will be compounded, and the strong, productive, and efficient will be forced to subsidize the weak, unproductive, and inefficient. It's ironic that businesses were bankrupted in the last depression because the prices of their products fell too low. This time, with the policies put into place after the 2008 market crash, it'll be because prices went too high.

THE UNEMPLOYED
1930s

If a man lost his job, he had to find another one as quickly as possible to keep from going hungry. A lot of other men in the same position competed desperately for what work was available, and an employer could hire those same men for much lower wages and expect them to work harder than what was the case before the Great Depression. As a result, the men could get jobs and the employer could stay in business.

Today

The average unemployed worker has many months of unemployment insurance available. After that, he can go on welfare if he can't find *suitable work*. Instead of taking whatever work is available, especially if it means that a white collar worker has to get his hands dirty, many will go on welfare. This will decrease the production of new wealth and delay the recovery. The worker no longer has to worry about entrepreneurs exploiting (i.e., employing) him at what he considers an unfair wage because the minimum wage laws, among others, precludes that possibility today. As a result, men remain unemployed and employers run the risk of going out of business.

THE WELFARE STATE
1930s

If hard times really put a man down and out, he had little recourse but to rely on his family, friends, or local social and church group. There was quite a bit of shame attached to that, and it was only a last resort. The breadlines set up by various government agencies were largely cosmetic measures to soothe the voting populic. Americans made do because they had to, and that meant radically reducing their standards of living and taking any job available at any wage. There were very few people on welfare during the Great Depression.

Today

There are insufficient Americans working today to support those who aren't. Entitlements in the U.S. are the primary cause of our ever-growing national debt. Half of Americans are on some form of government benefits—before the next Depression. But food stamps, aid to families with dependent children, Social Security, and local programs are already collapsing in prosperous times. And when the tidal wave hits, they'll be totally overwhelmed. There aren't going to be any breadlines because people who would be standing in them are going to be shopping in local supermarkets just like people who earned their money. Perhaps the most dangerous aspect of it is that people in general have come to think that these programs can just magically make wealth appear, and they expect them to be there, while a whole class of people have grown up never learning to survive without them. It's ironic, yet predictable, that the programs that were supposed to help those who are *entitled* to them will serve to devastate those very people.

BURDENSOME REGULATIONS

1930s

Most western economies have been fairly heavily regulated since the early 1900s, and those regulations caused distortions that added to the severity of the Great Depression. Rather than allow the economy to liquidate, in the case of the U.S., the Roosevelt administration added many more regulations fixing prices, wages, and the manner of doing business. It was largely because of these regulations that the Great Depression lingered on until World War II, which saved the economy only through its massive reinflation of the U.S. currency. Economists believe that had the government abolished most controls then in existence, instead of creating new ones, the Depression would have been less severe and much shorter.

Today

The scores of new agencies set up since the Great Depression have created far more severe distortions in the ways people relate than those of eighty years ago. Unless government restrictions and controls on wages, working conditions, energy consumption, safety, and such are removed, a dramatic economic turnaround during the next depression will be impossible.

TAX BURDEN

1930s

The income tax was new to the U.S. in 1913, and by 1929, although it took a maximum 23.1% bite, that was only at the $1 million level. The average family's income then was $2,335, and that put average families in the 1/10th of 1 percent bracket. At the time, there was no Social Security tax, no state income tax, no sales tax, and no estate tax. Furthermore, most people in the country didn't even pay the income tax because they earned less than the legal minimum. The government, therefore, had immense untapped sources of revenue to draw upon to fund its schemes to counteract effects of the Great Depression. Roosevelt was able to raise the average income tax from 1.35% to 16.56% during his terms in office—an increase of 1,100%.

Today

Everyone now pays an income tax in addition to all the other taxes levied by the federal, state, and local governments. In most Western countries, the total of direct and indirect taxes is over fifty percent. For that reason, it seems unlikely that direct taxes will go much higher. But inflation is constantly driving everyone into higher brackets and will have the same effect. A family must increase their income faster than inflation to compensate for taxes. Whatever taxes a man does pay will reduce his standard of living by just that much, and it's reasonable to expect tax evasion and the underground economy would boom in response.

PRICES OF GOODS AND SERVICES

1930s

Prices dropped radically because billions of dollars of inflationary currency were wiped out through the stock market crash, bond defaults, and bank failures. The government, however, somehow equated the high prices of the inflationary 1920s with prosperity and attempted to prevent a fall in prices by such things as slaughtering livestock, dumping milk in the gutter, and enacting price supports. Since the collapse wiped out money faster than it could be created, the government felt the destruction of real wealth was a more effective way to raise prices. In other words, if you can't increase the supply of money, decrease the supply of goods-basic Keynesian economics.

Nonetheless, the Great Depression was a deflationary collapse, a time when currency became worth more and prices dropped. Most Americans will assume—as a result of that experience—that *depression* means *deflation*. It's also perhaps the biggest single difference between this depression and the last one.

Today

Prices could drop as they did during the Great Depression, but the amount of power the government now has over the economy is far greater than what was the case eighty-five years ago. Instead of letting the economy cleanse itself by allowing the financial markets to collapse, governments will probably bail out insolvent banks, create government-backed debt to prop up real estate, the automobile industry, and education while the world's central banks will buy bonds to keep their currency values from plummeting. All of these actions mean that the total money supply will grow enormously. Trillions will be created to avoid deflation.

Consumer prices will probably skyrocket as a result, and the country will have an inflationary depression. Unlike the 1930s, when people who held dollars were king, by the end of the next depression, people holding dollars will be wiped out.

SOCIETAL COLLAPSE

1930s

The world was largely rural at the time of the Great Depression. Communications were slow, but people tended to trust the media. The government exercised considerable moral persuasion, and people tended to support it. The business of the country was business, as Calvin Coolidge said, and men who created wealth were esteemed. All told, if you were going to have a depression, it was a rather stable environment for it. Despite this *we're all in this together* mindset, however, there were still plenty of riots, marches, and societal unrest.

Today

The country is now urban and suburban, and although communications are rapid, there's little interpersonal contact. The mainstream media is suspect and viewed with contempt. The government is seen more as an adversary, or tyrannical, than as an arbitrator accepted by a consensus of concerned citizens. Businessmen are viewed as unscrupulous predators who take advantage of anyone weak enough to be exploited.

A major financial downturn in today's atmosphere could do a lot more than wipe out a few poorly positioned investors in the stock market and unemploy some workers, as occurred in the Great Depression. Some sectors of society are now ticking time bombs. How will Americans react to a notification that their banks are closed and their government entitlements are cut-off?

THE WAY PEOPLE WORK

1930s

Relatively slow transportation and communication localized economic conditions. The U.S. itself was somewhat insulated from the rest of the world, and parts of the nation were relatively self-contained. Workers were mostly involved in basic agriculture and industry, creating widgets and other tangible items. There wasn't a reliance on specialized training which made it easier for someone to move laterally from one occupation to the next, without extensive retraining, since people were more able to produce the basics of life on their own. Most women never joined the workforce, and the wife in a marriage acted as a *backup* should the husband lose his job.

Today

The whole world is interdependent, and a war in the Middle East or a military skirmish on the Korean Peninsula can have a direct and immediate effect on a retail store owner in Atlanta or Berlin. Since the whole economy is centrally controlled from Washington, a mistake there can be a national disaster. People generally aren't in a position to roll with the punches as more than half the people in the country belong to what is known as the *service economy*. That means, in most cases, they're better equipped to shuffle papers than make widgets. Even *necessary services* are often terminated when times get hard. Specialization is part of what an advanced industrial economy is all about, but if the economic order changes radically, it can prove a liability.

THE FINANCIAL MARKETS

1930s

The Great Depression is identified with the collapse of the stock market, which lost over ninety percent of its value from 1929 to 1933. A secure bond was the best possible investment as interest rates dropped radically. Commodities plummeted, reducing millions of farmers to near subsistence levels. Since most real estate was owned outright and taxes were low, a drop in price didn't make a lot of difference unless you had to sell. Land prices plummeted, but since people bought it to use, not for speculation, they didn't usually have to sell.

Today

In the current economic climate, both stocks and commodities are likely to increase in value. Real estate will be, next to bonds, the most devastated single area of the economy because no one will lend money long term. And real estate is built on the mortgage market, which will vanish.

The differences in the economic conditions of the Great Depression and the climate of today run deeper than this brief summary. The similarities can be summed up as follows: The crucial, obvious, and most important similarity, however, is that most people's standard of living will fall dramatically. Some economists believe the next depression is in its early stages. Most people don't know it because they can neither confront the thought nor understand the differences between this one and the 1930s version.

As the collapse approaches, perhaps exacerbated by a catastrophic event, many of the things that you've built your life around in the past are going to change dramatically. The ability to adjust to new conditions is the sign of a psychologically healthy person. Look for the opportunity side of the crisis. The Chinese symbol for *crisis* is a combination of two other symbols—one for danger and one for opportunity.

The risks that society will face in the years ahead are regrettable, but there's no point in allowing anxiety, frustration, or apathy to overcome you. Face the future with courage, curiosity, and optimism rather than fear. You can be a survivor of the coming economic collapse if you prepare carefully.

Could it happen again? Without a doubt.

CHAPTER FIFTEEN
THE GREATEST MARKET CRASHES

Economic collapse has occurred throughout history, but there are varying degrees of market crashes. It's important to identify the differences between crashes, corrections, and bubbles.

A stock market bubble is a rare event, but in today's 24/7 media cycle and entire networks being devoted just to the coverage of financial markets, the term gets overused. The media has a tendency to use the word bubble whenever they deem an asset to be overvalued.

An economic bubble occurs when fluctuations in market trading drive the equities' price above their value. Bubbles are also associated with human behavioral theory and their mentality. A bubble takes place when investors put so much demand on a stock that they drive the price beyond any accurate or reasonable measure of its actual value. Prudent investing dictates that a stock price should be determined by the performance of the underlying company. Like a helium filled balloon, market bubbles appear as though they will rise into space, but since they are not formed on any rational basis, they eventually pop. When the bubble bursts, the investment disappears.

A market crash is a sudden drop in the value of financial markets all across the spectrum, not just stocks, but also commodities, oil, and tulips. Yes, Tulipmania is commonly known as the first stock market crash.

Typically associated with the popping of a bubble, a market crash is a situation wherein the majority of investors are trying to flee the market at the same time, causing a massive loss in total market value. Attempting to avoid more losses, investors during a crash create panic selling, hoping to unload their declining stocks onto other investors. This panic selling contributes to the declining market, which eventually crashes and affects everyone. Throughout history, market crashes have been associated with an economic depression.

It is important to note the distinction between a crash and a correction, which can be a bit sticky at times. A correction is a warning sign to overly optimistic investors. A correction is a negative movement in the stock market of at least ten percent, but doesn't exceed a twenty percent loss of value. Surprisingly, some crashes have been erroneously labeled as corrections, including the terrifying crash of 1987. They are also considered temporary, lasting only days or weeks. A correction is also more substantial than the traditional *bear market*. A crash is characterized by a sudden and dramatic decline, across multiple markets, for a sustained period of time.

In addition to The Great Depression, here are some other market crashes of note.

Tulipmania: 1634, Holland

Over four hundred years ago, the entire country of Holland became obsessed with tulips. A flower native to Turkey, it became such a novelty that its price was driven higher and higher. Having been introduced into a non-native environment, the tulips contracted a rare virus called a *mosaic*. This virus did not kill the plant, but it altered the genetics of the flowers to create a beautiful array of colors to appear on the petals, much like a flame. The unusual color combinations and patterns only increased the desire of the Dutch for the tulip bulbs.

The rarity of this beautiful flower grew as demand skyrocketed. The bulbs, which were already selling at a premium, began to gain value according to their *mosaic* alterations. Soon, everyone in the country started dealing in the bulbs, creating a massive speculative market—a bubble.

Dutch bulb buyers, the predecessor to your local garden center, began to fill up inventories for the growing season, depleting the supply further and increasing scarcity and demand. Prices began rising so fast and high that people were trading their land, life savings, and anything else they could liquidate to get more tulip bulbs. Many

Dutch persisted in believing they would sell their hoard to hapless and unenlightened foreigners, thereby reaping enormous profits. During one period of trading, the already overpriced tulips gained twenty time their value—in one month!

The price swings were not caused by increases in production costs or an increased usage required for the greater good of the Dutch people. Tulipmania was a result of irrational, rampant speculation on a particular commodity. A bubble was created, artificially raising the value of the commodity, in this case tulips, and when the bubble burst, the value of the commodity crashed hard. A domino effect of progressively lower and lower prices took place as everyone tried to sell while demand was very low. The bubble was ready to explode because the prices were not an accurate reflection of the value of a tulip bulb.

The South Sea Bubble: 1711, United Kingdom

In the eighteenth century, the British Empire was the western world's largest trading partner. It was a period of growth and opulence for the British, especially the wealthy who had a significant amount of disposal income to invest. The South Sea Company was one of the few companies offering stock shares at the time. Along with the East India Company, the South Sea Company enjoyed favorable relationships with the British government, and its trading partners throughout Europe and the Mediterranean.

The first issue of stock available to the public was sold in days. Stories began to circulate that the company would be delivering goods to the Americas, which fueled the speculative activity. The South Sea Company issued more shares, which were quickly bought up by investors. When it was formally announced that the South Sea Company was granted a monopoly in trade with Spain's colonies in South America and the West Indies as part of a treaty made after the War of the Spanish Succession, investors were whipped into a fever pitch. They bid the South Sea Company's shares and the shares of similar trading companies to incredible heights in a typical speculative bubble fashion.

This spurred similar stock issues in companies that promised to reclaim sunshine from vegetables and to build floating mansions to extend Britain's landmass. The perceived successes of these new ventures stirred British pride, and, believing that British companies could not fail, investors were desperate to invest their money.

Not long after virtually all classes of British society were thoroughly engaged in wild stock speculation, the South Sea Bubble popped and stock prices violently collapsed, financially ruining their investors. Eventually, the officers and directors of the South Sea Company realized that the value of their personal shares in no way reflected the actual value of the company. In the summer of 1720, they sold their stocks and hoped no one would leak the failure of the company to the other shareholders. Like all bad news, however, the knowledge of the actions of management spread, and the panic selling of worthless certificates ensued. The value of the South Sea Company came crashing down.

A complete market crash was avoided due to the resilient economic position of the British Empire and the government's help in stabilizing the banking industry. As a result of the South Sea Bubble, the British government outlawed the issuing of stock certificates, a law that was not repealed for a hundred years.

The Florida Swamp Land: 1926, United States

In the 1920s, Florida was the site of a real estate bubble fueled by easy credit and advertisers promoting a lifestyle of sunshine and relaxation. The US economy was at the top of its game, growing on a par with the British Empire, two hundred years prior. It was natural that people were beginning to believe such prosperity was here to stay. Unlike the South Sea Company bubble, it wasn't the stock market that was the recipient of overinflated values. It was the real estate market.

By 1920, Florida became the popular U.S. destination for people who wanted to flee the cold of winter—the *snowbirds*. The population was growing steadily, and housing couldn't match the demand, causing prices to double and triple in some cases, which was not exactly unjustified at this point. But, news of anything doubling and tripling in price always attracts speculators. So, once people began pumping huge amounts of money into the Florida real estate market, it exploded. Soon everyone in Florida was either a real estate investor or a real estate agent.

Historical news reports describe a collective madness that consumed Florida land investors. Lots in Miami were bought and sold as many as ten times in a single day. Property that could be bought for $800,000 could, within a year, be resold for $4 million. People from the north were buying swamp land.

Land prices quadrupled in less than a year. Eventually, however, there became a shortage of investors for the Florida swamp land, and prices for the ridiculously overvalued properties began to adjust. Land speculators began to recognize that there was a limit to the craze and sold their properties to collect profits while they could. Other speculators also saw the writing on the wall, and panic selling ensued. With thousands of sellers and very few buyers, prices came down with a sickening thud.

The perceived wisdom holds that a 1926 hurricane helped burst the bubble, but house price indicators and historical construction data suggest that the boom and bust were in fact a nationwide phenomenon. The housing price downturn in 1926 led to a rise in the foreclosure rate of residential properties which also increased in 1926, rising steadily through the stock market bubble and peaking in 1933.

The Market Crash of 1987: United States

The Stock Market Crash of October 19th, 1987—*Black Monday*—was the largest one-day market crash in history. The Dow lost nearly twenty-three percent of its value, or $500 billion dollars.

Stock market investors enjoyed record profits in 1986 and 1987. These years were an extension of an incredibly powerful bull market that had started in the summer of 1982. This bull market had been fueled by low-interest rates, leveraged buyouts, and merger mania.

Institutional investors and large companies were scrambling to raise capital to buy each other out. The philosophy of the time was that businesses could grow exponentially simply by constantly acquiring other companies. In a leveraged buyout, a company would raise a massive amount of capital by selling junk bonds to the public.

Junk bonds are bonds that pay high-interest rates due to their high risk of default. The capital raised through selling junk bonds would go toward the purchase of the desired company.

IPOs were also becoming a commonplace driver of market excitement. An IPO or Initial Public Offering is when a company issues stock to the public for the first time.

The investing public eventually became caught up in a contagious euphoria which made investors, as usual, believe that the stock market would continue to rise. Then, in early 1987, there was a rash of SEC investigations into insider trading. For the most part, people were aware of the tendency of Wall Street to look out for itself, but the barrage of SEC investigations rattled investors. By October, investors decided to move out of the stock market and into the more stable environment offered by bonds or, in some cases, junk bonds.

During this time frame, inflation and an overheating economy became a concern due to the high rate of economic and credit growth. The Federal Reserve rapidly raised short-term interest rates to temper inflation, which had the desired effect of lowering some of stock investors' enthusiasm.

As interest rates rose, many institutional money managers scrambled to hedge their portfolios at the same time. On Black Monday, the stock index futures market was flooded with billions of dollars' worth of sell orders within minutes, causing both the futures and stock markets to crash. Also, many common stock investors attempted to sell simultaneously, which completely overwhelmed the stock exchanges.

$500 billion in market capitalization was evaporated from the Dow Jones stock index. Exchanges in nearly every country around the world plunged in a similar fashion. When individual investors heard that a massive stock market crash was occurring, they rushed to call their brokers to sell their stocks. This was unsuccessful because each broker had many clients.

Many people lost millions of dollars instantly. News reports began to surface of some unstable individuals who had lost significant amounts of money who went to their broker's office with a gun and started shooting. A few brokers were killed despite the fact they had no control over the markets.

The majority of investors who were selling did not know why they were selling except for the fact that everyone else was selling. This emotionally-charged behavior is one of the main reasons that the stock market crashed so dramatically. After the Black Monday plunge, many futures and stock exchanges were shut down for a day to allow reasonable minds to return.

Japan, The Lost Decade: 1989 - ?, Southeast Asia

Around the turn of the twenty-first century, the phrase *lost decade* began to be applied to Japan's economic performance over the course of the 1990s. The lost decade started with the popping of one of the greatest stock market bubbles in history.

The Japanese economy gained extreme strength after its long recovery from World War II. By joining other emerging Southeast Asian economies to form an unstoppable economic force, Japan seemed to have created an economic powerhouse. The phrase *Japan Inc.* was coined to describe how the Japanese economy, business, and government were intertwined. Businesses from all over the world were sending representatives to try and find out how Japan was gaining its success. In true business fashion, the Japanese built an industry around visitors with company expense accounts and profited off the corporate spies. Soon, the Asian economy became an alternative for investors who were recently bruised by the US market crash of 1987.

For decades, land prices in Japan appreciated by seventy times and stocks increased a hundred times over. Stock trading became a hobby for every Japanese investor, and the Japanese jumped into the market with more blind confidence than that of the Americans of the 1920s. During the eighties, large Tokyo trading firms were worth more individually than all their American counterparts combined.

Investors began to suspect Japan was becoming a market bubble, but it was thought that the high level of collusion between the Tokyo government and business interests could sustain the growth. Balance sheet manipulation began in the form of large real estate holding companies using the book value of their land to buy stocks that they, in turn, used to finance the purchase of American assets.

As the affluence of the Roman Empire, the prosperity of Japan proved to be its undoing as corruption began to spread throughout the political and business world.

The government sought to put a halt to the unrealistic growth of stocks and real estate by raising interest rates. This didn't have the slow, calming effect on the market that the Tokyo government hoped. Instead, it plunged the Nikkei index down over thirty thousand points. Japan's Nikkei 225 Index hit an all-time high of 38,916 in December 1989, and then began a sickening 80% crash to a low of 7,831 in April 2003.

The bursting of the Asian bubble nearly took out the American economy as well, but SEC measures enacted after 1987 stopped the avalanche of program trading.

But the lost decade included more than just stock market losses. Japan also saw crashing property values, falling interest rates, rising unemployment, declining and stagnant GDP, and the worst demographic profile of any major economy. In short, Japan exhibited all of the hallmarks of a depression of the kind not seen since the 1930s in the U.S.

As the term *lost decade* became widely used by economists, an interesting thing happened. Another decade passed and the Japanese economy was still in recession. Today, a full twenty-five years after the bubble burst in Japan, that country continues to struggle with deflation, zero interest rates, under-capitalized banks, adverse demographics, and periodic bouts of negative growth. Japan has endured a twenty-five year recession, and there is no end in sight.

The Dotcom Crash: 2000 - 2002, United States

During this period, the value of equity markets grew exponentially, with the technology-dominated Nasdaq index rising from under 1,000 in 1995, to 5,000 by the year 2000.

The dotcom bubble grew out of a combination of the presence of speculative, emotion-based investing, the abundance of venture capital funding for startups and the failure of dotcoms to turn a profit. Investors poured money into internet startups during the 1990s in the hope that those companies would one day become profitable, and many investors and venture capitalists abandoned a cautious approach for fear of not being able to cash in on the growing use of the internet.

The media filled investors with a rabid hunger for more. The IPOs of internet companies emerged with ferocity and frequency, sweeping the nation up in euphoria. Investors were blindly grabbing every new issue without even looking at a business plan to find out, for example, how long the company would take before making a profit, if ever.

In the year 1999, there were 457 IPOs, most of which were internet and technology related. Of those 457 IPOs, 117 doubled in price on the first day of trading. In 2001, the number of IPOs dwindled to 76, and none of them doubled on the first day of trading.

Obviously, there was a problem. The first pinpricks of this bubble came from the companies themselves. Many recipients of these hot IPOs reported huge losses and some folded outright within months of their offering. Many analysts argued that the dotcom boom and bust was a case of too much too fast. Companies were given millions of dollars and told to grow to Microsoft size by tomorrow.

The stock market crash of 2000–2002 caused the loss of $5 trillion in the market value of companies. The September 11, 2001, attacks accelerated the stock market drop causing the NYSE to suspend trading for four sessions.

Turning to the long-term legacy of the bubble, Fred Wilson, who was a venture capitalist during the rise and fall of the dotcom bubble, said:

"A friend of mine has a great line. He says 'Nothing important has ever been built without irrational exuberance'. Meaning that you need some of this mania to cause investors to open up their pocketbooks and finance the building of the railroads or the automobile or aerospace industry or whatever. And in this case, much of the capital invested was lost, but also, much of it was invested in a very high throughput backbone for the Internet, and lots of software that works, and databases and server structure. All that stuff has allowed what we have today, which has changed all our lives, that's what all this speculative mania built".

The Great Recession, Housing Bubble, & Credit Crisis: 2007, United States

The S&P 500 declined 57% from its high in October 2007 of 1576 to its low in March 2009 of 676.

Following the bursting of the tech bubble and the recession of the early 2000s, the Federal Reserve kept short-term interest rates low for an extended period of time. This coincided with a global savings glut, as developing countries and commodity producing nations accumulated large financial reserves. As these excess savings were invested, global interest rates declined to record low levels. Frustrated with low returns, investors began to assume more risk by seeking higher returns wherever they could be found. For several years, global financial markets entered a period which came to be called the *Great Moderation* due to the above-average returns and below-average volatility demonstrated by a wide variety of asset classes.

In the United States, the Great Moderation coincided with a housing boom, as prices soared (particularly on the two coasts and in cities such as Phoenix and Las Vegas.) Rising home prices led to rampant real estate speculation, and also fueled excessive consumer spending as people began to view their homes as *a piggy bank* that they could extract cash from to fuel discretionary purchases. As home prices soared and many homeowners stretched to make their mortgage payments, the possibility of a collapse grew. However, the true extent of the danger was hidden because so many mortgages had been securitized and turned into AAA-rated securities called *derivatives*.

When the long-held belief that home prices do not decline proved to be inaccurate, prices on mortgage-backed securities plunged, prompting massive losses for banks and other financial institutions. These losses soon spread to other asset classes, fueling a crisis of confidence in the health of many of the world's largest banks. Events reached their climax with the bankruptcy of Lehman Brothers in

September 2008, which resulted in a credit freeze that brought the global financial system to the brink of complete collapse.

Unprecedented central bank actions combined with fiscal stimulus (notably in the US and China) helped ease some of the panic in the marketplace, but by late winter 2009, widespread rumors surfaced that Citigroup, Bank of America, and other large banks would have to be nationalized if the global economy was to survive. Fortunately, the aggressive actions by governments around the world eventually helped avoid financial collapse, but the credit freeze forced the global economy into the worst recession since World War 2.

The credit crisis and accompanying recession caused unprecedented volatility in financial markets. Stocks fell fifty percent or more from their highs through March 2009 before rallying more than fifty percent once the crisis began to ease. In addition to stocks, most fixed income markets also displayed unprecedented volatility, with many corporate bond markets at one point forecasting bankruptcies at a level not seen since the Great Depression. Oil fell seventy percent, then doubled as the financial system stabilized.

The events of the housing bubble and credit crisis are likely to resonate with consumers and investors for years to come. In many countries (including the U.S.) consumers remain heavily leveraged, and many homeowners are *underwater*. As consumers deleverage and repair their finances, their purchasing patterns will be permanently altered. Many developed market countries have also seen a substantial deterioration in their fiscal position. While government actions helped prevent worst-case outcomes from the credit crisis, massive budget deficits now represent a structural problem that may take decades to solve.

Finally, investors have experienced the most volatile and frightening markets of their lives. Positive lessons, such as the importance of diversification and independent analysis can be taken from the crisis, but there are also emotional effects that must be considered. Investors that can incorporate the lessons of the credit crisis without having their emotions unduly influenced will be best positioned for future investment success.

As hindsight is always 20/20, we should take the time to highlight what we can learn from these past tragedies.

First off, we should point out that most market volatility is all our fault. In reality, people create most of the risk in the marketplace by inflating stock prices beyond the value of the underlying company. When stocks are flying through the stratosphere like rockets, it is usually a sign of a bubble. That's not to say that stocks cannot legitimately enjoy a huge leap in value, but this leap should be justified by the prospects of the underlying companies, not just by a mass of investors following each other. The unreasonable belief in the possibility of getting rich quick is the primary reason people get burned by market crashes. Remember that if you put your money into investments that have a high potential for returns, you must also be willing to bear a great chance of losing it all.

Another observation we should make is that regardless of our measures to correct the problems, the time between crashes has decreased. We had centuries of market crashes, then decades, and now years. We cannot say whether this foretells anything dire for the future, but the best thing you can do is keep yourself educated, informed, and well-prepared by doing research.

CHAPTER SIXTEEN
WHO'S NEXT?

There are as many as two dozen nations around the globe facing a full-blown debt crisis which puts them on the edge of economic collapse. Overall, the debt to GDP ratio around the world is nearly three hundred per cent. The total amount of debt outstanding is well over $200 Trillion. Nations have stopped looking for solutions and have actively pursued an easier alternative to dealing with their incredible debt. They delay. Let's take a look at some of the more prominent examples, followed by a dozen or more nations on the brink.

Latin America, especially Mexico, Venezuela, and Brazil

Falling oil prices and uncertainty in the world's largest economies appear to have hit the three biggest economies in Latin America hard. These economic struggles, when coupled with political instability, indicate that the region will face dire financial consequences into 2016.

Brazil is Deteriorating Rapidly

The largest economy in Latin America is a shadow of its former self. Economic activity is estimated to be shrinking at five percent per year. The hopes of a boost from the upcoming Olympic games have been doused as a result of Zika virus fears

According to economists, growth is unlikely to return before 2018—seven years of zero or negative growth for Latin America's largest economy.

At the beginning of August 2015, the Brazilian currency was trading against the U.S. dollar at its lowest level in years, and inflation has been predicted to surpass nine percent, which prompted a half-percentage-point hike in interest rates by the Brazilian central bank in

2015—the largest rate hike in a decade.

Activity in Brazil's service sector was at its lowest point since the world financial crisis of 2007-2009, and the unemployment rate grew to nearly nine percent in the second quarter of 2015, as nine million of the country's two hundred and four million people became jobless.

Consumer confidence has fallen to its lowest level since 2005 — when measurements began — and Moody's downgraded the country's bond rating to Baa3, with a negative outlook.

Economists at Moody's opined that the "combined output of the manufacturing and service sectors suffered the largest fall since early-2009. Weak demand, high-interest rates, fiscal tightening, strong inflation and rising unemployment are expected to continue to hamper activity."

The economic calamities facing Brazil has caused considerable political instability. This downturn would, on its own, likely be enough to imperil any government. But there's also a wide-ranging corruption scandal involving the state-owned oil company Petrobras that has ensnared many leading politicians, including President Dilma Rousseff, and has led to a wave of resignations and indictments.

The resiliency of Brazil's democratic institutions signals that the country may survive this contentious political atmosphere. If the government doesn't sink with the nation's economic ship, the independence of the judiciary and continued investigations by law enforcement suggest that, in the end, it may strengthen the quality of Brazil's democracy, forcing it to open up and become more accountable.

As for the economy, the jury is still out. Consider this recent reporting from CNN:

"Amid political chaos, Brazil's economic collapse is worse than its government once believed. In the midst of rising calls to impeach President Dilma Rousseff, Brazil's central bank announced Thursday that it now expects the country's economy to shrink 3.5% this year. That's worse than the central bank's previous estimate for a 1.9% contraction. The darker forecast matches what the International Monetary Fund projected for

Brazil — Latin America's largest country — and what many independent economists have suspected."

Mexico's Ailing Economy and a Crime-Filled Nation

Latin America's second-largest economy faces its broad set of challenges. Mexico opened 2015 with a GDP growth forecast that reached as high as four percent. Throughout the year, growth estimates shed percentage points, with the final number reflecting just one percent growth.

Some Mexican states, those with trade links to the US, have continued to grow, while others — ones with energy-focused economies, in particular — have slowed faster than expected.

Other national trends have stoked concern. The Mexico peso reached a value of seventeen to the dollar in late 2015, which was a new historical low signaling a fifteen percent depreciation over the previous year. Many Mexicans blamed the government for the tumble, and a majority, when polled, doubted it would recover.

Some economists have suggested a cheaper peso could boost exports, but depreciation in other national currencies appears to have stalled that increase. One Latin American expert on emerging markets, Carlos Petersen, cautioned, "The Central Bank of Mexico has argued that given the orderly depreciation of the peso, prices have not been affected, but this cannot be discarded from happening in the future."

Many other regional economists, however, claim that a weakening peso at a time of stagnant or negligible economic growth could trigger a debt crisis as the dollar-denominated debt held by Mexican corporations with peso-denominated operating income becomes increasingly difficult to service.

As a result of this economic downturn, Mexican workers have experienced growing poverty and a striking wealth gap. The numbers bear this out. By the end of 2012, more than half of all Mexicans were living in poverty. Two million more joined them by 2014. By the end of 2015, more than half the country reportedly fell short of the monthly minimum income level that is set by the Mexican government.

Mexicans also saw their purchasing power decline, and, between 1994 and 2012, wages grew just two percent when adjusted for inflation. Regarding real GDP growth, Mexico is eighteenth of twenty countries among Latin American economies.

On the other end of the spectrum, only twenty-five hundred Mexicans — about two-thousandths of a percent of the population — hold forty-three percent of the country's total individual wealth.

In addition to economic hardship, many Mexicans have also had to endure widespread violence. In 2015, a multitude of innocent Mexican citizens have been killed in suspected attacks by police, hundreds of migrants have been kidnapped or killed, journalists have been slain, and politicians have been assassinated without hesitation.

Despite the fact that Mexico faces a mixed economic outlook, the weakening currency has not yet led to inflation or higher prices. The goal of the weakened peso, a major boost to exports, has not materialized. Unlike the major economic nations of the world, the Mexican government has few tools to meaningfully boost growth, which is an indicator that its economy will only worsen in the years to come.

Venezuela is on the Verge of Economic Collapse

As of spring, 2016, the only question on economist's mind is whether Venezuela's government or its economy, will completely collapse first. At the start of 2014, economists at Barclays declared the economy of Venezuela to be beyond the point of no return and that a bankruptcy in 2016 will be near impossible to avoid.

Both the socialist government of Nicolas Maduro, and the economy which suffers under his rule, are under tremendous pressure. In recent elections, Venezuela's ruling party's losses gave the opposition a veto-proof majority. Recently the UK Independent added, "it's hard to see that getting any better for them anytime soon. Incumbents, after all, don't tend to do too well when, according to the IMF, their economy shrinks ten percent in one year, an additional six percent the next, and inflation explodes to 720 percent."

Bloomberg reported that the inflation rate for 2015 was in excess of 275 percent, and that the 2016 number will easily surpass 720 percent. It's no wonder, then, that markets expect Venezuela to default on its debt in the very near future. The country is technically bankrupt.

That's not an easy thing to do when you have the largest oil reserves in the world, but Venezuela has managed it. How? The first step was when Hugo Chávez's socialist government started spending more money on the poor, with everything from two-cent gasoline to free housing. The problem with these socialist policies is that the Venezuelan government didn't have the money. Despite having one of the planet's most precious commodities, oil, the Chavez government destroyed the economic potential of being a part of OPEC.

Chávez turned Petróleos de Venezuela, S.A. (PDVSA), the state-owned oil company from being professionally run to being barely run. People who knew what they were doing were replaced with people who were loyal to the regime, and profits came out but new investment didn't go in. The destruction of PDVSA was particularly devastating because Venezuela's extra-heavy crude needs to be blended or refined — neither of which is cheap — before it can be sold. So Venezuela just hasn't been able to churn out as much oil as it used to without upgraded or even maintained infrastructure. Specifically, oil production fell twenty-five percent between 1999 and 2013.

The rest is a familiar tale of fiscal woe. Even the triple-digit oil prices of summer, 2008, weren't enough to keep Venezuela out of the red when it was spending more on its people but producing less crude. So it did what all poorly run states do when the money runs out—it printed a lot more. When the crude oil prices started collapsing in mid-2014, Venezuela fired up the printing presses even more. The result of all this money-printing is that Venezuela's currency has lost over ninety percent of its value since 2014.

The Maduro government has tried to deny economic reality with price and currency controls. The Washington Post summed up the scheme this way:

"The idea was that it could stop inflation without having to stop printing money by telling businesses what they were allowed to charge, and then giving them dollars on cheap enough terms that they could actually afford to sell at those prices. The problem with that idea is that it's not profitable for unsubsidized companies to stock their shelves, and not profitable enough for subsidized ones to do so either when they can just sell their dollars in the black market instead of using them to import things. That's left Venezuela's supermarkets without enough food, its breweries without enough hops to make beer, and its factories without enough pulp to produce toilet paper. The only thing Venezuela is well-supplied with are lines."

The failed policies of Socialist President Maduro has hastened the collapse. He has changed the law so the opposition-controlled National Assembly can't remove the central bank governor or appoint a new one. Also, Maduro has picked a staunch socialist who doesn't believe in the concept of inflation but is a firm believer in *corporate greed*. During his first speech after being appointed by President Maduro, Governor Eudomar Tovar said:

"When a person goes to a shop and finds that prices have gone up, they are not in the presence of 'inflation,' but rather "parasitic" businesses that are trying to push up profits as much as possible."

According to the Governor's theory, printing too much money never causes inflation. And so Venezuela will continue to do so. If past examples of hyperinflationary periods are any guide, this will keep going until Venezuela can't afford to run its printing presses anymore, or until radical regime change takes place, whichever comes first. But for now, Venezuela is a modern day example of the failed economic policies followed by the Roman Empire, and others.

In the United States, there are still people who doubt that an economic crisis is happening. But in Mexico, Venezuela and Brazil there is no debate.

Unfortunately, what is happening in Venezuela and Brazil is also slowly starting to happen to most of the rest of the planet as well. It is just that they are a little farther down the road. Economic and financial bubbles are bursting all over the world.

"Deflationary tides are lapping the shores of countries across the world, and financial bubbles are set to burst everywhere," said Vikram Mansharamani, a lecturer at Yale University, during a CNBC interview at the Global Financial Markets Forum in Abu Dhabi in January 2016. He continued, "I think it all started with the China investment bubble that has burst and that brought with it commodities. That pushed deflation around the world and those ripples are landing on the shore of countries literally everywhere."

Russia

Despite outward appearances to the contrary, some economists argue that the days of Russian President Vladimir Putin's regime are numbered. As the countdown to Russia's economy demise begins, many experts are predicting chaos for Russia. The Russian economic conditions have been affecting a broad swath of Russians since the beginning of 2015 and the collapse of world oil prices.

HSBC economists report not only have wages in Russia not increased, but an increasingly large number of Russian firms have also started delaying payment of wages. The value of the Russian ruble is plummeting day by day, losing value to the US dollar consistently throughout 2015— to its lowest levels since the end of the 1990s.

The collapse of Russia's economy is explained by plummeting oil prices, which dropped to below $30 per barrel. Further, Russia's budget is in an unsustainable, high deficit condition, as it directly depends on rising oil prices.

Meanwhile, Russia's bank system is imploding, leaving Moscow without sufficient funds for its operations. With Western economic sanctions put in place during the Crimean and Ukrainian conflicts, Russia is limited in its options to seek assistance.

These sanctions have curtailed Russian access to funding based in dollar and euro currencies, leading to a contraction in access to cash for Russia-based companies that have a $44 billion amount of debt payment due in 2016. The Russian economy is heavily dependent on the energy sector, and plunging oil prices from the second half of 2015 onwards has hurt the Russian economy further.

The Ukraine crisis prompted a number of governments to apply sanctions against individuals and businesses from Russia and Ukraine starting in March 2014. Sanctions were approved by a combination of nations including the US, the European Union and numerous other countries and international organizations.

Russia has responded to this with sanctions of their own against a number of countries. These Russian sanctions now include a full ban on food imported from the EU, US, Norway, Canada and Australia. Both of these sets of sanctions applied to Russia and Russia's import bans in response have contributed to the collapse of the ruble and the 2014–16 Russian financial crisis.

As a result, businesses and investors have been leaving the nation — in particular there has been a flight of global banks out of Russia's borders. Along with these banks, there has been a reduction of capital, further exacerbating the fall in the ruble's value.

Faced with the economic downturn and its consequences, many of these banks have had to face up to the reality of their toxic-asset holdings, and this has forced them to close down or merge with other banks. The banking and financial-services sector has grown to a disproportionate, hard-to-control size. It appears that only those with the largest, most resilient balance sheets will be able to survive the turmoil that the Russian economy is suffering.

Economists predict that no matter what emergency measures Russia's leadership is willing to take, the outcome does not look good for the country. Russia's economy is approaching its demise.

Russia is on the brink of economic collapse, a British economist has warned. William Browder, CEO of Hermitage Capital (a Russian-focused investment firm) warned that Russia is approaching *chaos* due to global oil prices. While Moscow is hanging on, for now, Mr. Browder, a long-time critic of Putin's regime, warned that Russia is about to fall into a huge and deep hole of economic collapse. The investment manager explained that Russia's aggressive actions in Ukraine and Syria were to blame for Russia's current economic crisis, since the West imposed economic sanction on Putin's nation, destroying any hopes for economic growth.

This is exacerbating matters as oil prices worldwide have plummeted, hitting hard Russia's biggest export. "I don't think you can underestimate how bad the situation in Russia is right now. You've got oil below any measure where the budget can survive and you've got sanctions from the West. Russia is in what I'd call a real serious economic crisis," Mr. Browder told CNBC.

Russia's Central Bank is keeping the country's economy together for now, largely thanks to burning through cash reserves. "Eventually they're going to run out of that money and when they do, that's when the real trouble begins," Browder added in an interview with the UK Daily Mail. He also suggested that economic sufferings of Russia have led Putin to become a more nationalistic leader with a strong geopolitical position. As a result, the Russian President has oppressed his people and made a scapegoat of Western civilization.

Are the days of Putin's regime numbered?

Russia's ruble has depreciated by twelve percent in the first quarter of 2016. Its rise and fall can be directly attributed to crude oil prices. Russia has virtually no economy except its oil exports. Given the economic decline in China, the demand for oil has significantly decreased, but more importantly, there are more oil producers around the world, especially in the U.S.

Between the shale revolution, Saudi Arabia's refusal to cut down on oil production and lifting sanctions against Iran for its nuclear program, the production of oil on the global oil market reached one-and-a-half million barrels a day according to estimations made by the International Energy Agency. As a result – oil prices have decreased by $95 to as low as $30 per barrel.

If oil prices continue to fall, the ruble continues to depreciate, and Russian leadership takes no immediate emergency measures, Russia's days will be numbered. That's a bad sign for the future of Putin's crumbling regime.

Italy's Banking System, like the Greek banks before it, is on the verge of collapse.

Italy has the eighth largest economy in the world. By comparison, Greece's economy is small, ranking 44th. But when the Greek economy failed a few short years ago, the Eurozone struggled to avert the potential disaster to the Eurozone. Now, Italy, with its government debt to GDP ratio at 132 percent, is set to meltdown.

Europe does not have the financial ability to prevent the collapse of Italian banks. Shares of Italian banks have plummeted to start 2016 as non-performing loans consume their balance sheets. As some analysts have shown, Italian banks maintain an incredible thirty percent of its balance sheets in defaulted paper.

As a result, Italy's largest banks are being monitored for liquidity levels daily by the European Central Bank. With the news, Italians have begun a run on their deposits. A collapse of the Italian banking system would create a *domino* effect on other financially weak members of the Eurozone—namely, Greece, Portugal, Spain, and perhaps France. The repercussions on worldwide markets is unfathomable.

Puerto Rico

Closer to home (even more so than Mexico since Puerto Rico is a U.S. Territory), without the financial bailout it has requested, Puerto Rico is going broke.

A newly-released financial report for the U.S. commonwealth indicates that Puerto Rico does not have the means to overcome its massive debt. In 2015, Puerto Rican Governor Alejandro Garcia-Padilla acknowledged the island is not able to service its $70 billion debt load. Now, there is substantial doubt that San Juan's government can operate in the long-term.

The reports also reveal that Puerto Rico's Government Development Bank is in danger of missing upcoming debt payments. The island has a $70 billion deficit as of June 30, 2015, or $21 billion more than in 2014, so cash isn't available to pay down its loans. The $70 billion figure is higher than every US state except New York and California.

This huge increase in Puerto Rico's deficit has resulted in various American credit rating agencies to downgrade the government's debt to non-investment grade. In August 2015, San Juan defaulted on a $58 million bond payment to the Government Development Bank,

Puerto Rico's equivalent of a central bank.

In early 2016, the White House said Puerto Rican labor leaders and business executives met with senior Obama administration officials, including Treasury Secretary Jacob Lew, and Health and Human Services Secretary Sylvia Burwell. Lew acknowledged the extent of the crisis in the commonwealth, and administration officials repeated President Barack Obama's demand for Congress to give Puerto Rico a version of Chapter 9 bankruptcy protection. That would let the island create a process for its creditors to recoup some of the owed funding. But Obama's push has stalled in both the House and the Senate.

So have talks with Wall Street creditors, who want Puerto Rico's government to be more transparent about the state of its finances. Since the new documents were long delayed and didn't contain audited financial information for the Government Development Bank, nor for the government's largest pension fund, creditors will certainly remain on edge.

Puerto Rico's bonds are popular with municipal money managers because they are tax-free. The San Juan government has asked for a fifty percent write-off on their loans, which would allow Puerto Rico to pay far less than what it borrowed. So far, the creditors have refused.

Growing its way back to financial health is impossible. As of 2015, Puerto Rico has a forty-five percent poverty rate, and its tax base has shrunk. Its population, meanwhile, has left for the United States in droves, shrinking by about sixty thousand from 2010 to 2015—more than during the 1980s and 1990s combined.

Various proposals have been suggested in the United States Congress, but no solution has been adopted. With a lot of hutzpah, Governor Garcia-Padilla, the governor who has presided over this massive debt accumulation, recently demanded that Congress come to San Juan's rescue, and accused Republican lawmakers of *seeking an excuse for inaction.*

A recent analysis by the Heritage Foundation analyzed the proposals this way:

"Everyone is in agreement that the federal government needs to address Puerto Rico's insolvency sooner rather than later. What that would entail is where the consensus breaks down. The big battle to date has been whether the federal government extends some version of Chapter 9 bankruptcy to the island. Chapter 9 allows the states to authorize the reorganization of the debt of their municipalities and government agencies, but it does not allow states themselves to restructure their own debts.

The Treasury Department has agreed to not only allow Puerto Rico to avail itself of Chapter 9 protection but to expand the law so that it applies to the Commonwealth itself, essentially treating Puerto Rico like a municipality of the federal government. Puerto Rico's entire debt is $72 billion, of which roughly $20 billion belongs to the commonwealth itself, is backed by the full faith and credit of Puerto Rico, and is given absolute priority by the island's Constitution.

Limited government advocates have vociferously protested extending bankruptcy of any sort to Puerto Rico, arguing that doing so amounts to an unfair deal for the investors who bought the island's bonds thinking that the island had no recourse to Chapter 9. While that might be a solid conservative precept, the problem is that without some sort of haircut on the island's debt it's going to leave taxpayers on the hook to prop up the island's finances.

Proposed legislation in Congress does just that and more, by enabling a federally-appointed "Oversight Board" to, in essence, allow Puerto Rico to declare bankruptcy and restructure all of its debts, including those backed by the "full faith and credit" of the Commonwealth itself. This is, in effect, a "super" Chapter 9 bankruptcy, and just because it's not called that does not change the substance of the proposed restructuring regime

This is a truly problematic precedent: No state or territory has ever had the power to seek federal bankruptcy relief to compromise its own debts.

The trouble with allowing such a broad debt restructuring is the fact that there are a few states with their own fiscal problems - most notably Illinois, with a pension plan teetering on insolvency and a completely wrecked state budget - that are looking for a way to continue postponing making any difficult decisions. The prospect of the federal government allowing them to declare bankruptcy and trim their general obligation debts would take a lot of pressure off, allowing them to postpone reforms and potentially raising the cost of borrowing for all states."

More Nations on the Brink

A new report from Wells Fargo takes a look at developing economies and their potential exposure to a financial crisis. Economists at the bank ranked the 28 largest developing economies based on economic criteria that are associated with financial crises. These indicators include:

(1) Foreign exchange (FOREX) reserves
(2) The real exchange rate
(3) Growth in credit
(4) GDP growth
(5) The current account (as a percent of GDP)

Based on these criteria, the economists surmise, those countries that have low FOREX reserves, an appreciated exchange rate, rapid credit and GDP growth, coupled with current account deficits, tend to have the highest probabilities for a financial crisis.

Here is the list of countries to watch (in addition to the ones listed above):

South Africa, Pakistan, Egypt, India, Indonesia, Turkey, Chile, Peru, Colombia, and Argentina.

Note that the last four on the list round out the seven largest economies in Central and South America. Coupled with Puerto Rico, virtually every major economy in the Western Hemisphere is on the brink of collapse.

Does the United States belong on this list?

PART FOUR

IS ECONOMIC COLLAPSE A REALISTIC THREAT?

CHAPTER SEVENTEEN
TRIGGER EVENTS

The coming economic collapse, like those before it, may involve war, gold, or societal collapse. What is likely to play out in the next three years is financial warfare, deflation, hyperinflation, and market collapse. Due to the sheer magnitude of the world's debt levels, and the size of the economies in peril, the next financial collapse will resemble nothing in history.

This is the first time in modern history that all the central banks of the world have printed money simultaneously with the hope of propping up their nation's ailing economies. Many nations have convinced themselves that austerity measures are not the answer and that only additional stimulus will save the day. Many economists view our current situation to be Keynesian economics on display.

Four of the world's largest Central Banks have printed money in recent years at an unprecedented rate.

The Bank of Japan had already been printing money without compunction since their bubble economy burst in the early 1990s, resulting in the lost decade. When the debt crisis struck in 2008, the size of their balance sheet assets, which measure the cumulative total of a central bank's money printing operations, was already the largest in the world - twenty percent of their economy.

As the shock waves of the Lehman Brothers collapse rattled world markets, the Japanese stepped up their money printing operations further — to about thirty percent of GDP.

Other than Brazil in the 1970s or Germany in the 1920s, no other major nation — or group of nations — on the planet had ever printed money at that rate of GDP! (Until, that is, Europe. See below.)

Meanwhile, at the U.S. Federal Reserve, no Fed Chairman in history — not even notorious easy-money advocates like Arthur Burns or Allen Greenspan — had EVER run the money printing presses for any extended period.

But Fed Chairman Ben Bernanke surpassed all Keynesian expectations. Soon after the debt crisis hit in 2008, he nearly TRIPLED the size of the Fed's balance sheet from about six percent of GDP to almost seventeen percent of GDP. And in the years since, he has pumped it up even further to twenty percent of GDP!

On the European continent, The Bank of England has been expanding its balance sheet in lock step with the Federal Reserve.

But in the global race to print money, it's the European Central Bank which has been leading the pack recently, suddenly expanding their balance sheet from about thirteen percent of GDP to close to a massive thirty percent of GDP!

Since 2008, the four largest central banks have been artificially increasing the money supply to incredible levels at the same time. Not to be outdone, the central banks of China and India have been printing as well.

Central Banks will always be tempted to issue money, because their constituent governments can buy more with it, hire more people, pay more wages, and increase their standing with their citizens. On the other hand, printing too much money starts to push up prices. If people start expecting that prices will continue to rise, they may increase their own prices even faster. Unless the government acts to rein in expectations, trust in money will be eroded, and it may eventually become worthless.

What can Trigger an Economic Collapse?

Pick your poison. In the introduction to this book, we discuss the threats that we face as a nation. Any number of events can put a strain on our over-burdened government, or the financial markets. Cyber Warfare can undermine the reliability of markets. Natural disasters can cause economies to shrink rapidly, lowering GDP, and increase government debt ratios.

One thing is certain. Since 2008, the media has perpetuated the belief that the world's central banks solved the 2008 banking crisis by printing money. It defies common sense to believe that a world debt crisis can be solved by issuing more debt. The United States, and the world's economies, are heading for a crisis that will be far worse than the 2008 collapse triggered by Lehman Brothers. The next crisis will be triggered by the failure of the central banking system itself.

Watch for the following in the near future:

The Bond Market

Former Federal Reserve Chairman Alan Greenspan has been sounding the alarm about a bubble that he believes is forming in the bond market. Greenspan said interest rates may shoot higher in 2016 and derail the economy when the bubble bursts.

The former Fed Chairman says the current situation in the bond market is comparable to what happens in the stock market during an equity bubble. "If you turn the bond market around, and you look at the price of bonds relative to the interest received by those bonds that looks very much like the usual spread which would concern us if it were equities, and we should be concerned."

Economists recognize that interest rates are near record lows and that bond prices are inversely related to those rates. After the Federal Reserve ended its quantitative easing program, the Fed is now looking to begin raising short-term interest rates. Casual market watchers don't understand the extent of the risk which follows.

Similar to the environments leading up to the crashes in technology stocks and real estate years ago, most acknowledge the magnitude of a possible correction. As interest rates rise, watch for bonds to suffer in values. When the markets crashed in 2008, bond values were $80 trillion. Today, they are in excess of $100 trillion.

To add to the potential for collapse, the derivatives market that uses the value of these over-priced bonds as collateral is six times the actual bond market worth—nearly $600 trillion.

The Leveraging of our Corporations and Central Banks

A company's debt, reflected in the amount of corporate bonds it has issued, is at record highs in relation to GDP. In 2007, just prior to the market collapse that triggered the Great Recession, corporate bonds were valued at $3.5 trillion. Today, corporate bond issues exceed $7 trillion. That is an amount equal to half of the U.S. GDP.

When Lehman Brothers failed in 2008 which triggered the market collapse, the global financial firm was leveraged at a rate of thirty to one. Today, the European Central Bank is leveraged at twenty-six to one, and the Federal Reserve is a whopping seventy-eight to one.

A review of the minutes from the Federal Reserve in 2009 revealed that Janet Yellin, during her tenure as President of the Federal Reserve Bank of San Francisco, expressed concern about how the Fed would exit their quantitative easing strategies when the Fed's balance sheet was $1.3 trillion. Today, under her leadership as Chairman of the Fed, the balance sheet has expanded to $4.5 trillion.

Watch for signs of the bond market weakening. Follow debt levels of the Fed and the world's largest corporations. These are telltale signs that the Bond Market Bubble may burst.

Weak Bank Earnings

Most major financial institutions produce at least a third of their annual revenue during the first quarter of the calendar year. During the heart of the 2007 – 2008 financial crisis, banks reported dismal earnings and revenues. In hindsight, economists looked upon these results as a key indicator of trouble in the financial sector. Pay attention to earnings forecasts released by the major banks in the United States during the month of April, 2016.

Consumer Debt

Have we not learned anything as a nation? We appear to be making the same mistakes collectively, as we did in the last decade. U.S. consumers accumulated more new credit card debt during October, November, and December of 2015 than they did during the combined years of 2009 through 2011. Reports have also shown that nearly forty percent of American households carry over credit card balances from month to month. Credit cards feature very high rates of interest, which when combined with severe penalties and fees, can bury a family in debt beyond their means.

The Real Unemployment Rate

Economists look past the *main* unemployment number (also known as the "U-3 rate") to other indicators in the report that give a more accurate view of the employment situation. The Bureau of Labor Statistics puts out a slew of figures, each of which measures a different part of the economy.

One of those data points is the U-6 rate. Many experts prefer the U-6 rate to the U-3 rate because it captures those employees who have given up completely, and who may work part time but would like to be working full-time—the marginally employed. The BLS defines U-6 as "total unemployed, plus all persons marginally attached to the labor force, plus total employed part time for economic reasons, as a percent of the civilian labor force," plus all marginally attached workers.

In other words, a rate that remains stubbornly above pre-recession levels—the U-6 rate—currently hovers at ten percent, double the unemployment rate of five percent touted by the White House and the media. To put this in perspective, sixty-two percent of able-bodied Americans are currently unemployed, under-employed, or have given up looking for work. That is a staggering ninety-four million Americans. The U.S. ranks thirtieth worldwide. The percentage when the Federal Reserve began its quantitative easing program in January 2009 was over sixty-six percent. The total Americans not in the labor force at that time was eighty million. That's an increase of fourteen million people, most of which are now on some form of federal and state government assistance.

Finally, if you look at the figures for Americans aged twenty-five to fifty-five, in the prime of their lives, the unemployment numbers are alarming. Twenty-three percent of Americans of prime working age are unemployed.

Many economists believe that this marked increase in the number of unemployed is not sustainable. Only the period during the Great Depression rival these numbers. As the media reports the unemployment figures, look beyond the numbers and watch the change in the labor participation rate, and the U-6.

CHAPTER EIGHTEEN
THE DECLINE OF ECONOMIC FREEDOM

It has been said that economic freedom is the key to greater opportunity and an improved quality of life. It's the freedom to choose how to produce, sell, and use your resources, while respecting others' rights to do the same. While a simple concept, it is an engine that drives prosperity in the world and is the difference between why some societies thrive while others do not.

It is important because it affects every aspect of an individual's life. Living in a society with high levels of economic freedom leads to higher incomes, lower poverty, less unemployment, longer life expectancy, and cleaner environments, among a host of other benefits. It improves well-being and leads to a higher quality of life.

The Heritage Foundation performs an annual analysis of five subcomponents to measure a country's level of freedom. These subcomponents include the size of government based on expenditures and taxes, the legal structure and its protection of property rights, access to sound money, freedom to trade internationally, and regulation of credit, labor, and business.

For over twenty years, the Heritage Index of Economic Freedom has measured the impact of liberty and free markets around the globe and illustrates the positive relationship between economic freedom and progress. The findings are startling. With losses of economic freedom in seven of the past eight years, the U.S. has tied its worst score ever, effectively wiping out a decade of progress enjoyed from 2000 - 2007. Currently, the U.S. ranks eleventh, dropping out of the top ten for the first time.

The report finds that Americans continue to lose economic freedom. Leading the decline are ratings for labor freedom, business freedom, and fiscal freedom that have fallen precipitously, and the regulatory burden which has increased substantially. According to one economist's analysis of the report, the United States remains mired in the ranks of the *mostly free*, the second-tier economic freedom status into which it dropped in 2010.

America's historically vibrant entrepreneurial growth is significantly hampered by intrusive, expensive, and often ineffective government policies in areas ranging from healthcare to energy to education. Government favoritism toward entrenched interests has hurt innovation and contributed to a lackluster recovery and stagnant income growth.

The report states that the U.S. economy continues to underperform despite a private sector–led energy boom that has made the U.S. the world's largest producer of oil and natural gas. Uncertain responses to foreign policy challenges, particularly concerning the Middle East, have contributed to a loss of support for the President and strong gains for Republicans in Congress and state legislatures. Leading to a decline in CEO and consumer confidence are Political tensions related to racial, religious, and social issues have increased over the past year.

The conclusion of the report finds that the "regulatory burden continues to increase. Over 180 new major federal regulations have been imposed on business operations since early 2009 with estimated annual costs of nearly $80 billion. Labor regulations are not rigid, but other government policies, such as excessive occupational licensing, restrict growth in employment opportunities. Damaging monetary policies tangled webs of corporate welfare and various subsidies have bred economic distortions."

A thorough analysis of the report shows that America's economic freedom has been declining at an alarming pace. This is not something to cast aside as immaterial. Economic freedom is the foundation of our economic strength on the world stage, and the foundation of America's high living standards, military power and status as a world leader is directly related to our economic strength as well.

The risks that we face as a nation in decline by losing economic freedom are not fictional. Most economists agree that our economy has been performing far below its potential, with individuals, families, and entrepreneurs being squeezed by the proliferation of big-government bureaucracy and regulations.

Restoring economic freedom is a prerequisite to revitalizing and brightening America's future. We believe that it's necessary for patriotic Americans to reaffirm the principles of limited government, free enterprise, and the rule of law so that we can reconstitute the United States where freedom, opportunity, and prosperity flourish.

CHAPTER NINETEEN
CAN WE SURVIVE ANOTHER FINANCIAL CRISIS LIKE 2008?

Nations heal after terrorist attacks, pick themselves up after natural disasters, and rebuild after military conflicts. They can even handle years of economic uncertainty, stagnant wages, and sky-high unemployment. But many developed nations today could not possibly tolerate another wholesale banking crisis and global economic recession like 2008.

The world economic climate is too fragile, fiscally as well as psychologically. Our economies, cultures, and politics are still paying a heavy price for the Great Recession. Another financial collapse, especially were it to be accompanied by a new policy of banking bailouts by the taxpayer, might trigger a cataclysmic, uncontrollable backlash in this era of political populism.

The public, whose faith in political elites and the wealthy movers and shakers of the private sector, was shaken to its core after 2007-09. The public outcry for bank bailouts would be so explosive and all-encompassing, that it might threaten the very survival of free trade, of globalization and the free market-based economy. There would be calls for wage and price controls, punitive, ultra-progressive taxes, a war on the political class, and arbitrary jail sentences.

For fear of allowing extremist or populist parties through the door, mainstream politicians would end up adopting much of this radical backlash, with devastating implications for our nation's long-term prosperity. The Central Banks of the world, in desperation, would ramp up their money-printing. Some would propose, as they have in Scandinavian countries, to start giving consumers actual cash to spend, temporarily turbo-charging demand while destroying any remaining respect for the idea that money needs to be earned.

History never repeats itself exactly, but the last time a recession was met by pure, unadulterated populism was in the 1930s, when U.S. policymakers turned a stock market crash and a series of monetary policy blunders, into The Great Depression.

In early 2016, the volatility in the financial markets, and the increasingly worrying economic news may turn out to be a false alarm. It would certainly be ridiculously premature, at this stage, to refer to the U.S. economy as recessionary, let alone a financial crisis. But at the very least we are observing a significant dose of the dangerous cocktail of new threats, a development which will have political repercussions even if the economy eventually trudges through. Growth is slowing worldwide, and the monetary pump-priming of the past few years is looking increasingly ineffective.

Now, the Central Banks are recognizing that they are out of options to combat a future recession or deflation. There is increasing talk that negative interest rates could become necessary across the developed world, further crippling savers.

Imagine a bank that pays negative interest. Depositors are charged to keep their money in an account. Crazy as it sounds, several of Europe's central banks have cut key interest rates below zero and kept them there for more than a year. Now Japan is trying it, too.

Negative interest rates are an act of desperation, a signal that traditional policy options have proved ineffective and new limits need to be explored. They punish banks that hoard cash instead of extending loans to businesses, or to weaker lenders. Rates below zero have never been used before in an economy as large as the Eurozone. While it's still too early to tell if they will work, European Central Bank President Mario Draghi said in January 2016 that there are "no limits" on what he will do to meet his mandate, which is avoiding a deflationary period.

Europe's central bank chose to experiment with negative rates before turning to a bond-buying program like those used in the U.S. and Japan. Policy makers in both Europe and Japan are trying to prevent a slide back into deflation, or a spiral of falling prices that could derail the economic recovery. The Eurozone is also grappling with a shortage of credit and unemployment.

No positive spin can be put on any of the latest developments. Banking shares have taken a beating. China's slowdown continues. Maersk, the shipping giant, believes that conditions for world trade are worse than in 2008-09. Industrial production slumped worldwide in the fourth quarter of 2015. Energy prices are devastating Middle Eastern, Central American, and Russian economies.

Markets strive during periods of economic stability and predictability. It is always a sure sign that panic has broken out when financial markets respond badly to all possible scenarios. The prospect of higher interest rates? Sell, sell, sell. A chance of lower rates? Sell, sell and sell again. A rise in the price of oil is met with as much angst as a decline.

The world's financial markets remain addicted to assistance from Central Banks, which have become the globe's enabler. They are desperate for yet more interventions, regardless of the consequences on the pricing of risk, the allocation of resources or the creation of unsustainable bubbles that only enrich the owners of assets.

This type of monetary policy is unsustainable. Perhaps, another devastating market crash is not survivable.

CHAPTER TWENTY
ARE WE ON THE BRINK OF ECONOMIC COLLAPSE?

The United States is on the brink of an economic tsunami that could make the Great Depression look like a ripple on a serene lake. American economic history has shown us that every eighty years or so, we face incredible economic challenges. The American Revolution of 1776 transformed America as a fledgling nation found its way on the world's economic stage. The American Civil War of 1861 – 1865, was fought over state's rights but had undertones dealing with slavery and economic freedom. The Great Depression, which followed the stock market collapse of 1929, was the darkest period in American economic history. Historians and anthropologists have studied the generational cycles of economic collapse, world crisis, and revolutions. Is the eighty-year cycle or crisis going to be the norm for the United States?

To note this pattern of recurring crises is not to claim that some law of nature dictates a near-collapse of global capitalism every eighty years. It is, however, reasonable to recognize that democracy-based capitalism is an evolving system that responds to a crisis by transforming both economic relations and political institutions, sometimes in a knee-jerk manner.

One could see today's market instability as a predictable response to the breakdown of one incident of global capitalism in 2008. But, as we have shown, there have been several warning signs of something looming in the last thirty years, including the stock market crashes in 1987, 2000, and 2008. Are these tremors indicating a much larger, devastating economic earthquake that will shake the world's economy to its core? All over the world today, there is a sense of the end of an era, a deep foreboding about the disintegration of previously stable societies.

Many economists study charts and trends. Things like moving averages in the stock market mean a lot to stock traders, and the economists who work for major brokerage firms. Too many financial firms are suggesting cash positions to their clients. The trend is away from risky investments, and toward safe investments that are not subject to market swings.

As of early 2016, investors are seven years into a bull market that many believe has lasted too long already. The larger issue today is that itis difficult for investors to figure out where to put money. Interest income or cash flow on savings is virtually nonexistent, and investments in the stock market are thwarted because stock prices are at record highs, leaving a significant down-side risk. The situation is being made worse by events overseas, where one big country is wielding the monkey wrench.

China has been in a market bubble for twenty years. It has propped up the U.S. economy falsely. When China stops importing foreign goods, the world crashes with them. First to go will be commodity producers like Australia, Canada, and some African countries which will drag down the rest of the world's economies.

China has been throwing money at its banks to keep lending going, and debt quality at financial institutions is a constant theme among worried economists. It's likely Chinese banks will be at the forefront of the next market crash. How will our Federal Reserve react to a collapse of the Chinese economy?

One economist put it this way: "The big question is whether the Fed undertakes another round of quantitative easing—QE4. If we do, the stock market will come roaring back, but it's not rocket science. If we stop printing money, it crashes. If we print money, it goes up. But, eventually, it's all going to come down. This could be the last time they pull this stunt. The markets might really collapse at that point."

A lot of talk centers on the risks to stock market investors. What about the regular guy—the family that lives paycheck to paycheck? There are more of those, than there are stock market investors.

According to a 2016 study released by the Pew Charitable Trusts, average household spending increased by fourteen percent between 2004 and 2014, but median household income decreased by thirteen percent during that same period. In other words, the cost of living has steadily gone up, but your incomes have gone down. An analysis of the details of the Pew report finds that one-third of all Americans doesn't have enough income to pay for the basic staples—shelter, transportation, medical and food.

The middle class is gradually disappearing in favor of a burgeoning group of haves and have-nots. According to the Social Security Administration, fifty percent of all Americans make less than $30,000 per year. Half of people under the age of twenty-five still live at home with their parents. The study also indicates that most American households do not have one month of living expenses in savings. The majority of Americans across a broad age spectrum haven't saved a dime towards retirement. People tend to boost their retirement savings in their late fifties and sixties.

Perhaps the reason Americans aren't saving is they can't afford it. Americans spend more on taxes than their whole budget for food, clothing and housing.

The Tax Foundation defines Tax Freedom Day as the day when the nation has earned enough money to pay its total tax bill for the year and calculates it by taking all federal, state, and local taxes and dividing this by the nation's income. According to The Tax Foundation, that date for 2016 is April 24, or 114 days into the year.

"Tax Freedom Day gives us a vivid representation of how much federal, state, and local tax revenue is collected each year to pay for government goods and services," said Tax Foundation Analyst Scott Greenberg. "Arguments can be made that the tax bill is too high or too low, but in order to have an honest discussion, it's important for taxpayers to understand the cost of government. Tax Freedom Day helps people relate to that cost."

Here are some facts:

(1) Americans will spend more on taxes in 2016 than they will on food, clothing, and housing combined.

(2) Americans will pay $3.3 trillion in federal taxes and $1.6 trillion

in state and local taxes, for a total bill of almost $5.0 trillion, or 31 percent of the nation's income.

(3) If you include annual federal borrowing, which represents future taxes owed, Tax Freedom Day would occur 16 days later on May 10.

These trends are indicators of troubled economic times. Watch the trends, read the reports, and do the homework. Above all, get ready.

PART FIVE

PREPARING FOR ECONOMIC COLLAPSE

CHAPTER TWENTY-ONE
WAYS TO PROTECT YOURSELF

Every collapse event requires its unique level of preparedness. As we have written in other installments of the Prepping for Tomorrow series, preparing for a long-lasting, grid-down scenario provides you the ultimate level of preparedness. Under the present economic circumstances, it would be prudent to take some additional steps in the event of a significant downturn in the economy that doesn't become a full-blown depression or economic collapse.

We have identified several factors to consider. In the meantime, there are some financial actions a family can undertake to protect their savings, provide for their family, and preserve your assets in the event of a catastrophic drop in the markets which might leave you unemployed, or underemployed.

Convert to Liquidity—Cash in Hand

On Friday, March 15, 2013, residents of Cyprus went to bed just like it was any other day. The next morning, they woke up to a frightening scenario—their banking system collapsed. After suffering enormous losses, banks no longer had the liquidity to maintain customer balances and honor their deposits. Cyprians quickly realized that just because you can log onto the bank's website and see a positive balance doesn't mean the money is there for your withdrawal. To complicate matters in Cyprus, the government was bankrupt as well and was unable to bail out depositors.

This is what happens when a poorly structured banking system is coupled with an insolvent government. Western banking systems are extremely illiquid—thinly capitalized with minimal reserves. Deposit insurance funds lack the financial capacity to guarantee the deposits.

The governments that stand behind it all are insolvent as well. The information is published and is public knowledge. In the United States, banks maintain cash reserves amounting to just three and a half percent of its customer's deposits.

When it's clear that your government is broke, your deposit insurance fund is undercapitalized, and your bank is hazardously illiquid, it seems obvious that you shouldn't hold 100% of your savings in that banking system. There are a multitude of solutions to reduce this risk. The easiest option is to hold physical cash. Even if you're completely skeptical about everything you've just read, you won't be worse off for having cash instead of bank deposits.

Bank deposits pay you nothing. In fact, as we discussed above, the threat of negative interest rates where banks charge you for deposits is very real. The one percent you earn on a Certificate of Deposit is of no real value. The peace of mind of having cash on hand during a run on the banks, or a collapse of our critical infrastructure, is priceless. Create a variety of hidden compartments around your business and home. Withdraw money in small increments. Be especially mindful of the Structuring Laws established by the IRS. Withdrawing more than $10,000 at a time, or several withdrawals in close time proximity just under $10,000, can trigger a hold on your bank accounts, and confiscation of your funds by the FBI, Treasury, or the IRS.

Achieve True Freedom

To us, *true freedom* comes when you don't have to answer to anyone—whether it be your boss, a customer, a neighbor, or a lender. Consider the stories you read daily about a well-known figure who loses his job because he said something that was politically incorrect. The list is endless. By the same token, if you are heavily in debt, you aren't working for yourself and your family, you are working to stay afloat. How about the relationship with your employer? Do you find yourself being careful about your social media posts because you might be reprimanded for incorrect speech or political points of view?

This is not freedom. This is servitude. Not everyone is willing to make the sacrifices necessary to achieve *true freedom*. We are believers in down-sizing. Lower your standard living. Move to a rural area where the cost of living is much less. Although this requires a significant lifestyle change, a move provides more benefits to you than just financial. Look at it as moving to your bug-out location. It is a sage decision.

Focus on paying off your secured debt—mortgage loans, car loans, etc. If times get tough, and you have to pick who to pay, make sure you have the resources to pay the loans secured by collateral, not unsecured credit card debt, student loans, or other consumer debt. The key to retirement does not just have a big 401k. It's about being debt free. Imagine what your life would be like with no mortgage or car payments. That's what *true freedom* looks like. If your boss doesn't like your political posts on social media and demands you tone down the rhetoric, you can quote musician Johnny Paycheck—*Take this job and shove it*.

Practice Economic Situational Awareness

You've heard the saying—*Money can't buy happiness*. Well, we call bull shit on that one. We like to say that *there isn't much that time and money can't solve*. This is very true for most households. If the number one cause of family discord and divorce is financial disagreements, then clearly, money can buy happiness, to an extent.

The head of the household has an obligation to provide for their spouses, children, and anyone else living under their care. This requires planning, organization, and financial resources. You simply must study current affairs as it relates to the economy, and the politics impacting it. Read from several sources. Rest assured, you will not get the full picture from the mainstream media.

Maintain an Emergency Fund (cash and daily living requirements)

If you are not a prepper, you should be. One of the reasons we prep is the potential for a downturn in the economy that could result in a loss of income. If that happens, we not only have sufficient food, supplies, and medications on hand for a prolonged revenue loss, we also have cash on hand to pay our utilities. In the past, it was suggested that every household maintains three months of living expenses on hand as an emergency fund. The times have changed in the last eight years. The unemployed have experienced nine to twelve month periods of inactivity. Maintain nine months of utility payments, at a minimum. Keep sufficient funds on hand to make your car payments. Transportation is essential to finding a job. If you have to allow your mortgage payments to slide, contact the mortgage holder up front, before you're late. Mortgage holders have been more understanding in recent years than they were before 2008. Your mortgage company does not want to foreclose on your home. They've got enough of those in inventory already.

Adopt a Hunker Down Mindset

You're a prepper now. After TEOTWAWKI, in whatever form that takes, you must become a survivor. The days of McDonald's for breakfast, Applebee's for lunch and a Starbucks in between are over. Cut out all luxuries. Focus on nutrition, at the lowest cost. Eliminate high cable bills and find other ways to entertain yourself. Think about your everyday activities. How much money do you waste? Try to practice a *hunker down*, survival state of mind. Not only will this help you prepare for an economic collapse, but it will also help you realize how nice life can be without all of the excess clutter we heap upon our shoulders.

Remain calm and maintain a positive state of mind. A loss of a job is dreadful for anyone to suffer through. Imagine what economic collapse will look like. By being prepared in advance mentally and organizationally, you can avoid panic, which will in turn calm the nerves of everyone within your care. This will assist your chances of survival and recovery after the economic collapse passes.

Add an Additional Source of Income

Start a home business or adopt a new career as a second source of income. If you lose your job because of an economic collapse, it might be difficult or even impossible to find another job. Having an alternative source of income can help you. Choose your business idea based on skills that you have and things that you enjoy doing.

An economic collapse, or a deep recession, like the one in 2008, can have a devastating ripple effect across the world's economy.

When the economy starts to cool down, businesses tighten their purse strings. And when that happens, they begin to struggle and start laying off employees. That results in even tighter purse strings, leading to a downward spiral. During the Great Recession of 2008-09, some people fared better than others, mainly because of their skillsets, and the positions they held.

There are a handful of jobs that have proven to be recession proof. This means that even when things are tight and money isn't flowing as abundantly, certain goods and services are still going to be in demand. If you have one of those jobs, you should still be able to bring home a paycheck and keep your family protected.

Here are some suggestions of skills you can learn now that will also be useful after TEOTWAWKI.

(1) Paramedic. There will always be a need for emergency medical services, and we can't think of any greater post-SHTF skill to have than medical expertise. A collapsed economy does not mean that people will stop needing medical attention.

(2) Local Law Enforcement. Police officers will be in high demand during the societal unrest that necessarily follows an economic collapse. In addition, the contacts you make, and the training you receive, will be invaluable in dealing with a post-collapse world. Security guards will see an increase in work, and is an excellent skill to trade for shelter, water, and food.

(3) Farming. After shelter and water, food is the most important resource for preppers. You can't live more than three weeks without it. An economic collapse generally results in higher food prices. Local farmers will be able to compete with large food chains because they will not have the additional transportation expenses associated with stocking the shelves. After TEOTWAWKI, food becomes an excellent source of barter.

(4) Small engine repair. Once again, this is an opportunity to use your skills to assist the public. Learn how to repair power tools, chainsaws, ATV engines, etc. After TEOTWAWKI, having the tools, parts, and know-how to fix things will be very valuable.

(5) Gunsmithing and Ammunition Production. Many people

believe that after a collapse event, the government will take more control over their people, greatly limiting our access to guns and ammunition. Even if this weren't to occur, a lack of access to industrialized processes will bring the gun manufacturing industry to a halt. This will lead to a huge demand for gun repairs and homemade ammunition. Learning to be a gunsmith will keep you in demand and your arsenal stocked no matter what happens. We may not know the future, but we know that folks will always want guns!

(6) Leathercraft and Garment Making. We'll all lose a lot of weight after the SHTF. Also, the needs for holsters, belts, and shoe repair will need to be fulfilled.

(7) Blacksmith. Every town will have the need for a skilled blacksmith—someone who can work with wrought iron and steel, forging the metal into tools, weapons, farming equipment and much more. The blacksmith can also produce horse shoes which are sure to be a necessity post collapse.

(8) Butcher. With the absence of retail supermarkets and just in time delivery systems, the skills to slaughter and dress animals while minimizing waste and turning out cuts of meat for consumption will be in high demand in local communities.

Store Precious Metals for Investment and Barter

The topic of barter will be discussed extensively in the next chapter. But before collapse, precious metals are an excellent way to preserve your wealth from a market collapse. During a period of economic instability, investors often rush into precious metals. As panic sets in, the price of silver and gold can rise rapidly. There are a number of investment advisors who can argue for investing in gold over silver, and vice versa. Our opinion is that silver is preferable under current conditions, and post-SHTF. Either way, we recommend that you buy physical gold and silver in a form that is widely recognized.

We will not attempt to extol the virtues of one over the other as an investment tool. We will recommend that precious metals be a part of your investment portfolio as a hedge against inflation and market collapse. Owning physical gold and silver is the key;

otherwise, you might just end up owning a piece of paper when the grid goes down.

Chapter Twenty-Two
Barter

Bartering is the act of exchanging one commodity, goods or services for another, without the use of money. Bartering benefits individuals, companies, and countries that see a mutual benefit in exchanging goods and services rather than cash, and it enables those who are lacking hard currency to obtain goods and services.

When thinking about what you can barter to obtain a good or service you want, consider not only any possessions you might be willing to part with, but also any skills you have to offer. These skills might include what you do professionally, but they can also include any activity you're proficient at, from cleaning to babysitting to yard work to baking. Bartering exchanges can happen on a very small or large scale. Children exchanging items from their lunchboxes, for example, is a common form of barter exchange, but businesses may also barter for goods, advertising space or other commodities.

Before money became widespread, bartering was the way most people exchanged the things they had for the things they needed. Today bartering is not the most common means of exchange in any society, but it can still be a useful way of trading goods, particular when the economy is poor, there is a limited amount of money, or there is rapid inflation.

Bartering is a useful way for people with surplus or unwanted items to exchange them for items that would be more useful to them. Bartering may be less convenient than using money. Cash, or cash equivalents, are liquid, whereas bartering relies on the coincidence that two individuals will have exactly what the other wants, at the same time and in the right quantity. However, a growing number of websites are dedicated to connecting barterers and today there's a vast range of items to trade.

After an economic collapse or any significant collapse event, barter will become the new way to exchange goods and services. Barter is a favorite topic of preppers, and the views and opinions vary. Our opinion on barter can be reflected in a conversation I had with my wife regarding the purchase of pre-1964 silver for barter purposes.

Bobby: *I think we need to purchase some pre-1964 silver coins to use as barter after TEOTWAWKI.*

Danni: *Barter for what?*

Bobby: *Well, for something that we don't have.*

Danni: *Like what?*

Bobby: *I don't know. I guess we'll find out when the time comes.*

Danni: *Maybe it would be better to figure out what you might need, and get it now before the prices and availability become ridiculous. Instead of buying silver, go buy the stuff you'll need instead.*

The result of that conversation was an extensive prepper checklist, a link to which has been appended to this book as Exhibit C and is available as a free download at FreedomPreppers.com.

Of course, being a male, I purchased the silver coins anyway. Because you never know what you might have forgotten. Or perhaps there is a skill someone has that you don't. But my wife made an excellent point. If your resources are limited, focus on the prepper items on a well thought out checklist, and get them before TEOTWAWKI. Gold and silver will always have an intrinsic value, but when the economy collapses, or the grid goes down, covering the necessities of food, water, shelter, and security will be more important than your pile of silver quarters.

After the SHTF, marketplaces will begin to appear based upon barter exchange. These may be dangerous at first. Traveling to and from your secured location will certainly require planning. Also, it will take some period of time for prices to be established. Availability of goods will dictate the prices, but emotions may impact them as well. Until the economy returns to normal, the barter system will experience wide swings in pricing.

There are hundreds of articles and just as many opinions on the best items to have available for a barter exchange. We have only three suggestions:

(1) NEVER barter ammo or weapons. Why in the world would you want to trade away your security to a person who might come back and use it to kill you someday?

(2) NEVER create a barter exchange near your bug-out location. I don't care how many security personnel you have, there is always a greater force that can overcome you.

(3) Best form of barter exchange is something that you can replenish, such as heirloom seeds. If you've properly prepared, you'll have many years of heirloom seeds in storage. After each harvest, you can increase your supply of seeds. Most people have not stored seeds for long-term survival. You can help feed your community which in turn keeps them from looking at you and your food stores for survival.

(4) If you must, buy pre-1964 silver coins. It is recognizable to everyone. The last thing that you want to do is enter the newly formed barter marketplace and pull out a pocket of one ounce gold Krugerrands. What are you gonna do, ask for change?

One last suggestion. Don't enter the barter exchange looking like the President of the bank. Think poor and downtrodden. You don't want to be flashy. It'll get you killed.

CHAPTER TWENTY-THREE
WE ARE ALL PREPPERS NOW

The threats we face are many. At FreedomPreppers.com, Americans are urged to prepare for a worst-case scenario. If nothing happens, you've lost nothing. For the United States, short of nuclear annihilation, many consider the worst case scenario to be an extended grid down scenario.

The way you protect yourself isn't very high-tech. In fact, you're going to be better off going low-tech.

Where do you begin in formulating a Preparedness Plan? An entire preparedness guide, hundreds of pages long, may still not adequately cover the elements of a comprehensive preparedness plan. The numerous disaster preparedness guides, blogs, and professional videos are all excellent resources. But where does one start?

Essentially, it all boils down to:

Beans, Band-Aids & Bullets

Well, of course there is much more to developing a preparedness plan than the *big three*, but all preparedness experts know these are the basics. Many preppers are well organized and rely heavily upon checklists. We urge you to review Appendix B which provides a summary as well as a link to a free pdf download of an extensive preparedness checklist. Preppers constantly update their checklists to ensure they didn't overlook anything. You will as well.

As you review the following, keep in mind certain basic principles when preparing your plan.

The survival rule of threes: You can only live three minutes without air; three hours without shelter in extreme conditions; three days without water; and three weeks without food. This helps you prioritize your preps for a post-collapse survival situation.

The prepper rule of redundancy: Three is two, two is one, and one is none. When your prepper supplies run out, you can't drive down to Wal-Mart and restock.

Building your prepper supplies to an acceptable level for long term survival requires baby steps. Thus, survival planning starts with the perfect trinity of prepping—*beans, band-aids, and bullets*. Clearly, an oversimplification of what a preparedness plan entails, but it is a pretty good reflection of what you better have covered. This is a well-known expression within the prepper community as it outlines the essentials that you will need in the event of TEOTWAWKI—the end of the world as we know it.

In summary, *beans* will include your prepper supplies, the items in your prepper pantry and water. *Band-aids* will refer to all things medical. *Bullets* represent the weapons and ammunition necessary to protect yourself, your family and your preps.

Beans – Your Prepper Pantry

What's in your prepper pantry? Right now, honest assessment. How many days could your family survive on what's in your house right now? Most American households have less than seven days of food on hand.

Building a prepper pantry is one of those lifelines that take both time and planning to make it fully functional. Ideally, you want to store shelf stable foods that your family normally consumes, as well as find foods that serve multiple purposes. Stocking your prepper pantry should involve a combination of ready to eat food and beverages to last your family many months plus long term food storage for a year or more.

Overall, your prepper pantry should reflect an abundance of the foods that you eat on a regular basis. Utilize a first in, first out rotation. This is a mistake many new preppers make. They buy food they don't eat on a regular basis. Store foods that have a long shelf life that don't require refrigeration after opening, and that are easy to cook off the grid.

Our suggested preparedness plan includes non-perishable foods on our shelves to last us one year. Then we have canned vegetables, fruit, and meats created throughout the year. Finally, dried goods such as beans, rice, pasta, and oatmeal are stored utilizing Mylar Bags and desiccant packs (this technique is discussed in depth on the Freedom Preppers website) which can last for up to twenty years.

The following foods are all popular food staples that should be considered as essentials for your Prepper Pantry. The advantages to storing these items are they encompass all of the key consideration points listed above. Best of all, these items are very affordable and versatile, thus making them worthy of being on your storage shelves for extended emergencies. You'll find most of these items in your pantry already. Try to increase the quantity each week and place them into rotation. Use this list as a starting point on beginning or extending your Prepper Pantry. Always keep your family's food preferences and dietary needs in mind when investing in your food supply. This list is very basic, but a good start. The checklist in Appendix C is helpful as well.

- Dried legumes such as beans, lentils, and peas
- Rice, lots of rice
- Pasta and sauces
- Oatmeal, Cream of Wheat, and cereals
- Canned meat, fish, soups, fruits, and vegetables
- Peanut Butter
- Packaged Meals (macaroni and cheese, hamburger helper, Ramen noodles
- Seasonings and cooking oils
- Flour, salt, sugar, corn meal, and powdered cheeses
- Powdered drinks like milk, Tang, and Gatorade; Tea Bags

Here are some additional considerations.

Food - If you would like to start storing food there are some things to consider. How long will the food last? Is this something that you and your family will realistically eat? Will the food survive if there is a disaster and no electricity? How will you cook the food you have stored? The amount of food stored ultimately depends on the person that is storing it. But, keep in mind that you need to have enough food for the amount of time a foreseen disaster will last. If you are just preparing for a short term disaster then maybe only a few days to a week of food is necessary. If your preparations need to last after a massive break down of society or a major disaster, you may want to have a few months to multiple years of food stockpiled. Also you may want to raise your own livestock and have a fruit and vegetable garden. Hunting and Fishing are also a great way to get food. Just a note, all grocery stores combined in one city usually only have about 3 days' worth of food for the entire city. This is known as *just-in-time inventory*, and will be gone within hours when a collapse event becomes apparent.

Heirloom Seeds – While technically not food, yet, the ability to grow your food will be critical to sustain yourself after your food supplies run out. Besides, before the SHTF, *growing your own food is like printing your own money*. And, it's good practice.

Water – FEMA claims that each adult needs one gallon of water per person per day. This is wholly inadequate. While this quantity may keep you hydrated, it will not be sufficient to maintain your location. When there is no water coming out of the sink where will you find fresh, clean water? You may want to keep water stockpiled as well. There are a couple options for this.

The basic principles revolve around *water catchment, purification, and storage*. Again, water management is a subject for an entire book. But consider this. In third world countries, dysentery is one of the major causes of death. In a grid down scenario caused by a cyber attack, or otherwise, America will be set back into the nineteenth century from a technology standpoint. Drinking unclean water can kill you.

There are options. You can keep water bottles or gallon containers full. There are also water tanks that come in various sizes anywhere from under a hundred gallons up to thousands of gallons. If you are lucky enough to be near a river or lake, this may be a good source of water. There are many types and sizes of water filters that don't need electricity and make even the worst water safe to drink. There are also tablets that can be placed in water to purify it. A well would also be a fantastic water source, but can be quite pricey to build.

Ultimately, there are many options, but it is a good idea to know about the natural water sources in your area.

Pets - Finally, please do not forget your pets. They are family too and dogs, in particular, may be a useful asset in your home's defenses.

Bandaids – Your Armageddon Medicine Cabinet

After a collapse event, you will probably not have ready access to a dentist or doctor, much less a hospital. Available treatment will be scarce and required medicines even scarcer. When you become injured or sick, help will not be on the way. You will become the primary care physician for your prepper group.

Survival Medicine requires you to have a wellll-organized First Aid Kit, complete with over-the-counter and pharmacy medications. You'll need to gain the knowledge necessary to diagnose and treat a variety of illnesses and injuries, including dental care.

Preventative Medicine - Though not a conventional aspect of beans, bullets, and band-aids, staying in shape and being healthy is one of the best ways to prevent problems after any collapse event. When we are healthy we are able to work harder and more efficiently. Being healthy and in shape can also promote productivity. Some of the ways to prepare for an end of the world scenario are to eat right, exercise regularly, and keep an active lifestyle. Knowledge of minor medical procedures is also a great way to prepare.

Prescription Medications - If you need a certain prescription to maintain a productive lifestyle, make sure to have a surplus of them on hand. There are some doctors that will give extra prescriptions for the purpose of preparing and stockpiling, so the beans, bullets and band-aids theory suggests asking and explaining your situation to your physician. Additionally, there are some medicines that should be kept on hand; antibiotics are an important one. We suggest stockpiling fish antibiotics as they are some of the most useful to treat infections. But don't forget the many over the counter medicines that are used regularly. These can include aspirin, allergy medicines, cold or flu remedies, diarrhea medicines, stool softeners among many more. Medical supplies such as those found in a first aid or trauma kit are very important. For instance, how will you dress a wound or set a broken bone? It is good to have bandaids, bandages, braces, splints, and thermometers on hand. The more you know and have increases the chances of surviving.

Hygiene - Maintaining personal hygiene and sanitation after the collapse event is critical. Ingesting bacteria may kill you without access to proper medical care. Consider this: How many rolls of toilet paper do your family use a day? What will you use as an alternative when you run out? Where do you plan to poop when the SHTF? Got the picture?

Prepping for hygiene may be as simple as obtaining multiples of everyday household items. Savvy preppers know they need to stockpile a supply of food and water, but hygiene products are essential to decrease the spread of disease and illness. It also helps you to maintain a sense of normalcy.

In a post-SHTF world, sanitation and hygiene will be important to keep yourself and your family healthy. Running water may no longer be an option or a healthy choice, and you need to know how to practice good hygiene, proper sanitation and keep your environment healthy. These are all very important considerations in a SHTF situation. Due to a lack of available medical facilities or treatment, health and disease prevention are going to be more important and more difficult to treat than ever after the TEOTWAWKI.

Sanitation items are easy to gather. You may prefer a pre-assembled emergency kit which already contains necessary items for grooming and sanitation. Because many kit items are sold as a unit, you may find that purchasing a kit is an inexpensive and convenient way to prepare all that you'll need during an emergency. Another option may be to assemble your own emergency kit so you can choose brands or items your family is accustomed to using. Often, you can purchase your favorite brand of soap, toothpaste, shampoo, toilet paper, deodorant and other items in bulk or extra saving packages so you can afford to set some aside for your emergency kit.

Here are some items to consider:

Toilet Paper - When it comes to emergencies, any kind of toilet paper is a luxury. By preparing ahead of time, you can ensure that you don't experience unneeded discomfort by having to get used to a new texture of paper. Also keep in mind that it is common for those in emergency situations to develop stress and diet related stomach problems that can intensify your sanitation difficulties.

Toothbrush + Oral Hygiene - People with sensitive teeth may want to store their preferred brand of toothbrush in their emergency kit. It is probably a wise idea to store several toothbrushes to give away to someone who neglected to store one. It may also have another useful purpose such as cleaning or scrubbing.

Toothpaste, Mouthwash, and Breath Fresheners - Emergencies present stressful situations where human communication is crucial. Sometimes water is scarce or unavailable which causes dryness in your mouth. A breath freshener may be a nice addition to your preparedness supplies.

Feminine Hygiene Products - It is important to be prepared in all areas. These items are definitely important to have available in any emergency situation.

Deodorant - With several choices of deodorants including anti-perspirants, made-for-a-woman brands, gelled, etc., you may want to decide ahead of time what you'll need during an emergency.

Air fresheners or deodorants may also increase your level of comfort during an emergency.

Hair Supplies Shampoo, conditioner, hairspray, combs, brushes, and other items may not be necessary for survival, but they can help make an emergency situation more comfortable and clean. Be sure to store smaller sanitation items in your emergency kit and be aware that you can overstuff your emergency kit. If it is too heavy, you may not be able to leave with it during an emergency.

Medications for diarrhea, constipation, headaches, allergy and other minor conditions should also be included in kits for added comfort.

Laundry Detergent and Soap - During some emergencies, you may be required to evacuate the area or may be stranded in some remote area. Because you won't have lots of clothing, you will want detergent to clean your clothes and soap for bathing and for washing utensils.

Hand sanitizers are essential to keep in your bug out bag as well.

Bathing - You can prevent illness by washing your hands often; before eating, after using the bathroom, after you change a diaper, and any other time you may need to freshen up. Because water is such a precious commodity during an emergency, you should remember to use purified drinking water first for drinking, cooking, washing dishes and then for other purposes. Be organized and choose a designated bathing area. If you wash in a river or stream use biodegradable soap and always be aware of others who may be down stream. With a little soap you can also wash yourself in the rain. Other washing alternatives include moist towelettes, a spray bottle, sanitizing lotions, or a wet washcloth. Be sure to wear shoes to prevent parasitic infections and to protect you from cuts and puncture wounds that can easily become infected.

Sanitation Area - Choosing the right location for your sanitation needs is as important as staying clean. Your waste place must be located downhill from any usable water source. It should also be a few hundred feet from any river, stream, or lake. It also helps to have your waste place downwind from your living area, and yet not too far from your camp that the distance discourages people from using it.

Luggable Loo - With a little preparation, you can have a decent emergency toilet. If you have a five gallon plastic bucket lined with a heavy-duty garbage bag, you have a toilet. Don't forget to add deodorized cat litter to assist with the odor. Make sure you have a lid to cover it. A plastic toilet seat can be purchased to fit on the bucket for a more comfortable seat. If you don't have an extra plastic bucket available, you can make a latrine by digging a long trench approximately one foot wide and 12 to 18 inches deep and cover as you go. When you dig too deep a latrine it can slow the bacterial breakdown process. The long latrine approach is appropriate for large groups camping in one spot for a long period.

Getting Rid of Refuse - If you cannot dispose of refuse properly you should always bury biodegradable garbage and human waste to avoid the spread of disease by rats and insects. Dig a pit 12 to 18 inches deep and at least 50 feet but preferably 200 plus feet downhill and away from any well, spring, or water supply. Fill the pit with the refuse and cover with dirt. For back-country hikers, packing out all solid waste is always appropriate, and some authorities at high-use rivers usually require this process. You can make a seat for your latrine by laying logs across the hole, leaving an area open for you to use. After use, cover the waste with small amounts of dirt to decrease the odor. A covered toilet reduces more of the odor than an open one. Make a toilet cover with wood or a large leaf. If the odor becomes unbearable, fill in the latrine completely with dirt and dig a new one. Build a new seat and burn the old wood that you used for the last toilet.

Keeping Food Sanitary - All food scraps should be either burned or buried in a pit far from your living area to keep bears and other wild animals away from you. Keep all your food covered and off the ground. You may keep your food in a tree, but be sure tree dwelling creatures can't get into it. Replace all lids on water bottles and other containers immediately after use. Do not wash your dishes in the area where you get your drinking water supply. Instead, wash your dishes away from a stream. Use clean plates or eat out of the original food containers to prevent the spread of germs. Wash and peel all fruits and vegetables before eating. Prepare only as much as will be eaten at each meal.

Bullets – Your SHTF Defense Tools
Bottom Line: If you can't defend it, it isn't yours.

Conceptually, preparation without security is meaningless. It doesn't matter if you hate guns. Perhaps your political or religious beliefs prevent you from committing acts of violence, or self-defense. After TEOTWAWKI, the world will become a brutal place. The world we live in will not be unicorns and rainbows. Unless you are prepared to give up your preps, or even your life, all preppers need a security plan.

Actual security countermeasures can be quite complex, but they generally conform to the five principles of prepper security. A security plan involves the five D's:

Deter ~ Deny ~ Detect ~ Delay ~ Defend

The first *D* is *deter*. The first goal is to deter an attack by giving the appearance of a robust security program and substantial physical barriers. Deterrence also comes from aggressive defensive positioning. Countermeasures include an alert security force, vehicle checkpoints & searches, guard towers, visible weapons positions, lighting and armed patrols pushing out from the immediate perimeter.

The second principle is to *deny* access through physical barriers and security forces. The types of physical barriers include trenches, fences, concertina wire, razor ribbon, Hesco baskets and concrete barriers. In the absence of construction resources, security guard forces can be positioned to deny access. However, the fewer the physical barriers in place, the greater the security forces required to deny access into your perimeter.

The third *D* is *detect*. Early detection of an attempted intrusion or breach of your perimeter is critical to an effective defensive response. Detection is best achieved through open ground, cleared area, and alert security personnel. Assuming a *grid down* scenario, this can be augmented with guard dogs, trip flares, battery operated alarm systems and other noise or light generating devices.

The fourth principle is to *delay* your aggressor. When your physical barriers or security forces cannot stop an attack, they should at least be positioned to delay the approach. Additional barriers allow your security forces the time to regroup, reassess and re-engage the approaching attack. An effective delaying tactic will allow for reinforcements of your perimeter security forces.

The fifth *D* is *defend*, or as some might say—*destroy*. To put it bluntly, *kill or be killed*. Without rule of law—WROL—the Rules of Engagement with your adversaries will change. Make no mistake, *defend*, or the concept of *self-defense*, will be defined differently after a collapse event. The best defense is to destroy your enemy with whatever weapons are available to you. Otherwise, the sixth *D* results—*deceased*.

But, if you follow proper OPSEC, Operational Security, discussed at length below, you can minimize the number of threats that you face—especially if you follow disciplined OPSEC prior to the collapse event. Otherwise, you will face the sixth *D*.

Protection - Having a way to protect you and your family is very important during trying times as people in desperate situations will take desperate measures. Guns are a very important part of protection and may be able to diffuse a situation where talking and negotiating do not solve the situation. There are many different types of guns and many theories on which ones to own. Of course, any gun is better than no gun, but remember, each type of gun has different uses in a variety of situations. If your target is relatively close, a shotgun or pistol may be the best option. If your target is 60 yards or more away, a rifle is probably the best option. However, protection is not just limited to guns. Reusable and quiet weapons such as bows or knives are great to have because you constantly run the risk of depleting your bullet stockpile. Protection could also be in the form of a fence or barbed wire outside your home that deters thieves and other mischievous people.

Hunting- This also goes into the food category of beans, bullets and band-aids. In order to hunt efficiently and effectively, you need to know which hunting weapons to purchase and use. A .22 rifle would be much better for squirrel and varmint hunting than an AR-15. However, a .308 caliber rifle would be more effective for hunting deer or other big game animals. A bow may be better in any situation, as it is silent and will not arouse attention like a gun. Another great idea is the use of traps. These are reusable and are semi-passive ways of finding food. They can also protect your home from intruders. In the forest and plains areas, squirrels, elk, deer, birds, turkeys and waterfowl are all great sources of protein.

Finally, a word about *operational security*—***OPSEC***. This brings us to another important axiom of prepping:

Tell No One About Your Preps!

The Prepper's Creed begins:

If you don't talk, no one will hear and if no one else hears, no one else will know.

Operational Security, or OPSEC, for Preppers is a discipline, a mindset. It is simply denying an adversary, present or future, vital information that could harm you or benefit them.

Prior to collapse, OPSEC involves curtailing your activities on social media or not bragging about your weapons cache.

As kids we found comfort in our homes with our families, maybe hiding under the covers or with a fave blankie. As we grow up, our concerns may focus on job security, financial security and general home security. Now we are big boys and girls—preparing for TEOTWAWKI. Security takes on a whole new meaning when you have to fear armed marauders streaming down your driveway to take your preps, or worst. Your favorite blankie won't help you.

Once there is a life changing collapse event you may take comfort in knowing you're well prepped with all the beans, band-aids, and bullets a well prepared family could need. Well, guess what? Your failure to abide by OPSEC guidelines will quickly make you a target. There are relatively simple SOP—standard operating procedures—for survival groups who've advanced their level of preparation. How can you avoid armed confrontations with the marauders? What should you do prior to the collapse event in order to keep your preps hidden from the world?

Pre-Collapse: Getting Others to Prep

Getting other people to prep is far easier said than done. If it were easy to convince people to spend their hard earned money on a possible bad future, then we'd all be prepared, and there wouldn't be a fear of looting and raiding. But it isn't easy, and those threats are real.

When first talking to someone about prepping, you need to understand your audience. This means that if you're talking to a hard-core outdoorsman, you can bring up far more *survival-esque* components to prepping while a friend that is just talking about a natural disaster should be eased into it more.

Secondly, it's important to focus on the need to prep over the possible reasons. People don't like thinking about or cyber warfare, so instead of hearing you talk about prepping, those people will instead argue the finer points of why those things can't happen. If you focus on the possibility of something making food, water, or essentials like toilet paper hard to get, it only makes sense to prepare for that possibility. Whatever the case, getting people on board by scaring them doesn't work, but getting them to understand their lives without the essentials is a sure fire way to get them signed up.

Once you get friends and family on board with prepping for them, it's easier to talk with them and for everyone to help each other. There's something to be said for acting alone—*the lone wolf prepper*, but a little help will never hurt. If you make the determination to form a group, you can proceed with caution.

Pre-Collapse: Forming a prepper group

As preppers, you face a conundrum. Should you be part of a prepper group or should you be a lone wolf prepper? There are benefits and detriments to both options. Here are some considerations in forming a prepper group.

One of the first things a new prepper typically wants to do is reach out to other like-minded people in their area about prepping and trying to form a prepper group. Unless there is an established and open group in the area, it's often very difficult to form a post-collapse team. Preppers are naturally cautious about discussing prepping with people they don't already know. Unless the group is actively looking for new members, you might not even know about a group in your area.

If you are serious about preparing then you have probably come to the realization that you will not be able to do everything yourself when SHTF. Just the day-to-day chores of collecting firewood, sanitation issues, cooking, food procurement, and cleaning without modern technology, will be overwhelming for a family but when you have the added issue of providing your own security you quickly realize you will need help in maintaining security.

A prepper group is an association of people that have agreed to help each other out after a collapse event. The level of help depends on the scenario, the people involved, and the community. Some prepper groups encompass an entire small town or community. Typically, the residents intend to stay in their own homes but agree to provide mutual security and aid on a community-wide scale. Because of their size, these types of groups are rare, and formed post-collapse.

The most common type of group is a loosely organized group of people that may or may not live close to each other but have general plans to provide mutual aid. They might meet together on a regular basis to discuss different scenarios, take classes together, and combine orders for bulk purchasing. Some are well organized while others just pay lip service to the concept. A prepper group like this might be beneficial during the planning stage, but in an actual event the distance between them will make mutual aid impossible.

The next prepper group is a collaboration of several like-minded individuals that have made a plan, practiced their plan, and have a mutually agreed upon location to execute that plan as a group. They live fairly close to each other but instead of trying to stay in their various locations recognize the importance of being together to provide strength in numbers. This is the best case scenario.

Putting together a prepper group does not mean you find a group of survivalists and band together, there are several things you need to consider when deciding if someone is right for your group. Factors include:

1. What are they prepping for?
2. What skills or supplies do they bring to the table?
3. How many in their group and their relationship to each other
4. How committed are they?

When we look at forming our prepping group we have to consider if the people are like-minded, their skills, commitment, and who they bring with them. Later, for recruiting purposes, we also need to consider how many people we will need to accomplish what needs to be done

Recently, a Prepper in the Tampa, Florida area learned a hard lesson in choosing members for his preppers group. Many of the newest members had prior felonies which prohibited them from owning or possessing firearms. Further, this Florida prepper engaged in questionable conduct such as building pipe bombs and making veiled threats against law enforcement. When one of his new members of the group was arrested on unrelated charges, they turned snitch and wore a wire during the prepper's group meetings. The end result—the leader of the group is going to prison while the snitch walks free.

The debate will always rage as to whether you should be a member of a preppers group or a lone wolf prepper. Regardless of how you define your preppers group, there are common issues when determining who to let into *The Club*. It is a private membership which should always practice OPSEC due to the sensitive information everyone in the group has access to. You need to give careful consideration to the people becoming part of your group. In general, this is not an easy topic, as there are no fast and simple rules. The average human being is a complex bag of emotions and logic, to which fields of science have been dedicated to understanding. Therefore, it is not surprising when the person you thought to be a stable individual turns out to be not much more than a basket case.

Consider this. Choosing members of a preppers group is a lot like courting; you cannot really tell if they are right for you from just a few dates. Sure, we've all heard of love at first sight. However, given time, a person's true colors shine through. Being part of a group is not much different. There will be differences, arguments, heated debates, betrayals, and various other emotional conflicts. All of which need to be addressed, particularly since this group is supposed to be like a second family to you.

One very important aspect to keep in mind is what happens when someone stops being a group member. Though it may seem like many people would make a good group member, most will turn out to be incompatible with you and your group. Some people are very good at hiding who they really are, even after knowing someone for years. What has the newly ejected member learned about you, your family, and your preparedness plan? They may get kicked out of the group or they may decide to leave voluntarily. Either way, this person becomes a security risk.

When looking at group preparedness, remember that a long-term crisis scenario will require large amounts of labor for survival. Therefore, unless you are creating a specific paramilitary team, no one should be automatically discounted because of any disabilities or shortcomings (such as having a lack of gear). Look at each prospective member on a case-by-case basis, weighing their strengths and weaknesses, while keeping in mind that everyone has something to contribute. Finding group members is a tedious process, but the gains accomplished by having a group of people you can depend on are immeasurable.

Your survival may depend on it.

Post-collapse: How to Assimilate with your neighbors to form a group

These are all considerations of OPSEC for preppers that can be implemented prior to the collapse event. After TEOTWAWKI, when other factors like a grid down scenario come into play, OPSEC becomes less technology oriented.

After collapse, OPSEC will require you to resist the urge to step up and be the new leader of any newly formed survival group. One of the biggest mistakes preppers can make is to tell the wrong person or people about it. While helping people in a time of need is one of the most selfless things you can do, if you're the only person prepared in your neighborhood and everyone comes looking to you for help, all your pre-collapse OPSEC will be wasted as desperate people attempt to take the things you've worked so hard to save. We believe that it is better to be safe, keep our preparedness plans to ourselves, than to be sorry.

While you don't want to tell the world about your plans, it's expected that you want to share with close friends, family and possibly trusted coworkers. To help you understand who you should tell and who you shouldn't, we've put together a few points.

Complete privacy is nearly impossible to keep, especially when you will surely need help with something at some point. It will be very difficult to survive on your own. The biggest reason to form a survival group in our opinion is to maintain security. After collapse, your world will become much smaller. Your neighborhood will become your universe. Focus on establishing a group of neighbors first, and then look outward for like-minded thinkers.

The goal is to survive and if possible looters know what you have, that survival will be a big challenge. Within days if not hours of the collapse event, your neighbors will begin to gather to seek information. You will have a decision to make. Step up and be the leader of the group, or lay back and observe. We are in favor of continuing your OPSEC practice after collapse, and avoid a leadership role at first.

Here are the steps we recommend you take after a collapse event:

1. Take a day to gather information and assess the extent of the collapse. Observe your neighbors to gauge their reaction.

2. Maintain a heightened state of awareness. Every action and reaction of your neighbors should be observed, and not dismissed.

3. Be polite to everyone you deal with, but do so with confidence. You do not want to be perceived as weak.

4. Learn about the people around you from reliable sources. Immediately attempt to identify troublemakers.

5. Identify cliques within your neighborhood, and seek out individuals or families to approach. You have to establish trust.

6. Initially, don't worry about ascertaining the level of other people's preps. Avoid suspicion by not being to inquisitive.

7. If a neighborhood meeting is called, determine who the organizers are. Typically, these individuals will be type A, overbearing tEconomic Collapseeraments.

8. Don't make waves. Better to remain quiet, than to argue. Your job is not to take control, or provide information.

9. Conceal your weapons, and do not discuss your preps, ever.

In summary, focus on your immediate family. You shouldn't tell anyone else your plan. This means if you tell your parents that live outside your house (which of course you will) you need to save supplies for them as well. If you tell your close friends, you need food and water for them, too. If you tell anyone they immediately become part of your plan. This is why the final step is getting those special people in your life to prep as well. This way, you now have a network of trusted preppers that can help one another now and when times get tough. Once you have them all at your location, then you can begin to take a more active role in your neighborhood survival group. Your close-knit group of family and friends can defend your preps in case there is an uprising amongst your neighbors.

So the big question is *who should I tell about my prepping?* The answer is anyone you feel comfortable surviving TEOTWAWKI with. If you want to house enough supplies for all your neighbors to come enjoy, tell them at your own risk. Even then you run the risk of them telling their friends and so on until you have 100 people at your door looking for a handout. Help people with knowledge and never let on to the size of your prep or the weapons you have. Getting to know your neighbors will be a big help. You will be able to determine who has the will and aptitude to survive a collapse event. After collapse, cautiously approach those neighbors to form alliances and encourage them to use their skills to help them and your group.

This is only a start to the concept of beans, bullets and band-aids. The one thing I haven't discussed yet is the importance of research and knowledge. If money is an issue, this is a great place to start. This necessary step to survival just happens to be free. There are many great books and tutorials online that will teach you anything from CPR and fishing to gardening at no cost. Now that you know about beans, bullets and bandaids, you can start preparing for any scenario you see fit.

John F. Kennedy once said *the time to repair the roof is when the sun is shining.* Because you never know when the day before—is the day before. Prepare for tomorrow.

Thanks for reading!

SIGN UP to Bobby Akart's mailing list to receive your FREE copy of Bobby Akart's #1 bestseller— *Seeds of Liberty.* You'll also be one of the first to receive news about new releases in The Boston Brahmin series and the Prepping for Tomorrow series—which includes three Amazon #1 Bestsellers in 23 different non-fiction genres.

Sign up here:
http://eepurl.com/bk7i_9

Visit Bobby Akart's website for informative blog entries on preparedness, writing and his latest contribution to the American Preppers Network.

www.BobbyAkart.com

Stop by the Boston Brahmin website to dig deeper into the history, characters and real-life events that inspired the series.

www.TheBostonBrahmin.com

Visit the Freedom Preppers website to learn about all aspects of preparedness and the threats we face.

www.FreedomPreppers.com

APPENDIX A

AN EXCERPT FROM THE LOYAL NINE BY AMAZON
BEST-SELLING AUTHOR BOBBY AKART

Chapter 25

February 8, 2016
Harvard Kennedy School of Government
Cambridge, Massachusetts

Sarge was late for class. A massive pileup on the Mass Turnpike, near the Beacon Park rail yard, forced him to drive the long way, via Beacon Hill and East Cambridge. Ordinarily, he would enjoy the change of scenery, but he had already been running late. He and Julia had a sleepover—devoid of much sleep.

He entered the classroom to a round of throat clearing, followed by sarcastic applause. He gathered his thoughts and brought up the first slide on the screen:

ALL EMPIRES COLLAPSE EVENTUALLY

He turned to the class and took a moment to gauge their reaction. *Let's see what they think about this topic.*

"Okay, guys, what do you think I mean by this?" asked Sarge.

A few hands shot up. Sarge pointed at a meek student in the back of the room. *Time to come out of your shell.*

"Mr. Lin, what say you?"

"Professor Sargent, I believe that in the history of mankind, every civilization ever formed has eventually disappeared or been replaced," said Lin.

"How does this come about, Mr. Lin?" asked Sarge.

"They either go broke or get their asses kicked," said Lin.

This elicited a round of laughter from his classmates. Sarge was also amused. *So much for Mr. Lin's shell.*

"Thank you, Mr. Lin, for that concise, articulate answer," Sarge chuckled. "All empires collapse eventually when they are defeated by a more powerful enemy or when their funding runs out."

"Ladies and Gentlemen, there have been no exceptions in the history of mankind. Empires are not typically the result of conscious thought. Empires form when a group of people is large enough and powerful enough to impose its will on others—or *kick their asses,*" said Sarge with a nod and smile to Lin.

"But Empires are expensive," continued Sarge. "Throughout history, how did the mighty empires of the world finance themselves?"

Sarge saw the hands pop up. He chose Miss Crepeau.

"To the victor go the spoils," she replied.

"Exactly. Thank you, Miss Crepeau," said Sarge. "In the early

1800s, this phrase was coined by a New York politician, but we have President Andrew Jackson to thank for the modern-day patronage system, which is so prevalent in our government today. President Jackson believed it was healthy to clear out the prior administration's workers and bring in fresh faces. This patronage policy resulted in many *Jacksonian Democrats*, his political supporters, being placed into important government positions."

Sarge allowed the playful banter between warring political factions in the class to settle down before interrupting.

"Before the Republicans point fingers, I will remind you—the Southern Democrats of the early nineteenth century are the political equivalent of today's Southern Republican base," said Sarge.

The class erupted in another round of political posturing.

"So," said Sarge, pausing to bring the class back to attention, "to Miss Crepeau's point, Empires have historically financed their governments through force and theft. The great Empires conquer their lesser opponents, take everything they have, and extort protection money out of the conquered citizens. This is how all of the great Empires of the world were formed.

"Some might argue that the United States is different—and in some respects it is," said Sarge. "America was not formed by conquering another, less powerful opponent, although the Native Americans might disagree. The Founding Fathers sought independence from what they considered oppressive rule from Great Britain. But the formation of the great American Empire, if you will, is only part of the equation."

Sarge brought up a new screen.

Who's going to pay for this new Empire?

"Part two of the formation of a new Empire involves financing its operations," said Sarge. "America didn't conquer another nation and plunder its wealth. The premise of the American Revolutionary War included a revolt against the implementation of taxes on the citizenry.

Clearly, there wasn't a stomach for that. What did they do to pay for this new government?"

The young law student, Ocampo, eagerly raised his hand.

"Mr. Ocampo," said Sarge, "what do you think?"

"They fired up the printing presses, sir," said Ocampo.

"That's true to an extent," said Sarge. "The Constitution provided in Article One that the federal government had the sole power *to coin money and regulate the value thereof.* But the Constitution was devoid of reference to paper money. You see, the Founding Fathers had some experience with paper money. The Continental Congress, as Ocampo suggested, fired up the printing presses and financed the American Revolution with a newly minted currency — *continentals.* Unfortunately, although I would argue predictably, the *continentals* became worthless by the end of the war—to the point they were never spoken of again.

"It wasn't until the Civil War when the National Banking Act was passed that the paper dollar became the fully accepted currency of the land," said Sarge. "The United States adopted a gold standard, and its currency value became universally accepted. This leads us to one of the most important acts of participation by our country in global governance in its history—the Bretton Woods Conference."

Sarge changed the slide.

"After the conclusion of World War II, delegates from the forty-four Allied nations participated in the UN Financial and Monetary Conference in Bretton Woods, New Hampshire. This conference produced the International Monetary Fund and the World Bank," said Sarge. "At the time, the United States was the world's greatest economic power and had a lot of influence on the agreements reached. Study the history and background of the Bretton Woods system. This is a prime example of the impact of global governance." Sarge changed the slide again.

The Nixon Shock

"Welcome to the Nixon Shock, the mother of all government

economic intervention," said Sarge. "In essence, among other things, President Nixon abandoned the gold standard and the United States dollar became strictly a fiat currency. This is when we fired up the printing presses, Mr. Ocampo, and we haven't stopped since.

"You see, America never grasped the whole concept of being an empire. We conquered, but we did not take anything like our predecessors. In fact, history will show that we lose money on every conquest. Typically, after destroying another country in battle, we then move in and pay to fix it back. We lose money every time," said Sarge, returning to a previous slide.

Who's going to pay for this?

"So how does a nation that conquers without obtaining the spoils of victory sustain itself?" asked Sarge. "They do it with debt. No other Empire has ever tried to finance itself by borrowing from others. No other nation has ever tried to borrow its own currency, which it prints any time it chooses. As we have seen in recent years, if the burden of repaying this debt is too high, the Federal Reserve simply prints more dollars to satisfy its creditors. They call this Ponzi scheme *quantitative easing*. The United States government is paying its prior debt obligations by issuance of new debt obligations or the printing of new money out of thin air. There are people sitting in Federal Prison for this exact type of scheme.

"Today, our national debt, the amount we owe our creditors, is twenty trillion dollars. Every year, we add another one point two trillion to this total," said Sarge. "Many argue that this trend is unsustainable, which leads us back to our original premise." Sarge changed the slide back to the beginning. He had come full circle.

ALL EMPIRES COLLAPSE EVENTUALLY

"All empires collapse when they are defeated by a more vigorous empire, such as China, Russia or any of a number of rogue nations who possess nuclear capabilities," said Sarge. "Or Empires collapse when their financing runs out. America has built up a tremendous amount of debt that is owed to countries that do not like us very much—like China and Russia.

"I want you to consider this. Should China and Russia elect to devalue our currency, resulting in our allies such as Germany and Japan becoming skittish about purchasing more of our debt, what would be the fate of the almighty dollar?" asked Sarge rhetorically. "If the United States cannot continue to finance itself via debt instruments, then it must tax its citizenry at an unprecedented rate. I submit to you that there isn't enough income or wealth in this country to cover the bill."

Sarge pointed to the screen.

"I will leave you with this. If all empires eventually collapse, does this premise also apply to the United States? If so, is this the beginning of the end?"

APPENDIX B

PREPAREDNESS CHECKLIST

Provided by www.FreedomPreppers.com

Go here for
PREPPERS CHECKLIST

www.freedompreppers.com/preppers-checklist-free-pdf-
download.htm

APPENDIX C

By Eamonn Butler in association with the Adam Smith Organization Reprinted with Permission from AdamSmith.org.

Adam Smith's The Wealth of Nations is one of the most important books ever written. Smith recognised that economic specialization and cooperation was the key to improving living standards. He shattered old ways of thinking about trade, commerce and public policy, and led to the foundation of a new field of study: economics.

And yet, his book is rarely read today. It is written in a dense and archaic style that is inaccessible to many modern readers. The Condensed Wealth of Nations condenses Smith's work and explains the key concepts in The Wealth of Nations clearly. It is accessible and readable to any intelligent layman.

This appendix also contains a primer on The Theory of Moral Sentiments, Adam Smith's other great work that explores the nature of ethics.

Chapter 1 Introduction by Eamonn Butler

Adam Smith's pioneering book on economics, The Wealth of Nations published in 1776, is around 950 pages long. Modern readers find it almost impenetrable: its language is flowery, its terminology is outmoded, it wanders into digressions, including one seventy pages in length, and its numerous eighteenth-century examples often puzzle rather than enlighten us today.

And yet, The Wealth of Nations is one of the world's most

important books. It did for economics what Newton did for physics and Darwin did for biology. It took the outdated, received wisdom about trade, commerce, and public policy, and re-stated them according to completely new principles that we still use fruitfully today. Smith outlined the concept of gross domestic product as the measurement of national wealth; he identified the huge productivity gains made possible by specialization; he recognized that both sides benefited from trade, not just the seller; he realized that the market was an automatic mechanism that allocated resources with great efficiency; he understood the wide and fertile collaboration between different producers that this mechanism made possible. All these ideas remain part of the basic fabric of economic science, over two centuries later.

So The Wealth of Nations is worth reading, but nearly impossible to read. What we need today is a much shorter version: one that presents Smith's ideas, not filtered through some modern commentator, but in modern language. This book aims to do precisely that, updating the language and the technical terms, with just enough of Smith's examples and quotations to provide a sense of colour, and with marginal notes to explain how today's economic concepts have developed from Smith's early ideas.

The same treatment is given to The Theory of Moral Sentiments (1759) – Smith's other great book, and the one that made him famous. A product of the philosophy course that Smith taught at Glasgow University, it explained morality in terms of our nature as social creatures. It so impressed the young Duke of Buccleuch's stepfather that he promptly hired Smith (on a handsome lifetime salary) to tutor the boy, and escort him on an educational journey through Europe. With time on his hands, and new insights gleaned on these travels, Smith began sketching out the book that would become The Wealth of Nations. He spent another decade writing and polishing the text at his home in Scotland, and debating his ideas with the leading intellectuals of the age in London. The finished book was another huge commercial success, rapidly going into several editions and translations.

It was revolutionary stuff. It hit squarely at the prevailing idea that nations had to protect their trade from other countries. It showed that free trade between nations, and between individuals at home too, left both sides better off. It argued that when governments interfered with that freedom with controls, tariffs or taxes, they made their people poorer rather than richer.

Smith's ideas influenced the politicians and changed events. They led to trade treaties, tax reform, and an unwinding of tariffs and subsidies that in turn unleashed the great nineteenth-century era of free trade and growing world prosperity.

Chapter 2 The Condensed Wealth of Nations

A nation's wealth is its per capita national product – the amount that the average person actually produces. For any given mix of natural resources that a country might possess, the size of this per capita product will depend on the proportion of the population who are in productive work. But it also depends, much more importantly, on the skill and efficiency with which this productive labour is employed.

At the time, this idea was a huge innovation. The prevailing wisdom was that wealth consisted in money – in precious metals like gold and silver. Smith insists that real wealth is in fact what money buys – namely, the 'annual produce of the land and labour of the society'. It is what we know today as gross national product or GNP, and is used as the measure of different countries' prosperity.

Wealth of Nations examines the mechanism by which this productive efficiency comes to be improved. Productive employment depends (it will be shown) on how and how much capital is in use. The Wealth of Nations is divided into five 'books' which are in turn divided into chapters. Where Smith writes 'stock' we would normally use 'capital' today. Book II explores this. National product is also greatly influenced by public policy, which Book III considers. Book IV appraises different theories of economics in the light of all these considerations. Book V then identifies the proper role of government, the principles of taxation, and the impact of government on the economy.

Book I: Economic efficiency and the factors of production

Specialization and productivity

The key to economic efficiency is specialisation – the division of labour. Take even the trifling manufacture of pin making, for example. Most of us would be hard pressed to make even one pin in a day, even if the metal were already mined and smelted for us. We could certainly not make twenty. And yet ten people in a pin factory can make 48,000 pins a day. That is because they each specialise in different parts of the operation. One draws out the wire, another straightens it, a third cuts it, a fourth points it, a fifth grinds the top to receive the head.

Making and applying the head require further specialist operations; whitening the pins and packaging them still more. Specialisation has made the process thousands of times more productive. This enormous gain in productivity has led to specialisation being introduced, not just within trades, but between them. Farming, for instance, becomes much more efficient if farmers can spend all their time tending their land, their crops and their livestock, rather than pausing to tool up and make their own household items too.

Likewise, ironmongers and furniture-makers can produce far more of these household goods if they do not have to dissipate their effort on growing their own food too. Even whole countries specialise, exporting the goods they make best and importing the other commodities that they need.

The greatest improvement in the productive power of labour, and the greater part of the skill, dexterity, and judgment with which it is anywhere directed, or applied, seems to have been the effects of the division of labour.

Three factors explain the enormous rise in efficiency which specialisation makes possible.

• First is the increased skill which people gain when they do the same task over and over again. The rapidity with which skilled workers can do a task is sometimes amazing.

• Second, less time is wasted in moving from one task to the next. A weaver who cultivates a smallholding has to break off weaving, fetch the farming tools, and walk out to the field. It takes time for people to get in the right frame of mind when they turn from one task to another, and back again. The importance of such disruptions should not be underestimated.

• Third, specialisation allows the use of dedicated machinery, which dramatically cuts the time and effort needed in manufactures. Often, workers themselves have invented labour-saving devices, while other improvements have come from the machine-makers, who are now a specialist set of trades themselves.

The division of labour clearly requires an advanced degree of cooperation between all those who are involved in the manufactures concerned. Indeed, the production of even the simplest object harnesses the cooperation of many thousands of people. A woollen coat, for example, requires the work of shepherds, sorters, carders, dyers, spinners, weavers, and many more. Even the shears needed to cut the wool will have required the work of miners and ironworkers. And the transportation of the wool will have required sailors, shipwrights, and sail-makers. The list is endless.

The woollen coat, for example, which covers the day-labourer, as coarse and rough as it may appear, is the product of the joint labour of a great multitude of workmen. The shepherd, the sorter of the wool, the wool-comber or carder, the dyer, the scribbler, the spinner, the weaver, the fuller, the dresser, with many others, must all join their different arts in order to complete even this homely production.

This collaboration of thousands of highly efficient specialists is a very advanced economic system: and it is, in fact, the source of the developed countries' great wealth. It means that things are produced far more efficiently, making them cheaper. Even the poorest members of society thereby gain access to a wide variety of products and services that would be completely unaffordable in the absence of specialisation.

The mutual gains from exchange Specialisation developed out of the natural human tendency to barter and exchange. When we see people who have things that we want, we know that they are unlikely to give them to us out of the goodness of their hearts. But then we might have something which they want, and which we would be prepared to give them in return.

It is not from the benevolence of the butcher, the brewer, or the baker, that we expect our dinner, but from their regard to their own interest. We address ourselves, not to their humanity but to their self-love, and never talk to them of our own necessities but of their advantages.

By 'self-love' or 'self-interest', Smith does not imply 'greed' or 'selfishness'. He has in mind a concern for our own welfare that is entirely natural and proper indeed, in The Theory of Moral Sentiments he calls it 'prudence'. And he stresses that 'justice' – not harming others – is fundamental to a healthy human society.

And this in fact is how we acquire most of the things we need – through exchange, rather than trying to make everything ourselves. And the trade has made both of us better off. We have each sacrificed something we value less for something we value more.

This is another crucial insight. In Smith's world, like ours, most goods were exchanged for money rather than bartered for other goods. Since money was regarded as wealth, it seemed that only the seller could benefit from the process. It is a notion that led to the creation of a vast web of restrictions on trade, in the attempt to prevent money leaking out of a country, a town, or even a profession. But Smith shows that the benefit of exchange is mutual, so no such restrictions are needed.

These gains from exchange, and our natural willingness to do it, stimulate the division of labour. It is worth us building up a surplus of what we personally make well in order to have something to trade with other people. To take it at its simplest, imagine a primitive society where, through some particular mental or physical talents, one person is better than others at making arrows, or building houses, or dressing skins, or working metal. If, through that specialist skill, they make more of these things than they have personal need for, it gives them something they can exchange with others. So each can then focus on their efficient specialist production, and get the other things they need from exchange with other efficient producers. The smith trades surplus knives for the fletcher's surplus arrows, the tanner trades clothing for the builder's shelter. Each ends up with the mix of things they want, all of them expertly and efficiently produced.

Even the most dissimilar people can thus cooperate – though they do not do so from any great feelings of benevolence, but because both sides see a personal benefit from the exchanges that they make. Wider markets bring bigger gains The benefit that we get from exchange is what drives us to specialise, and so increase the surplus that we maintain to exchange with others. Just how far that specialisation can go depends on the extent to which exchange is possible – that is, on the extent of the market.

Some trades – the profession of a porter, for example – are possible only in large towns, where there are enough customers to provide constant work. At the other end of the scale, though, each family in the remote Highlands of Scotland must be its own farmer, butcher, baker, brewer and carpenter. In between, a country smith must deal in every sort of ironwork, and a country carpenter must be a joiner, a cabinetmaker, carver, wheelwright and wagon-maker all at once.

Money and value

One thing that definitely does extend the market is money. In a commercial society, where specialisation is strong, we make few of our own needs, and rely on our exchanges with others to supply our wants. But exchange would be difficult if, for example, hungry brewers always had to search out thirsty bakers. Rather than everyone having to rely on finding some person with exactly the inverse of their own needs, ancient human societies therefore strove to find some medium of exchange – some third commodity that most people would be happy to trade for their own product, and could then trade with others.

In Homer's time it was cattle; in Abyssinia it is salt; shells serve the purpose in India, dried cod in Newfoundland, tobacco in Virginia, and sugar in the West Indies. But over time, metal became the standard currency. It is durable, and (unlike cattle) can be divided without loss into small amounts, then reassembled into larger amounts again, according to the need. Originally, simple bars of copper served as money in ancient Rome; but these were variable, and the quantity had to be weighed each time they were used. So eventually, stamps were devised, showing the standard of weight and fineness of the metal – the first coins.

But, whether exchange is mediated through money or not, what is it that determines the rate at which different products are exchanged? The word value has two meanings – one is value in use, the other is value in exchange. Water is extremely useful, but has almost no exchange value, while a diamond is largely useless but has enormous exchange value.

Explaining the principles that determine exchange value, the components of this price, and the factors that cause it to fluctuate, was no easy matter. Indeed it is not. It takes Smith several chapters of The Wealth of Nations to do it, specifically Book I, Chapters V–XI. Today we might solve the diamonds and water problem with marginal utility theory: since diamonds are so rare, an additional one is a great prize, but since water is so plentiful, an extra cupful is actually of little use to us. Or we might use demand analysis. But such tools did not exist in Smith's time.

The real measure of the exchangeable value of all commodities is the labour put into their production. The reason why we put effort into creating the product we sell is precisely to spare ourselves the effort of creating the things we buy. When we trade, what we are buying is the labour of others. Ultimately, wealth is not money – it is the amount of other people's labour that we can command, or purchase. (Of course, some sorts of labour might be more difficult, or require more ingenuity than others. But these things will be adjusted by the bargaining in the marketplace.)

For many commentators, this looks uncomfortably like a crude labour theory of value, which focuses on production costs and overlooks demand. Some argue that it led Karl Marx into his appalling errors about labour. One could defend Smith as just trying to simplify things by talking about an age before land or capital ownership, where labour was the sole production cost, and temporarily ignoring other factors such as land and capital, and also ignoring demand, all of which he goes into later. At best his words are misleading, at worst they are mistaken: but then he was breaking new ground.

Usually, of course, we estimate exchange value in terms of money, because money is far more tangible and easy to measure than labour. But it is not a perfect measure. The metals we use for coinage, such as gold and silver, fluctuate in value over the long term, depending, say, on the productivity of the mines and the cost of transportation. Labour remains the real price: money prices are just nominal prices. We buy in from others things that it would cost us more toil and trouble to do for ourselves. The real wealth that we obtain from exchanging with others is their labour, not their money.

Labour, capital, and land

In a primitive, hunting society where there is no stock and land is free, labour is the only factor of production. Since there is no point in anyone buying something they could make with less effort themselves, prices should always reflect the labour involved. If it costs twice the labour to kill a beaver than it does to kill a deer, one beaver should exchange for two deer (though the difficulty or dexterity of the required labour will be reflected in market prices).

In the hunting society, the whole product of labour belongs to the labourer. It is different, though, when people acquire capital and employ others to work with it. Then, the product must be shared between them – in the wages of the labourer and the profit of the employer. Profits, though, are different from wages: they reflect not the work of the employer, but the value of the capital that is employed in the production.

In the earlier chapters of The Wealth of Nations, Smith uses the word 'stock' rather than 'capital'. He later explains that 'stock' includes fixed and circulating capital, as well as materials being used in the process of manufacture, finished goods that are still unsold, and goods being held for later consumption. And then he starts talking more about 'capital'. Normally today we would call all these things 'capital', including any 'stock' of semifinished, unsold or unconsumed goods; it seems easier to use this term.

When land is taken into private ownership, a third group shares in the national product, namely the landlords. Food, fuel, and minerals are now no longer available merely for the labour of collecting them. The landlords demand that part of the product must now be remitted to them as rent.

Thus there are three factors of production, remunerated by different principles. The price of wheat comprises partly the rent of the landlord, partly the wages of the labourers, and partly the profit of the farmer who provides the money and the equipment to run the business. In the price of flour, the profits of the miller and the wages of the miller's workers must be added; and in the price of bread, similarly, the profits of the baker and the wages of the baker's staff. However many people are involved in a productive process, the costs always resolve themselves into some or other of these three elements.

Of course, it is possible for two or more of these revenue streams to belong to the same person. A planter may combine the roles of landlord and farmer, and a farmer may combine the roles of farmer and labourer: so some mixture of rent, profit and wages then comes to the same person.

Production costs and market prices

The wages and profits in any production process tend to an average rate that depends on the market. When the price of a commodity exactly matches the cost (rent, profit, wages) of producing it and bringing it to market, we might call it the natural price. If it sells at more than that, the seller makes a profit. If it sells at less, the seller makes a loss. The language is antiquated, but by 'natural price' Smith means no more than the cost of production, including a 'normal' rate of profit under competition.

This is in line with his view that value has more to do with what goes into a product, whereas today we would talk about supply and demand. This makes the term 'natural price' difficult to render in modern language, but it seems sensible to use simply 'cost of production'. The price at which products are actually sold is called the market price. This depends on supply and demand – the quantity of the product that sellers bring to market, and the size of the demand from potential buyers. When supply falls short of demand, there is competition between buyers, and the price is bid up. If a town is blockaded, for example, the prices of essential goods rise enormously. By contrast, when there is a glut and supply exceeds demand, sellers have to drop their price – particularly if the product is perishable, like fruit, and cannot be brought back to market later.

When supply and demand match exactly, however, the natural and market price are equal, and the market exactly clears. If a market is overstocked and prices are below the cost of production, landlords will withdraw their land, employers their stock, and workers their labour, rather than suffer continued losses in this line of production. So the quantity supplied will fall, and market prices will be bid up again to the natural price, at which the market is cleared. If, by contrast, a market is understocked and prices are high, producers will commit more resources to this profitable line of production. So the quantity supplied will rise, and market prices will be bid down again to the natural, market-clearing price.

The market is therefore self-regulating. Prices are always gravitating towards the cost of production under competition, and producers are always aiming to supply the amount of their product that exactly matches customers' demand.

Here is yet another hugely important insight from Smith. The market is a completely inevitable system. In their natural pursuit of profit, sellers steer their resources to where the demand, and therefore price, is highest, thereby Smith calls this effectual demand, pointing out that some people who would like a product cannot actually afford it. Today this is understood, and we would say simply resources are drawn to their most valued application, without the need for any central direction.

Specific price factors

Of course, market prices still fluctuate above or below the cost of production. Because harvests are variable, for example, the same labour may produce more wheat, wine, oil or hops in one year than in another, and the market price will fall or rise accordingly. The production of other goods, such as linen and woollen cloth, suffers less variation of this sort, and prices are more stable. But a public mourning will raise the price of black cloth, for example, along with the wages of journeymen tailors.

When demand increases and the market price of a commodity rises above its cost of production, suppliers naturally try to conceal the fact that they are making extraordinary profits. They do not want to alert their competitors. So prices may remain high for a while. But such secrets cannot be kept for long.

Manufacturing secrets may last longer. A dyer, for example, who finds a way of producing a particular colour at half the usual cost, might enjoy extraordinary profits for many years before competitors also discover it. So here the market price may diverge from the natural price for a long time.

Other special circumstances can have the same effect. The favourable soil and situation of particular French vineyards, for example, may raise their rent well above others in the same neighbourhood. Or again, a supplier who is granted a monopoly can keep prices up, simply by restricting supply. Likewise, laws that limit apprenticeships, or restrict the number of people who can enter a trade, enable particular professions to keep their prices high.

As a result of such accidents, natural causes, and regulations, the market price of a product may remain above the production cost for some time. But it cannot long remain below it. In that case, suppliers would simply withdraw, rather than face continued losses (assuming they are free to do so – unlike ancient Egypt, for example, where boys were forced to follow their father's trade).

Wages depend on economic growth

As we have seen, in an age before land is appropriated by owners, and capital is accumulated by employers, the whole produce of labour belongs to the labourer. But as soon as land is appropriated, landlords demand a share of any production that uses their land, and as soon as capital is accumulated, employers demand the same.

There are a few workers who own all the stock needed for their own production activities, but this is uncommon. Usually, workers are employees of other people, who own productive assets. How the product is shared, then, is a matter of contract between workers and employers: but the employers usually have the upper hand.

Since there are fewer of them, they can combine more easily to rig the labour market and keep down wages. They have greater resources with which to sit out a trade dispute. And while the law forbids combinations of workers, the collusion of employers is everywhere.

Throughout his writings, Smith shows great sympathy for the ordinary working people of the time, and little for the merchants and employers, whom he sees as trying to rig markets in their own favour. This often comes as a shock to people who assume that Smith, as a believer in markets and free trade, must be on the side of the bosses. Smith believes that free and competitive markets are the best way to spread wealth, and in particular, to spread it to the poor – and that the efforts of politicians and business people to diminish competition and freedom should therefore be resisted.

When the demand for labour is rising, however, the workers have the advantage, and competition between employers bids up wages. But the demand for labour can rise only when gross national product rises, since wages can only be paid out of income or capital. When wealthy landlords have spare revenue, for example, they hire more servants; when weavers or shoemakers have surplus stock, they hire more journeymen. Wages cannot rise if the national product is static or falling.

China has long been a rich, fertile, industrious and populous country; but there seems to have been little or no development there since Marco Polo visited it five hundred years ago. The land is still cultivated and not neglected, but China's economy is not growing. That is why the poverty of the poorest labourers in China is greater than in even the poorest nations of Europe.

Bengal is also a fertile country, but poverty is so rife that hundreds of thousands of people die of hunger each year. Clearly, the national product that is needed to maintain the labouring poor is in fact shrinking (for which we can blame the oppression of the East India Company).

Factors affecting wage rates

In growing economies such as that of Great Britain, however, wages are above subsistence, though they do vary. Summer wages, for example, are higher, because workers need to save for the winter, when wages are lower but costs are higher. Wages also vary from place to place. The usual price of labour in London is about eighteen pence a day; in Edinburgh it is ten pence; in rural Scotland it is eight pence. And yet, grain – the food of the common people – is dearer in Scotland than in England, where it grows better. If working people in Scotland can sustain themselves on these low wages and with high grain prices, it suggests that the working people in England must be living in some affluence.

Though wages are rising in Great Britain, prices are generally falling as a result of the rising productivity brought on by specialisation. Potatoes, turnips, carrots and cabbages, for example, cost half of what they did forty years ago. Linen and woollen cloth is cheaper, as is ironmongery and furniture. We should welcome the fact that the working poor are becoming better off: a country where most people live in poverty can hardly be called rich and happy. (It is true that soap, salt, candles, leather and alcohol have become more expensive – though mainly because of the taxes on them. But these are luxuries which do not feature in the budgets of most working people.)

No society can surely be flourishing and happy, of which the far greater part of the members are poor and miserable. Decent wages are essential for the well-being of labourers and their families. But to pay decent wages is in the interests of employers, too. When wages are high, workers are better fed and stronger. They also have the prospect of saving and improving their condition, which makes them more inclined to work diligently. And when workers are given sufficient rest, they are likely to be healthier and more productive.

Capital and profits

The profit which employers derive from capital is even more variable and hard to measure than the wages of labour. It depends on market prices, on how competitors are faring, and on the many problems that can occur in the production, transportation and storage of goods. Interest rates, however, provide a rough index of profitability: if people can make a good profit from the use of money, they will be prepared to pay well to borrow it.

As we have seen, an increase in capital allows more business to take place, and so tends to raise wages. But it also tends to reduce profits. The greater supply of capital increases the competition between its owners, and bids down the rate of return that it can generate, and the interest rates that borrowers will be prepared to pay for its use.

However, there are exceptions in particular circumstances. In the North American and West Indian colonies, for example, wages are high, and so are interest rates. So those are indicators that profits are high too. The reason is that there is plenty of fertile land in these territories, but as yet there aren't enough people or capital to cultivate it. Workers and equipment are in great demand, and therefore they command high prices. This, of course, does not last forever: as new colonies grow, they have to bring more marginal land into production, and profits gradually fall.

Another special case might be where a country has become as rich as its soil and situation can sustain, and could grow no further. Being fully populated, there would be great competition and wages would be low; and being fully capitalised, the competition between employers would be great, and profits would be low as well. But no country has yet reached this degree of wealth.

Today we see no limit to economic growth. Our capital and technology give rise to all kinds of new business sectors and opportunities for employment. In Smith's time, however, the economy was dominated by agriculture, and he mistakenly sees the impossibility of developing land beyond its fertility as a limit to economic growth.

Market wage rates

In any locality, the net benefits of employing labour or capital should tend to equalise across all uses. If they did not, and there were higher wages or profits to be made in some particular industry, workers or employers would flood into that employment – whereupon wages or profits would be bid back down towards the norm. In reality, however, it is obvious that the financial rewards that are actually achieved in different lines of work and industry vary widely. But in saying that the rewards of employment tend to equality, the non-pecuniary costs and benefits of different industries must be considered too, along with the purely financial returns. There are several such factors:

• First, some professions may be easier, cleaner, or more respectable than others. A weaver earns more than a tailor because the work is harder, a smith more than a weaver because the work is dirtier. A collier earns still more because that work is dark, dirty and dangerous. Butchers are well paid because the work is brutal and odious; and in the case of public executioners, even more so.

• Second, some professions are difficult or expensive to learn. The time and effort spent in learning them has to be recovered through the price of the work done. Hence a skilled labourer is better paid than an unskilled one.

• Third, some trades are seasonal. A builder cannot work in frost or hard weather, and has to earn enough in good seasons to provide for the dearth of work in the bad. Common labourers earn four or five shillings a week, but, for this reason, builders earn seven or eight shillings a week during the seasons when they can work.

• Fourth, earnings are higher in trades that require a large degree of trust, such as goldsmiths, lawyers or doctors. Their honesty and competence commands a premium from their customers.

• Fifth, earnings reflect the probability of success in any profession. Lawyers are well paid because very few of those who go into the law actually succeed in it. Their customers are paying the costs of those who fail, along with those who succeed. The exorbitant rewards of actors, singers, dancers and so on reflect not only this, but the rarity and beauty of their talents – and the discredit of employing them in such professions.

Other special circumstances can also make a difference to wage and profit rates. For example:

• First, it depends on how established the trade is. Entrepreneurs will have to pay more to attract workers from established trades into new ones. Employment in the new trade may be seen as less secure, or more dependent on the fickleness of fashion.

• Second, there might be a particular shift in supply or demand. In time of war, for example, merchant sailors' wages rise from twenty-one or twenty-seven shillings a month to more like forty or sixty shillings. And in different years, harvests of wheat, wine, hops, sugar, tobacco and other crops can vary greatly, and the profits made by the dealers will necessarily vary too.

• Third, pay can vary when people have more than one job: cottagers in Scotland commonly receive an acre or two of land, and two pecks of oatmeal a week in return for their occasional labour to the farmer. This they consider as their salary: and they are willing to work for others in their spare time for very little.

Wages and politics

It is not just the economic character of different employments that can lead to discrepancies in wages and profits. Political factors can be critical too.

First, there are regulations that restrict entry into certain professions. The fewer people who are allowed to practise in a particular trade, the more they can charge for their services. And the professions have exploited this by promoting various rules governing apprenticeships. Bye-laws forbid master cutlers in Sheffield, for example, from having more than one apprentice at a time, while Norfolk weavers, English hatters and London silk weavers are not allowed more than two. Apprenticeships are also very long, usually seven years. This is supposed to protect the public from shoddy work. In fact it does no such thing, but like the limit on apprentice numbers, it again serves to keep up the wages of the relevant professions. Unfortunately, this gain for the producers is achieved only by forcing the public to pay more, and by denying others the right to use the sacred property of their own labour as they choose.

It is perfectly natural that the professional guilds should try to expand their markets and limit the competition – and thereby promote their own interest against that of the general public. Unfortunately, they have been aided in this by the law, which grants them special privileges. The establishment of a public register of a profession's members, for example, makes it easier for them to come together (and, of course, talk about how to raise their prices or restrict the market still further). Laws that allow professions to levy compulsory welfare funds for the benefit of their own members make it inevitable that they have to come together. And allowing trades to decide policy by a majority vote will limit competition more effectively and durably than any voluntary collusion whatever.

People of the same trade seldom meet together, even for merriment and diversion, but the conversation ends in a conspiracy against the public, or in some contrivance to raise prices. The only truly effective discipline over businesses is their fear of losing customers. A competitive market in which customers are sovereign is a surer way to regulate their behaviour than any number of official rules – which so often produce the opposite of their avowed intention.

Secondly, public policy can sometimes depress the earnings of a trade by over-encouraging entry into them. Public pensions, scholarships, bursaries and so on may have this effect.

Third, the law obstructs the circulation of labour and capital from trade to trade and from place to place. For example, the arts of weaving linen, silk and wool are not very different. If one of these industries faced hard times, its members could quickly re-train and move into another. But the other trades have secured legal powers, such as rules on apprenticeships, that enable them to exclude these workers. Similarly, the poor laws, which made each parish responsible for the support its own poor, made parishes unwilling to allow poor people to move in from other areas, even if they were willing to look for new work.

Land and Rents

The third factor of production is land, and rent is what is paid for its contribution to the national product. Rent is different from wages, which must be laboured for, or the profits of capital, which must be carefully accumulated and managed. It is derived merely on account of ownership, rather than any care and effort of the landlord. Indeed, rent is charged even on unimproved land.

Scottish landlords whose estates are bounded by kelp shores charge a rent to those who harvest this useful seaweed that washes up naturally – just as surely as they charge a rent for their wheat fields.

In his discussions of landlords, Smith has principally in mind the Scottish chiefs and nobles who dominated huge tracts of land there. Much of it was being enclosed; and forfeited Jacobite estates were being handed over to new owners. Hence, perhaps, Smith's scornful view of landlords as an avaricious class who 'love to reap where they never sowed'.

Landlords take as much rent as they can get; when wages or profits are high, rents naturally follow. Fortunately for them, almost any land can produce more food than is required for the subsistence of those who work it. Even the deserted moors of Norway and Scotland produce pasture for cattle, which provide more than ample milk and meat for the few people who are needed to tend them. In other words, land always produces some surplus that can provide a rent to the landlord. Land that is very fertile, or well situated (close to a town and its markets, for example) will produce an even higher rent.

As well as food, of course, land provides clothing and living space. Once again, land can always provide a surplus of clothing, from the skins of animals, for example. The natives of North America probably had so many pelts that they would be thrown away as being of no value – until the Europeans arrived, eager to trade these things for blankets, guns and brandy.

A rich family consumes no more food than a poor one – though it may be of better quality. But the landowners who have command of more food than they can eat – either through growing it themselves or in the form of rent from tenants – nevertheless seem to have a boundless appetite for clothing, housing and showy equipage.

Compare the spacious palaces and great wardrobes of the rich with the hovels and the few rags of the poor. The rich are always willing to exchange their surplus for luxuries of this kind, and the poor are equally willing to supply this demand in order to get the basics that they need by way of exchange. The poor compete and specialise to supply the rich, which boosts the efficiency of production, raises incomes, and creates a growing demand for buildings, dress, furniture, fuel, minerals, precious stones – every convenience that the land can produce. But still the landlords take their share, of course, because all those farms, forests and mines produce a rent for them.

On the basis of his principle that every part of a nation's production reflects rent, wages and profits, Smith has shown that all the various actors in an economy – landowners, workers and employers – are in fact interdependent. Indeed, their interdependence goes beyond production: since goods are produced to be exchanged, they are all crucially involved in the valuation and distribution of that product too. In other words, they are parts of a seamless system of flows in which goods are created, valued, exchanged, used and replaced – and resources are pulled to their best use – all quite automatically, within a functioning economic system. This is, essentially, the modern understanding that we call the market economy. It was a huge theoretical innovation.

Nevertheless, this interdependence does not prevent some economic agents from trying to take advantage of others, as Smith now goes on to explain.

Self-interest of the different factors

Laws and regulations, as we have seen, can promote or damage the interests of particular groups, and indeed, of the public. But it is the employers of capital who do best out of this. Landlords are unlikely to understand the consequences of such measures: the fact that income derives from mere ownership, rather than the application of physical or mental effort, leaves them too idle and ignorant to think about such things.

As far as those who live by wages are concerned, the general interest of society is crucial. Labourers suffer most cruelly when business is in decline. They benefit when society prospers. But as a result of poor education and their lack of access to information, they are incapable of understanding how society's interests affect their own. Struggling merely to survive, they have no time or energy to spend thinking about public policy. And the voice of the common people does not carry far in the public debate.

Those whose income derives from capital, however, are quite different. Their interests do not coincide with those of other people, because their profits are squeezed when the economy flourishes. Their interest lies in widening the market and narrowing the competition, and they are skilled at achieving this end. Since planning and management is fundamental to their business, they have the knowledge, contacts and mental acuity to promote measures that they know will benefit them.

But this private benefit comes at the expense of the public, who suffer when markets are distorted and competition is reduced. When the owners of capital propose a new regulation, therefore, it should be given the utmost scrutiny. It comes from a group whose interest does not coincide with that of the public, and who can and do gain by deceiving them.

The proposal of any new law or regulation of commerce which comes from this order, ought always to be listened to with great precaution, and ought never to be adopted till after having been long and carefully examined, not only with the most scrupulous, but with the most suspicious attention. It comes from an order of men, whose interest is never exactly the same with that of the public, who have generally an interest to deceive and even oppress the public, and who accordingly have, upon many occasions, both deceived and oppressed it.

Book II: The accumulation of capital

In an advanced economy, most of our needs are supplied not through what we make ourselves, but through our voluntary exchange with others. But this means that we have to produce, and sell, our own surplus before we can acquire the products we need in return. Weavers, for example, need sufficient capital to buy or rent their weaving frame, for tools and materials, and to have enough to live on until their cloth is finished, transported to market and sold.

Capital has to be accumulated, in other words, before people can embark on specialist trades – and capture the large gains in productivity that result from it. And the greater the specialisation in the economy, the more capital is required to maintain it. The accumulation of capital thus feeds economic growth. It is a virtuous circle: the growth of capital promotes specialisation, which creates even larger surpluses, and these in turn can be reinvested into new equipment that makes yet further specialisation and growth possible.

Division of capital

Capital has two parts to it. One is that part which is expected to produce future income. This can be fixed capital, which stays with the owner, or circulating capital, which does not. The other part is that which supplies immediate consumption: this includes stocks of goods that are intended for consumption, income from whatever source, and stocks of goods such as clothes or furniture, which are not yet completely consumed.

Smith in fact says 'stock' is divided into 'capital' and the other 'stocks'. It is not easy to render this in modern terminology; 'capital' seems the best general term. Also, Smith's definition includes revenue, which modern economists would not, though cash in hand, work in progress and fixed and moveable assets are regarded as capital items today.

Money

Though we commonly express a person's income in money terms, as a particular quantity of gold or silver pieces, money itself has no intrinsic value. Money is only a tool of exchange, a highway that helps get the nation's product to market, but produces none itself. Real wealth resides in what that money can buy, not in the coins themselves.

The fact that wealth and money are separate things can be shown quite easily. After all, a person who receives a guinea of income today may spend that same guinea tomorrow, thus providing the income of a second; and that person may spend the same guinea on the next day, providing the income of a third. So the amount of money in circulation is clearly much less than the total income of the nation. National income is the quantity of goods bought and sold, not the metal pieces that happen to be used to facilitate the exchange of that product.

Smith is again taking on the mercantilists here, and trying to dispel the myth that money is wealth. This, he believes, causes many policy errors as nations try to limit the outflow of money by restricting trade, while in fact wealth is increased when trade is vibrant and free.

Yet money does have some important effects. It renders capital active and productive. The cash which dealers are obliged to keep aside for occasional needs is dead capital, which produces nothing. But efficient banking can make it move faster and work harder. Where banks substitute paper banknotes for gold and silver, it allows this dead capital to be brought back to life and into use more easily than before – speeding up the commercial highway and increasing the productivity of the country's industry.

There may be a temptation among banks to over-issue their notes beyond what their stocks of gold and silver will bear. This risk can be reduced if banks are not allowed to issue small notes. Otherwise, competition between banks safeguards the public, forcing banks to be careful about the scale of their note issue, limiting the possibility of a run on any one bank doing widespread damage, and focusing them on the needs of their customers to avoid them defecting to others.

Smith was writing in an age before fiat currency – notes and coin that governments simply declare to be legal tender and (somehow) get the public to accept as such. In his day, banks could issue notes as receipts for customers' gold, and using those in transactions was far more efficient than having to move around the real metals. The banks could even issue more notes than they had gold in their vaults, relying on the probability that not all the note holders would demand their bit of gold all at once. If a bank over-issued notes beyond this comfortable level, however, it could lead to a run on the bank as note holders rushed to cash in their notes before the bank's reserves ran out. There was a major Scottish banking crisis of this sort shortly before Smith wrote: hence his sensitivities on the matter. He believes that competition will generally keep banks prudent, but that there still needs to be regulation to protect the public. He has no problem with a general regulation in the public interest: it is just regulations that favour special interest that he objects to.

Productive and unproductive labour

Some labour adds to the value of what is worked on – the labour of a manufacturer, for example, works to add value to an item which can then be sold at a profit. This we can call productive labour. It produces something marketable that lasts for some time afterwards. Other labour – such as the labour of a menial servant – does not add value to anything. It is consumed immediately, and leaves nothing vendible behind. This we can call unproductive labour.

A man grows rich by employing a multitude of manufacturers: he grows poor by maintaining a multitude of menial servants. This kind of labour still has value, which is rewarded accordingly. The army and judiciary, for example, serve the public, and their professions are honourable, but their labour of today purchases nothing tomorrow. This year, the army may maintain security in some hostile region; but next year they still have to be there to continue the same task. In the same category of unproductive workers are churchmen, lawyers, physicians, actors, buffoons, musicians and dancers. What they do expires as soon as they do it, leaving nothing saleable behind. Unproductive labour is supported mostly from the rent of land and the profits of stock. Common workmen have scant wage, and little time to spend on them.

The realisation that services have value, as well as manufactures or agricultural products, is another Smith innovation, and one we recognize today, when service industries have grown enormously important. But the fact that they add value makes it rather misleading to call them 'unproductive'. It might be that the menial servants of the rich landowner are a pure consumption. But the services of teachers, writers, composers, doctors, and even lawyers can last and be enjoyed for some time after the service is performed. It may be that the knowledge, ideas, music, health and laws they produce are intangible and cannot be sold, but today we would hardly call that 'unproductive'.

Once again, Smith is breaking new ground, so the fact that he struggles to pin down these concepts is understandable. The more such services are consumed, the less income and capital are we left with for future investment. And therefore, the lower will be the next year's national product. Future income depends on the extent of our capital, and the only way to accumulate capital is by saving. Indeed, just to maintain capital we need to save, because materials and equipment must be repaired and replaced all the time. If instead of saving, we consume our current revenues on unproductive hands, then we are eating into our capital for the purpose of current consumption. This is prodigality, and if it persists, must lead to ruin.

The mercantilist view is that such dis-saving does not matter provided all the spending is done at home in the domestic economy, and that no gold or silver is therefore sent abroad. If the quantity of money in the country has not fallen, they say, then no wealth has been lost. But in fact, even though the quantity of money in the country does not change, real damage is being done.

Capital is being consumed instead of maintained. Since future income growth depends on the accumulation of capital, future income will necessarily be lower.

Capital can also be wasted through bad investment decisions. Again, this does not affect the nation's gold and silver deposits, but it certainly reduces its future productive capacity. Every failed project in agriculture, mining, fisheries, trade or manufactures uses up some of the country's productive funds.

However, nations are never ruined by the prodigality or injudicious investment of private individuals: only by that of public institutions. Ordinary people know that they must save and invest if they are to improve their condition and boost their future incomes. But most of government's income is spent on maintaining unproductive hands – a numerous and splendid court, the religious establishment, great fleets and armies – all of which subsist on the product of taxpayers' labour. Governments see little reason to save and invest for themselves. Unfortunately, when such public spending becomes so large that taxpayers have to eat into their capital in order to continue to pay for it, then future incomes are necessarily diminished. Even so, the free economy is remarkably robust. People's constant effort to better themselves, the mainspring of progress, is often enough to keep the economy growing, despite the extravagance and errors of government.

It is the highest impertinence and presumption...in kings and ministers, to pretend to watch over the economy of private people.... They are themselves always, and without any exception, the greatest spendthrifts in the society.... If their own extravagance does not ruin the state, that of their subjects never will.

The total national product can grow only through a growth in the number of productive workers, or through a rise in their productivity. Productivity can be increased only through better management of labour and capital resources, or through the use of more or better machines and equipment – each of which usually requires new capital investment. Greater production, therefore, usually indicates that a greater quantity of capital has been invested. If we see a country's lands becoming better cultivated, its manufactures more numerous, and its trade more extensive, we can be sure that its capital has increased. And that increased capital accumulation can be attributed to the private saving and investment of individuals, together with the legal security that enables them to accumulate their capitals without fear of them being stolen, and the liberty that encourages them to save, invest, and so better their own condition.

Interest

People lend to others in the expectation that the capital they advance to the borrower will eventually be returned to them, and that the borrower will pay a kind of rent for the use of it. Borrowers expect that they can use this capital for productive uses that will be so profitable that they can more than repay both capital and interest. Again, though, we should remember that what the borrower wants is not the money, but what the money will buy. The loan, in other words, represents some small part of the national product being assigned over from the lender to the borrower. When there is more capital available in any country, there is more competition between its holders, and borrowers can offer a lower price for it. In other words, the more capital there is, the lower the rate of interest that can be charged. The growth of capital, and its lower cost, will boost productive industry: more labour will be hired, and wages will be bid up. So employers will be paying less for their borrowed capital – though they will see their profit rates being eroded too.

Some people argue that it is the increase in the quantity of gold and silver, which resulted from mining discoveries in the Spanish West Indies, that has lowered interest rates. But this cannot be true. If everything else stays the same, then an increase in the quantity of silver has no effect other than to diminish the value of that particular metal – like every other commodity that is in plentiful supply. The effect of this is that money prices would appear to rise. But this rise in prices is purely nominal, rather than real. Prices would rise, but nothing, including interest rates, would really have changed.

Here, Smith is countering the mercantilist view with a quantity theory view of money – that the more money there is in circulation, the less it is worth. In other words, inflation. His intuitive view is that all prices are affected, and that nothing real changes. Today we recognise that inflation does have some distorting effects because the new money enters the economy in particular places and that price rises spread out from there, with the differences causing real misallocations on the way.

Some countries have attempted to outlaw the lending of money at interest. But this has simply increased the evil of usury, rather than preventing it. People still want to borrow money, but now they have to pay not just the interest, but a premium for the risk that the creditor runs in lending illegally. Government efforts to peg interest rates below their market price have the same effects. Creditors will not lend their money for less than the use of it is worth: so borrowers have to offer them a risk premium in order to get it at its full value.

This is a classic example of price controls leading to a black market. Where prices are artificially held down below market rates, suppliers may simply turn to other markets where they can make more money, creating shortages. Or they may continue to deal illegally: but in this case, customers will have to pay even more than the market price to compensate sellers for their risk. The same arguments apply to rent controls, wage controls and other price restrictions.

Further reflections on capital

Capital can be used in four different ways. Some assets (such as farms or fisheries) yield raw produce for immediate consumption or for processing. Some (such as machinery and equipment) are used to prepare raw materials for consumption. Some (such as carts and ships) are used to transport raw or manufactured products to market.

Lastly, capital is used in retailing – to divide raw or manufactured goods into smaller amounts that match consumers' needs. If there were no butchers, for example, people would be obliged to purchase a whole ox or sheep at a time, which would be an inconvenience to the rich and an impossibility to the poor.

Smith here is taking on a view common in his time that retailers contributed nothing, and that they required regulation because competition was cut-throat, causing some to fail as others pushed customers into buying what they did not need.

The current political prejudice against shopkeepers is therefore misplaced. They do add value, and they serve the public. The competition between them might force some out of business, but it can never hurt the consumer. Competition pressurizes them to keep down their prices – a pressure which monopolists do not experience. The argument that, without regulation, some retailers might dupe customers into buying things they do not need is a specious one. For example, it is not the widespread prevalence of alehouses that causes people to drink to excess. Rather, it is the disposition to drink that gives employment to the alehouses. Retail trades, like any other, follow the demand.

The capital that is employed in agriculture seems to be the most productive. That is because nature works alongside the human labour, bringing the crop to fruition. The American colonies have grown rapidly largely because their capital is focused on this highly productive sector. They let others provide the capital for the (less profitable) trading and manufacturing sectors they need. America's manufactures are almost entirely imported, in a trade financed by the capital of merchants in Great Britain. Even the Virginia and Maryland stores and warehouses employed in this transatlantic trade are British owned. If, as a result of the present disagreements, the Americans were to call a halt to this trade and divert their capital into domestic manufacture, the effective monopoly that would be given to their domestic producers, and the increased costs they faced, would make them worse off.

Economic progress stems only from countries producing a surplus that they can then exchange with others. Countries are better off if they do not try to remain self-sufficient and raise trade barriers against others.

Book III: The progress of economic growth

The principal commerce of an advanced society is that which takes place between the country and the towns. In a sense, the towns acquire their whole wealth from the country. But that does not mean that their wealth comes at the expense of the country. Both sides benefit. Farmers need town artisans to make their tools and household goods, and towns need markets for their produce. The greater the wealth and population of a town, the bigger is the market, and the more the country benefits.

Priority of agriculture

Since subsistence is prior to convenience and luxury, the cultivation and improvement of the country must have taken place prior to the growth of towns; and towns could only grow insofar as the country produced surpluses. If the profits were equal, people would generally prefer to live from land, rather than manufactures or foreign trade. Land, and rent, seems much more secure than manufactures or trade, which are liable to many accidents and uncertainties, and landowners enjoy the beauty and peace of the countryside. Yet farmers still need artificers such as smiths, carpenters, wheelwrights and ploughwrights, masons and bricklayers, tanners, shoemakers and tailors. These people in return need food and raw materials. The inhabitants of the town and the country are mutually dependent; nevertheless, the towns could only grow in proportion to the prosperity of and the demand from the countryside.

When people are allocating their capital, therefore, they prefer to put it first into land, then into manufactures, and only then into foreign trade, with its many risks. Where land is extensive and fertile, such as the North American colonies, capital goes predominantly into agricultural improvement. In countries where the land is fully improved, more capital is diverted into manufacturing. In either case, the import-export business is generally left to other countries, where manufacturing is advanced. In fact, North America has grown fast precisely because its capital has gone into agriculture, while its trade has been financed by British merchants. The wealth of ancient Egypt, and of China and Indostan, demonstrate that nations can prosper even though their trade is financed mostly by foreigners.

The rise of the towns

The towns may depend on the country, but they also help to improve it. First, they provide large markets for the produce of the country. Second, rich people in the towns buy and improve land in the country. Wealthy merchants fancy themselves as country gentlemen – though they are also businesslike improvers of agriculture. Thirdly, the commerce of the towns promotes order and good government – principles which spread out to the country.

Townspeople achieved their freedom and independence before those in the country. Gradually they won privileges and self-government – helped in part by the desire of weak kings to make them allies against the rich landowning barons, who despised both kings and merchants. Order and government, security and liberty thus arose in the towns, and manufacturing and trade expanded.

In the age before manufactures, however, great landowners had nothing for which they could exchange their surplus. All they could do was use their wealth to maintain a large following of retainers and dependants. This gave them a vast authority, and they – rather than any distant king – naturally became the chief lawgivers and administrators. But such power can be arbitrary, and the introduction of the feudal law was an attempt to restrain it by creating a comprehensive system of rights and duties, from the king down to the smallest landholder.

The feudal law still could not curb the arbitrary power of the great lords. But the rise of manufacturing and commerce did. Once manufactured goods became available, the lords at last had something for which they could exchange their surplus. They started to spend their wealth on comforts and impressive luxuries, rather than on maintaining thousands of retainers.

As a result, however, the great landlords lost the source of their whole power and authority. For merchants are not as dependent on their customers as retainers are on their lord. They have other customers too: their loyalty is more divided.

For a pair of diamond buckles perhaps, or for something as frivolous and useless, they exchanged the maintenance, or what is the same thing, the price of the maintenance of a thousand men for a year, and with it the whole weight and authority which it could give them.

As the number of retainers diminished, farms were enlarged and became more efficient and productive. This prompted landlords to raise their rents, but in return the tenants demanded more security. Tenants became more independent, landlords lost their arbitrary power, and an orderly system of justice developed. The commerce and manufactures of the cities had been the cause of the improvement and cultivation of the country.

This history is speculative, and yet the breakdown of the traditional feudal power of the great Scottish chiefs may have given Smith real examples from his own time.

Tenancy law and agricultural efficiency

In England, the considerable security that is given to tenants has contributed to the agricultural success and grandeur of the nation. In other parts of Europe, leases have been too short to encourage improvements, or entailed unspecified services to be delivered to the landlord, or invited taxes (French farmers who produce a surplus find it almost all confiscated in the taille).

Small proprietors have a much more direct interest in managing their land than large ones, and so are more successful and productive. But in Europe, the persistence of primogeniture has still prevented the division of great estates. Land was considered, not just as a source of income and enjoyment, but as the basis of power, patronage, and protection: so in the dangerous times that followed the fall of Rome, it was thought better for land to be kept intact. This tradition has persisted, and as a result, land rarely comes to market – perhaps a third of the land area of Scotland is entailed under this system – and where it does come to market, it is sold only at a high, monopoly price. The system makes land use inefficient: cost-effective improvement of land takes the same close attention to detail and to profit as any other business, but the grand proprietors of large estates have much less interest in these things than those who cultivate their own small landholdings. Such is the inefficiency of this system that in Europe it takes over five hundred years for the population to double.

In North America, where primogeniture does not prevail, the population doubles every twenty-five years. There is an open market in land, and fifty or sixty pounds is enough to begin a plantation. If European landholdings were divided equally among the children on the death of the proprietor, the estate would generally be sold, more land would come onto the market, prices would moderate and the productivity of the land would rise.

Slavery, however, is another factor that limits agricultural efficiency. In Russia, Poland, Hungary, Bohemia, Moravia and other parts of Germany, serfs are tied to the land and can be bought and sold with it. But a serf or slave who can acquire no personal property has no interest other than to eat as much, and to labour as little as possible: productive work has to be forced out of them. Though slave labour looks cheap it is therefore the least cost-effective sort of labour. Slavery is common in the sugar and tobacco plantations of the British colonies, but only because the extent and fertility of the land makes the expense of slavery affordable.

Book IV: Economic theory and policy

Economics is about how to generate income for the people and to supply a revenue for the state. There are presently two principal theories, the mercantile system and the agricultural system.

The mercantile system

The mercantile system holds that wealth consists in money – gold and silver. A rich person, or a rich country, is one with plenty of money. Under this view, therefore, policy should focus on heaping up large quantities of money, seeking it out from colonies, welcoming it into the country, but preventing it from leaving.

As an illustration of this attitude, when the Spaniards discovered America, their first question was whether gold or silver could be found locally, such was the prevalence of this view and the assumed importance of these metals. For the same reasons, Spain and Portugal have severe prohibitions, or heavy taxes, on the exportation of gold and silver. Even some old Scottish laws prevented their exportation.

Traders, of course, found these restrictions very inconvenient. So they argued that by allowing them to pay for some imports with gold and silver, they could actually make more money for the country by processing the imports and exporting them elsewhere, getting back even more gold and silver. This led to some easing of the rules: the prohibition on gold and silver exports from France and England was confined to coin, not bullion. Holland even dropped the coin restriction.

So attention then fixed on the balance of foreign trade, since this is what would determine the net inflows and outflows of gold and silver if they could be moved freely across borders. By contrast, domestic trade – though far more important – was ignored, on the grounds that no money came into or left the country as a result of it, so it could never make the country richer or poorer. But in fact the preoccupation with international trade is inappropriate. Very little of a country's trade comprises foreign trade, with gold or silver being imported or exported: most wealth is created and consumed domestically. Cross-border movements of gold and silver are hardly likely to ruin a great nation.

And it is a mistake to imagine that wealth resides only in money. Money is just a medium of exchange. It is useful, because everyone accepts it. Yet what people actually want when they do accept it is not the money, but the things that they can buy with the money.

Certainly, gold and silver have the merit of being more durable than some other commodities, and this adds to their usefulness as a store of value. But durability is not everything: we are perfectly happy to import wine from France and send them hardware in exchange.

Nevertheless, the French are not so stupid as to amass more pots and pans than they need to cook their food, just because they are more durable. It would be a complete waste of resources. By the same token, neither we, nor any country, should seek to amass more gold and silver than is needed to facilitate trade. It would be a waste too – dead capital that would come out of the available resources we need to feed, clothe, maintain and employ the people.

Money is a utensil, just like pots and pans

Having thus shown the error of the mercantilist belief that money equals wealth, Smith now moves on to attacking the trade restrictions that the mercantilists have erected, in the name of preventing money

228

from leaking abroad. Prohibitions or high duties against imports – motivated by the mercantilist confusion about money – mean that the country's domestic producers are given an effective monopoly of the home market. Bans on the importation of live cattle, for example, give domestic graziers a monopoly on the supply of butcher's meat; woollen manufacturers benefit from bans on woollen imports, and silk manufacture has recently secured the same advantage, as have many other trades.

But, as explained earlier, the number of people who can be employed in a developed country is proportional to the capital that is mobilised there. Regulations such as these cannot possibly increase employment beyond what the available capital can maintain. All they do is to divert industry from one employment to another. But businesspeople naturally invest their capitals where they believe they can generate most value. Indeed, they are likely to be much better judges of this, understanding more about the local situation, than some distant regulator; and giving regulators such great economic power is dangerous in itself.

The only mention of the Invisible Hand in The Wealth of Nations occurs at this point above. However, while the invisible hand idea – a functioning social order produced by the private and indeed self-interested action of individuals – pervades Smith's work, this particular reference to it is rather elliptical.

If foreign goods are no cheaper than domestic ones, then giving a monopoly of the home market to domestic producers is evidently pointless. If, on the contrary, foreign goods are in fact cheaper, then the regulation is harmful, because it is wasteful to make at home what you can buy cheaper elsewhere. The tailor does not attempt to make his own shoes, nor the shoemaker his own clothes: and countries too should make what they can make cheaper, and buy in what would cost them more to produce.

By means of glasses, hotbeds, and hotwalls, very good grapes can be raised in Scotland, and very good wine too can be made of them at about thirty times the expense for which at least equally good can be brought from foreign countries. Would it be a reasonable law to prohibit the importation of all foreign wines, merely to encourage the making of claret and burgundy in Scotland?

Trade restrictions are also defended as a tool to prevent an adverse balance of trade. But as we have seen, foreign trade is relatively insignificant. And as long as a country is producing more than it consumes, it is saving and adding to its capital. Such a country could still import more than it exports – an adverse trade balance – and nevertheless continue to produce surpluses and grow richer.

Justified and unjustified trade barriers

Trade restrictions are a tax on the whole country. But they are often defended as being necessary to deal with 'special cases'. British tariffs on foreign wine and beer, for example, are justified on the grounds that they reduce drunkenness. It is a remarkable claim, since the wine producing countries such as France, Italy and Spain are among the soberest peoples in Europe. Certainly, alcohol may sometimes be abused, but it is still better if we can buy it – like anything else – more cheaply than we can brew it ourselves. And in any case, the fact that the tariffs favour Portugal, which British merchants say is a better customer for their manufactures, over France, gives the lie to their supposed justification. It is an example of how interest groups can pervert the policy of a great country.

In any event, we cannot prosper by trying to impoverish our neighbours. A nation is more likely to grow rich from trade if its neighbours are also rich, industrious, commercial nations, than if they are poor.

Here, Smith is attacking the common assumption that in any exchange there must be a winner and a loser. In terms of international trade policy, this led to the idea that a country could become rich only by taking money off others and making them poorer. Smith, of course, champions the modern view, that both sides benefit from voluntary trade, so the assumption is wrong and the policy is counterproductive. But Smith concedes that there can be some justification for at least temporary restrictions on foreign trade in limited circumstances, which he now enumerates.

A case can be made for tariffs when some particular industry is vital for the defence of the country, of course. The Navigation Acts, which aimed at reducing the naval power of Holland, are an example. But there is a cost; if foreigners are hindered from coming to sell into our markets, they may not come to buy, either. The embargo may make them less wealthy, or they may form trading alliances with other nations, and buy in their markets instead.

There is, too, a case for imposing a tax on imported articles if the same articles produced at home are taxed for some reason – as are soap, salt, leather and candles. This levels the competition between domestic and foreign producers. However, we should not let this policy be expanded, as domestic producers would like it to be, into imposing taxes on all foreign imports that might happen to compete with home industries. Taxes raise the prices of things, imposing a burden on consumers; and taxes on necessities are a particular evil.

There might be a case for retaliatory import tariffs or prohibitions as a way of forcing other countries to drop their trade restrictions against us. It is up to those insidious and crafty animals, the politicians, to negotiate and decide if such a policy is likely to work.

But if there is no chance of it working, why add further injury to ourselves by imposing tariffs? Some people argue that if trade has been interrupted by tariffs or prohibitions, it should be restored only slowly; that a sudden restoration of free trade would be disruptive. In fact, though, foreign trade is a small part of a country's industry, and any disruption would be small. Most of the people affected would easily find other employments – especially if labour-market restrictions were eased.

And in the process, the whole country would be the gainer. Drawbacks, bounties, price controls and trade preferences. Drawbacks – where an exporter can claim back tax paid at home, or where import duties can be reclaimed upon re-export – cannot boost industry beyond its natural level. In principle, they merely restore activity to where it would have been in the absence of the tax. However, the specific rules on these tax concessions are so complicated that they do distort things, and often invite fraud.

Bounties – subsidies on exports – are designed to boost our foreign trade in lines of industry that could not profitably be exported without them. But again, if merchants did not receive the bounty, they would employ their capital in other, more profitable, industries.

Subsidies of any sort merely force the country's trade into a different, less advantageous direction. They are a double tax on the public: the public have to pay tax to finance the subsidy, then they have to pay more than they need for a commodity that could be bought cheaper from another source.

Subsidies are also open to fraud. The subsidy to the white herring industry, for example, is set according to the tonnage of the ship, rather than its crew's diligence or success in fishing. Not surprisingly, ships equip themselves for the purpose of maximizing their subsidy, rather than maximising their catch. In the process, the subsidy has ruined the local coastal fisheries and driven up the price of essential equipment (barrels, for example, have doubled in price from three shillings to six shillings).

The bounty to the white-herring fishery is a tonnage bounty; and is proportioned to the burden of the ship, not to her diligence or success in the fishery; and it has, I am afraid, been too common for vessels to fit out for the sole purpose of catching, not the fish, but the bounty.

Another form of intervention is price controls. The production of grain is an industry that has been subject to such controls. When harvests are poor, the price naturally rises. But when governments then try to help consumers by imposing price limits, it discourages the producers from bringing grain to market, or encourages consumers to buy it up so fast, that the season will surely end in shortages and famine. Bad harvests cannot be prevented: but the best way to temper them is to maintain the unlimited and unrestrained freedom of the farmers and merchants.

Another intervention in markets is import preferences, where particular countries are given the sole right to bring in particular goods, or the right to bring them in at a lower rate of tariff than faced by others. An example is the treaty that allows Portugal to import wines to England at two-thirds of the normal tariff. But while import preferences are obviously advantageous to the merchants and manufacturers of the exporting country, they are inevitably disadvantageous to the receiving country – which thereby denies itself access to world competition and ends up paying more to the monopoly importer.

Colonial trade restrictions

Countries even impose trade restrictions on their own colonies. In line with the mercantilist view, the usual motivation for founding colonies is the prospect of finding gold and silver. Since Columbus, the pious purpose of converting native peoples to Christianity might have sanctified the project, but the real motive was the hope of treasure. That is what carried Ojeda, Nicuesa, and Vasco Nuñes de Balboa to Darien, Cortez to Mexico, and Almagro and Pizarro to Chile and Peru. But the search of treasure is an uncertain and ruinous exercise. It was over a hundred years after the Brazils were first settled, before any silver, gold or diamond deposits were discovered there.

But there are compensations. Colonies that are planted on waste or thinly inhabited land advance more rapidly to wealth and greatness than any other society. The colonists bring with them agricultural and other useful skills. They have the habits of regular government, with the legal system and administration to support it. They have no rent to pay, and few taxes. But the land is so extensive, that even with every available hand, it is unlikely that any owner could make it produce even a tenth of what it is capable of producing.

Owners are eager, therefore, to collect more labourers, and are prepared to reward them liberally for their work. But these high wages, combined with the cheapness of the land, soon enable the labourers to set themselves up as landlords, who will seek to attract workers of their own, paying them equally liberally; and so the cycle continues.

For a new colony to prosper, the key seems to be plenty of good land, and the liberty to manage their own affairs. The English colonies in North America have grown faster than any: land is so cheap, and labour consequently so dear, that they can import from Britain almost all of the manufactures they need. The fact that Britain prohibits them from making certain manufactures in order to maintain a monopoly for its own producers therefore does them little practical harm. As their economy develops, however, such prohibitions could become really oppressive and insupportable.

The policy of forcing the North American colonies to trade only with the home country poses dangers to Britain too. It has drawn Britain's capital away from other markets and concentrated it in the colony trade. An unnaturally large proportion of Britain's industry is therefore at risk in this overgrown market. The threat of the trade being disrupted has accordingly filled the people of Britain with more terror than they ever felt for a Spanish armada or a French invasion.

The only solution to this is to relax the laws that give Britain the monopoly on trade with the colonies, and let other countries trade with them. Capital would then return to the many other uses that the monopoly has starved of it. To avoid doing permanent damage, this trade liberalisation would have to be gradual: for example, the sudden loss of trade to the ships which carry the 82,000 hogsheads of tobacco that Britain then re-exports to other countries, would in itself be a major economic shock.

But such is the mercantile system: it produces large distortions that are then very hard to remedy. The colonial trade monopoly has not boosted industry: indeed, by diverting industry into a market where the returns are slow and distant rather than frequent and near, it has made Britain's capital work less productively and has actually depressed incomes.

Since capital can only come out of income or savings, this means that Britain's capital is accumulated more slowly, and future incomes are lower than they would otherwise have been. Rents too are depressed by the monopoly, since by raising manufacturing profits, it discourages capital from going into land improvement.

And since it also depresses capital accumulation, in the long run, the amount of income earned as profits is smaller as well. In other words, wages, rent and profits are all damaged by the monopoly – just for the benefit of a few manufacturers.

Unnaturally high rates of profit, like those that come from monopoly, seem to destroy merchants' natural thrift. Instead of saving and reinvesting, they spend instead on expensive luxuries, and the capital of the country is consumed rather than accumulated. The exorbitant profits of the merchants in Cadiz or Lisbon, for example, have not augmented the capital of Spain or Portugal, nor promoted the industry or alleviated the poverty of those two beggarly countries.

London merchants enjoy lower rates of profit, but still seem better off. Profit rates in Amsterdam are even slimmer, but its attentive and parsimonious burghers are even wealthier than those in London.

Smith's interest in colonial policy is not entirely academic. He is writing just before the American colonists declared independence from Britain. He wants to advise the British authorities that only greater freedom of trade and more proportionate political representation can head off the crisis.

Unfortunately, his advice came too late. Ancient Rome's refusal to grant the privileges of citizenship to allies who had borne the cost of defending her precipitated the social war. Now, Britain insists on taxing its American colonists, but refuses them parliamentary representation. This has precipitated discontent, and turned the Americans from peaceful tradesmen into militant politicians. The only solution is for Britain to grant representation to the colonies, in proportion to what they contribute to the public finances.

As the colonies grow stronger, it becomes harder for home nations to unjustly usurp the whole benefit of the trade with them. All they end up with is the expense of maintaining their authority. In the mercantilist system, producer interests come to dominate. But the whole purpose of production is actually consumption, and it is consumer interests that should rightly prevail.

Consumption is the sole end and purpose of all production; and the interest of the producer ought to be attended to, only so far as it may be necessary for promoting that of the consumer.

The agricultural system

The second theoretical system of economics suggests that the product of land is the sole source of national wealth and income. It divides society into three groups: first, the proprietors of land; second, the farmers and farm workers; and third, the artificers, manufacturers and merchants – whom they see as an unproductive class.

Proprietors, they argue, contribute to national income through the expense that they lay out on land improvement, such as buildings, drains and enclosures. Farmers too contribute to national income through their expenditures on husbandry, seed, livestock and the maintenance of farm workers. But in this system, the overall contribution of manufacturers is zero. The benefit of their labour is precisely offset by the cost of their wages, materials, and tools.

They may indeed be useful, adding value to particular parts of what the landowners and farmers produce, but they consume the same amount from elsewhere. They provide the equipment needed to grow wheat or raise cattle, for example, but they consume wheat and cattle products too.

Though unproductive, in the sense that they merely rearrange wealth, this class is still nevertheless very useful to the producers, providing them with markets, equipment and manufactures. The producers have no reason to oppress them: quite the opposite, in fact, since the more liberty they enjoy, the more competition there is between them, and the lower the cost of what they supply. Likewise, the more liberty enjoyed by the other two classes, the greater the surplus that their land produces, and the more there is available for the unproductive class. The best policy for promoting prosperity, according to this system, is one of perfect liberty.

This view probably overstates the need for liberty to be perfect.

By way of analogy, it seems that the human body can remain perfectly healthy despite a variable and sometimes unwholesome diet.

Similarly, the economy seems capable of surviving, despite illiberal public policies. It may be slowed, but it is hard to stop. Turgot, the leading advocate of this view, was not only a pioneering economist but also physician to Marie Antoinette. Smith's comparison of the economic system to the human body therefore rebuts Turgot's philosophy in terms he could well understand.

However, the main error of the agricultural system is to see the artificers, manufacturers and merchants as a barren or unproductive class. First, the theory accepts that this class covers its own cost. This is hardly barren. Second, they do actually attach value to things that endure and which can later be sold: this is clearly productive labour.

Despite these imperfections, this theoretical system is among the better ones. It recognises that wealth consists not in money, but in a country's production; and it sees perfect liberty as the best way to maximise this. In the absence of trade restraints or preferences, people are left free to pursue their own interests, and to bring their capital and labour into competition with others, subject only to the rules of justice. Capital and labour flow into their most advantageous uses, and the state is spared any need to supervise and direct economic life. Indeed, the system of perfect liberty leaves the state only three duties to attend to: defence, justice and certain public works.

The sovereign is completely discharged from a duty [for which] no human wisdom or knowledge could ever be sufficient; the duty of superintending the industry of private people, and of directing it towards the employments most suitable to the interest of the society.

Book V: The role of government

Defence expenditure

The first duty, and necessary expense, of the state is defence: protecting the society from the violence or invasion of others.

Among nations of hunters, such as the native tribes of North America, people have to be warriors as well as hunters. They must live off their own labour, even when they are at war. There is no king or commonwealth with the resources to maintain them.

Nations of nomadic shepherds, such as the Tartars and Arabs, all have chiefs, but warriors must still live off their flocks. These, and the whole nation, go along with them. But then there is the prospect of capturing booty from vanquished enemies.

In an agricultural age, people are settled. Farms cannot simply be abandoned, so the men of military age go to war, and others stay behind. As long as the seeds are in the ground, they can be spared; nature will do most of the work.

In the manufacturing age, things are different. When people quit their work as smiths, carpenters, or weavers, their income immediately dries up; when they take to the field to defend their nation, they cannot maintain themselves, and must necessarily be maintained from the public purse – all the more so because modern military campaigns can last for months on end. Also, military equipment has become more complex and more frightening, which requires a specialist and disciplined force. For all these reasons, the defence of advanced countries must be financed by the state.

Justice

Just as the state must protect people from foreign enemies, so must it protect them against domestic ones. Among nations of hunters, there is hardly any property. People usually have nothing to gain from injuring others, and there is little need for any formal administration of justice. But where property exists, things are otherwise. There are potential gains from theft.

The avarice and ambition of the rich, or the desire for ease and enjoyment among the poor, can lead to private property being invaded. The acquisition of valuable property – which may take years to build up – necessarily requires the establishment of a civil government and a magistracy to preserve order and justice.

The affluence of the rich excites the indignation of the poor, who are often both driven by want, and prompted by envy, to invade his possessions. It is only under the shelter of the civil magistrate that the owner of that valuable property, which is acquired by the labour of many years, or perhaps of many successive generations, can sleep a single night in security.

It is obviously useful if, as a rational matter, everyone accepts the authority of independent judges. But there is also a natural respect for authority among humans that makes this acceptance more likely. People respect personal qualities such as strength, wisdom, prudence and virtue; and they respect maturity and age. Wealth is another factor which promotes deference, particularly so in the age of shepherds, where great proprietors have nothing else to spend their fortunes on other than maintaining thousands of retainers. That is why the authority of an Arabian sharif is very great, and that of a Tartar khan altogether despotic.

A fourth cause of human deference is the inequality of birth: though this is the result of an inequality of wealth. In the age of hunters, there are no major wealth inequalities; the son of a wise or brave man may be more respected than most, but the differences are unlikely to be great. In nations of shepherds, by contrast, wealth can stay within families for generations, and birth is greatly revered. It is in this age that great inequalities of wealth start to emerge. Alongside this wealth emerges civil government – an institution designed to protect those who have property against those who do not.

Civil government, so far as it is instituted for the security of property, is in reality instituted for the defence of the rich against the poor, or of those who have some property against those who have none at all.

Smith's argument that law and government are institutions devised by the rich to prevent them being robbed by the poor does not mean that it is a bad system. He has already remarked earlier that for people to accumulate capital, they must have confidence that their property, which may take years of effort to acquire, will not be stolen from them. And this capital accumulation is essential for economic growth.

Public works

The third role for the state is to build and maintain public works that could never yield a profit to individuals: institutions to facilitate commerce, the education of the young and the instruction of people of all ages. As the commerce of a country increases, so does its need for public works such as roads, bridges, canals and harbours. Most such facilities can be financed out of tolls or charges, without any burden being imposed on the public finances. The coinage, which also facilitates commerce, generally defrays its own expense and indeed provides a small seignorage to the state; the post office generates a very large profit.

The greater part of such public works may easily be so managed, as to afford a particular revenue sufficient for defraying their own expense, without bringing any burden upon the general revenue of the society. Public works which cannot produce such revenues, but which benefit some particular locality, are better maintained by a locally raised and administered tax. London streets, for example, would not be so well lit and paved if the cost of the lighting and paving fell upon the Treasury; and instead of being a tax on the particular street, parish, or district of London, the expense would be a tax on all citizens, most of whom would gain no benefit at all.

Some supporters of greater public expenditure take comfort from Smith's remarks on public works and education (below), but it is a false comfort.

First, Smith limits his remarks to projects that are essential for commerce, such as infrastructure and education. He does not support public projects as a substitute for private commerce. There is an unbridgeable distance between this limited support for public works and the numerous and large undertakings of the modern state. Second, even where Smith accepts that public expenditure may be necessary to get infrastructure projects built, he thinks that this cost should be repaid by charges on the users, rather than direct taxation. If charges are impossible, it should be the local beneficiaries who should pay the tax. Third, in Smith's time there were few companies large enough to finance large-scale infrastructure projects (except a few joint-stock companies, of which he was very suspicious for other reasons): this has changed. And ways of collecting tolls and charges are much more sophisticated today. Private build and operation of public infrastructure projects is therefore more practical than in Smith's time.

The object of these public works is to facilitate commerce generally. But some particular branches of commerce, such as that carried on with barbarous and uncivilised nations, require extraordinary protection. An ordinary store or counting-house could give little security to the goods of the merchants who trade with West Africa, or Indostan. The interests of commerce have often made it necessary to post ambassadors to foreign countries: the commerce of the Turkey Company prompted the establishment of an ambassador in Constantinople; the first English embassies to Russia were entirely for commercial interests.

It seems reasonable that such extraordinary expense should be paid by a moderate tax on those in the particular trades affected. It also seems reasonable that, when merchants undertake to establish a new trade with some remote and barbarous nation, they might be granted a temporary monopoly. Like the patents on new machines, this is the easiest way for the state to recompense them for a risk that should afterwards deliver benefit to the general public.

National policy has been inconsistent, however, and sometimes this protection of trade has been contracted out to private companies, but these companies have either mismanaged or restricted the trade. They include regulated companies like the Hamburgh, Russia, Eastland, Turkey and African Companies, which any qualified person can join on payment of a fee; in other words, they are rather like the trade guilds, and behave like them too. They include joint stock companies established by government, such as the South Sea, Hudson's Bay, and Royal African Companies, which have been granted exclusive privileges in foreign trade. But such privileges have not prevented such companies from failing, and perpetual monopolies to them are an absurd tax on the public.

Joint stock companies may succeed, without special privileges, in repetitive trades like banking or insurance, or in building utilities such as canals. Other forms of business, however, move too quickly and require risk-taking and attention to changing details.

A company governed by a board of directors moves too slowly to succeed in such industries. Smith is commonly construed as being opposed to joint stock companies – the kind of arrangement that dominates big business today. But in fact he is principally against the special privileges that had been granted to particular companies; and he believes that companies governed by a large board of director-shareholders could not move quickly enough to succeed in most lines of business. Today, however, shareholders elect a small board of directors who in turn rely on a small executive group to run things, making it possible for large companies to operate quite nimbly.

Education of the young

Despite the clear benefit of economic efficiency that it delivers to society, specialisation can have harmful effects on the individual. The person who spends years performing the same simple operation has no opportunity for innovative thinking. Unless the government takes steps to prevent it, the labouring poor will fall into mental torpor, narrow-mindedness, and a fear of change and the unknown.

Smith here anticipates Karl Marx's idea of 'alienation' among workers who do repetitive tasks with little interest in their final product. In barbarous countries, of hunters or shepherds, the variety of people's occupations and the everyday problems they have to overcome keeps their minds and their judgement sharp.

The man whose whole life is spent in performing a few simple operations, of which the effects too are, perhaps, always the same, or very nearly the same, has no occasion to exert his understanding, or to exercise his invention in finding out expedients for removing difficulties which never occur.

In civilised countries, however, the education of the common people requires particular attention. Wealthier people are more willing and able to pay for their children's education; and they tend to have more varied jobs, so their minds are less likely to grow torpid through want of exercise. The common people, however, have little money for education – and little time, too, since in order to eke out a living for the family, their children have to start work as soon as they are able to do so.

But the essential elements of education can be acquired very young. And for a very small cost, the public can encourage, or even impose, the requirement to acquire this basic learning on almost everyone. It could do this by establishing local schools where children can be taught for such moderate fees that even a common labourer could afford them. The masters could be paid partly from the public purse (though they should not be paid wholly, nor even mainly, from this source, because they would then soon neglect their students). In Scotland, the establishment of such parish schools has taught almost all the common people to read, and many of them to write and account. In England, charity schools have had something of the same effect.

The endowments of schools and colleges have necessarily diminished more or less the necessity of application in the teachers. Their subsistence [is] altogether independent of their success and reputation in their particular professions. Smith himself was educated at one of these local, publicly supported schools in Scotland. But his policy recommendations, while generously motivated, are not wholly consistent. He argues for some state finance for school buildings, but only partial state support for teachers; and at the same time he praises the private schools that teach dancing and other arts.

Certainly, he was not contemplating comprehensive state education as is common in many countries today. Schoolbooks could of course be more instructive: and instead of Latin, elementary geometry and mechanics would be more useful to the common people. Public awards for educational achievement could help too. And there could be an examination before anyone was allowed to join a trade.

This is how the Greek and Roman republics maintained the

martial spirit of their citizens. They instituted gymnasia for their practice, appointed teachers (who were paid by their students) and awarded badges of distinction to those who excelled in these exercises.

Today, only a few people are trained in this martial spirit, except perhaps in Switzerland, and the spread of cowardice and the lack of a sense of self-worth, is as big a danger as ignorance and stupidity. Fostering self-worth and promoting knowledge are a benefit to society, promoting decency and good order.

Religious education

The institutions for the instruction of all ages are chiefly those for religious instruction. The ministers of established religions, being supported by estates or tithes, grow complacent, and are often eclipsed by the zeal and industry of new ones. They fall back on the law to protect their position: the Roman Catholic clergy, for example, used the law to persecute the heretics, and were in turn persecuted by the Church of England.

Moral systems can be austere or liberal. People of fashion veer to the liberal system, and indulge luxury, disorderly mirth, and within reason, intemperance. But then they can afford such laxity. The wiser folk among the common people, by contrast, abhor such excesses, which they know are potentially ruinous to them. Their moral problem is particularly acute in the cities, where anonymity allows people to fall more easily into self-neglect and profligacy, unless they are picked up by one of the small, austere, often unsocial religious sects.

The first remedy for this problem is the study of science and philosophy, which the state could spread, not by giving salaries to teachers (which would make them negligent and idle), but by requiring people to learn them before going into a trade. The second is to amuse and divert people by promoting the arts.

Funding state expenditures

Some expense is needed to support the dignity of the monarch, who as the chief magistrate must command general respect. The cost of the criminal justice system is likewise an expense that the whole society should bear. The expense of civil proceedings, however, is better defrayed by those who benefit from it – that is, its users. Indeed, as a general principle, public servants should be paid by results.

Public services are never better performed than when their reward comes in consequence of their being performed, and is proportioned to the diligence employed in performing them. Local or provincial expenditures which have a local or provincial benefit should be paid out of local or provincial taxes, rather than a tax on the whole society. The cost of good roads and communications, however, may justly be financed out of general taxation. But much of the cost can be recovered by user fees, such as the turnpike tolls in Engand or the peages in other countries.

The expense of education may also fall legitimately on general taxation; but again it is equally proper and perhaps advantageous if it is paid for by those who receive the immediate benefit. In other cases, where public works benefit the entire society but cannot be paid for by specific users, the shortfall must usually be found from general taxation.

Governments may try to raise money from commercial projects, but they are generally unsuccessful traders. Public servants regard the public purse as almost inexhaustible, spend unnecessarily and pay themselves well, while successful businesspeople are careful and parsimonious at managing their limited resources. Some governments, likewise, raise revenue from their land holdings, but these are generally insufficient to pay for all the demands on the public purse, and moreover, state assets are generally less well managed than private holdings.

When the crown lands had become private property, they would, in the course of a few years, become well-improved and well-cultivated... the revenue which the crown derives from the duties of customs and excise, would necessarily increase with the revenue and consumption of the people.

The principles of taxation There are four principles that should guide legislators in the design of taxation. There is no art which one government sooner learns of another than that of draining money from the pockets of the people. First, people ought to contribute, as far as possible, in proportion to the income that they derive under the protection of the state.

Second, taxes ought to be certain, and not arbitrary. The time and manner of payment should be clear to everyone. Otherwise, it gives excessive and arbitrary power to tax gatherers, and can lead to corruption and intimidation.

Third, taxes should be levied at a convenient time. Taxes on rents or houses, for example, should be payable when rents are paid. Taxes on consumable goods are convenient too, because they are paid little by little, as goods are bought.

Fourth, taxes should cost no more than necessary. They should not require a great number of expensive officers to collect. They should not discourage industry nor destroy capital. They should not encourage evasion (as high excise taxes encourage smuggling) nor should the penalties ruin those who are driven to evasion. And they should not require frequent, odious and vexatious visits from tax gatherers in order to collect them.

These principles of taxation would seem entirely natural today. The fact that he has to state them indicates how arbitrary and unjust were the taxes of his day. However, there are inconsistencies in Smith's other tax proposals. He opposes taxes on consumption, but supports a tax on luxuries (including things that we would think rather basic today, like poultry). He says that people should pay tax in proportion to their income, but wants the rich to pay 'something more than in that proportion'.

Taxes on land

If taxes are levied on the rent of land, it requires periodic reassessment, since rents do vary from time to time, and the tax would otherwise become unequal and unfair. This of course requires a certain bureaucracy – rent agreements would have to be declared and registered (and indeed, policed) to prevent any fraudulent collusion between landlord and tenant to evade the tax.

Taxes on the produce of land, such as tithes, are very unfair. They fall harder on those who own and farm less productive land. And they discourage landlords from improving their land, or farmers from investing in better cultivation, when the church or state shares none of the expense but takes part of the profit.

House rents can be divided into building rent – the profit on the capital used to build the house – and ground rent – the rent derived from the ownership of the land it is built on. Taxes on house rents would fall most heavily on the rich, which is perhaps not unreasonable, and rents would be very easy to ascertain. Taxes on ground rent would have the advantage of being a tax on land ownership and not discouraging improvement and building, but then it is harder to ascertain what part of the total rent should be considered as ground rent.

Such difficulties have led legislators to adopt easier ways of estimating the rent. Now, for example, taxes are levied in proportion to the number of windows in each house. Unfortunately, the low rent house of a poor family in the country can have more windows than the high-rent house of a rich family in town, and this tax is accordingly very unfair and unequal in its impact.

Taxes on capital and profits

There are two kinds of income generated by capital, namely interest and profit. Profit is not a good object of taxation, because it is the compensation for the risk and trouble of employing capital, and if it were taxed, employers would have to increase their profit margins (making their products dearer for consumers), or reduce the interest they pay to lenders (making those with savings worse off).

Interest would appear to be as easily taxed as rents, but this is not so. First, loans and repayments are much easier to conceal than land and rents; monitoring them would require an intrusive bureaucracy. Second, capital is very mobile, and owners can avoid the tax (and the vexations of the tax-gatherers) simply by moving their capital abroad. And that robs domestic industry of the capital it needs to grow.

The proprietor of stock is properly a citizen of the world, and is not necessarily attached to any particular country. He would be apt to abandon the country in which he was exposed to a vexatious inquisition, in order to be assessed to a burdensome tax, and would remove his stock to some other country where he could either carry on his business, or enjoy his fortune more at his ease.

Some countries have taxed the profits of particular trades – such as hawkers and peddlers, and hackney coaches and sedan-chairs. The licence to sell alcohol is another form of taxation. However, such taxes always fall ultimately on the consumers, rather than the dealers, who simply raise their profit margins to compensate for the tax.

Tax can also be levied when property is transferred – such as death duties or stamp taxes. But such taxes eat into the nation's capital. They transfer it into the current consumption of public expenditure, and leave less to be invested in productive enterprises.

Taxes on wages, individuals and goods

Just as producers, in order to maintain their margins, pass on taxes to consumers, so are taxes on wages ultimately paid by the employers – and therefore, once again, by the consumers.

Absurd and destructive as such taxes are, they still occur in many countries. Wealth taxes are arbitrary and unfair, given that a person's wealth varies from moment to moment. Capitation taxes are unfair because they fall most heavily on the poor: like income taxes, they simply push up wages and therefore, ultimately, consumer prices.

Taxes on the necessities of life (such as salt, leather, soap and candles) do the same. Taxes on luxuries raise only the price of those luxuries, but like customs duties, they are very expensive to collect. They discourage particular industries, and heavy taxes of this sort prompt people into evading them, requiring an intrusive bureaucracy to police them.

Public debts

When the costs of running the public sector are financed through borrowing, it consumes some of the capital that has been built up within the country. Private capital that is intended for the maintenance of productive labour is diverted into the support of unproductive labour.

Smith is not exactly arguing that public servants are 'unproductive' in the sense we would understand the word today (though he does think that public services tend to be less efficient and well-managed than private businesses): rather, he is saying that most public services are a form of consumption. If they are financed by debt, this amounts to consuming the capital of the nation.

On the other hand, the more that is borrowed, the less has to be raised in taxation, and borrowing can be a rational way to finance a large, lengthy and costly expenditure, such as a war. Private capitals would certainly suffer greatly if all the costs of a war had to be raised through tax rises at the time (though it might make wars

shorter, less popular, and less likely to happen).

And yet, when the principle of government borrowing has become entrenched, the number of taxes that come with it still put a burden on the public that makes it hard for them to maintain their capitals. As a result of the debt, Britain's peacetime public budget is now more than £10m – which would be enough to fight a war, under conventional tax-based financing.

People argue that the public debt is simply a transfer from one set of pockets to another; no money goes abroad, and the country is not a farthing poorer. But this is not true. The Dutch, for example, own a very large part of our public debt. Furthermore, the debt diverts capital from landowners and employers, towards the government's creditors. With less capital, land is less improved, and agriculture declines; the same is true of manufactures. They face the further vexation and cost of the necessary visits from the tax gatherers. So capital is being transferred from people who have a keen interest in using it productively to those, mere creditors, who have no interest in the condition of land or the good management of the capital stock at all.

Borrowing has enfeebled every state that has done it. Genoa and Venice are the only Italian republics that remain independent. Spain seems to have learnt the practice from Italy, and was deeply in debt by the end of the sixteenth century, before England owed a shilling.

France too suffers a large debt burden. It may be that England's military expenditure, and tax burden, have been light enough that private capital has been strong enough to repair all the breaches which the waste and extravagance of government has made in it, but another war may yet compromise it.

And we should remember than when public debts have been run up, there is scarcely any example of their being fairly and completely repaid.

The cost to Britain of maintaining its colonies has been large. The last war cost upwards of £90m. The Spanish war of 1739, undertaken mainly on account of the colonies, cost above £40m.

Had it not been for these wars, the public debt might well have been completely extinguished by now. It is argued that the colonies must be protected, as they are

provinces of the British empire. But they contribute neither revenue nor military force to the empire, they are merely showy appendages of the empire. And if the empire can no longer support the expense of maintaining these appendages, it should let them go, save the expense, and live within its modest means.

Chapter 3 The Incredibly Condensed Theory
of Moral Sentiments

Natural empathy as the basis of virtue

Human beings all have a natural feeling for others. Even the worst of us feels some pity when others suffer. We flinch when we see someone about to be struck, and writhe when we watch the slackrope artist. And we share the happiness of others too. Let us call it sympathy.

How selfish soever man may be supposed, there are evidently some principles in his nature, which interest him in the fortune of others, and render their happiness necessary to him, though he derives nothing from it, except the pleasure of seeing it.

Yet there are limits. We sympathise only when the actions and emotions of others seem appropriate to their circumstance. When we see someone consumed with grief, we want to know what has befallen them: it is not their emotions that excite our sympathy, so Smith says sympathy, so we will stick with that, but empathy might be a more accurately descriptive word today.

On the other hand, we do feel a genuine pleasure when someone else exactly shares our emotions and opinions. We unburden ourselves onto friends, and their sympathy makes us feel better. We consider the views of those who agree with us as just, proper and appropriate. But when we do not share the emotions of others, or disapprove of their actions and opinions, we think them at fault, and it distresses both of us.

Even so, as mere spectators, we cannot really share the full ferocity of another person's emotions – the fierce anger of someone who has been wronged, say, or the profound grief of someone recently bereaved. Our sympathetic feelings, though genuine, are inevitably weaker.

But these other people are spectators of our emotions too. They will see that we feel less strongly than they. This discord will distress them, and prompt them to restrain their emotions in order to bring themselves more into line with our view of their predicament.

Gradually we learn what emotions and actions seem proper to others. We try to temper them to the point where an impartial spectator would fully share our sentiments and regard them as appropriate. Indeed, we are prompted to go further and show real concern for others, because we know that an impartial spectator would approve, and we take pleasure from that.

And hence it is, that to feel much for others and little for ourselves, that to restrain our selfish, and to indulge our benevolent affections, constitutes the perfection of human nature; and can alone produce among mankind that harmony of sentiments and passions in which consists their whole grace and propriety.

Smith's explanation of the source of human morality is completely novel. Many philosophers, from the ancients such as Zeno to the moderns such as David Hume, had sought to explain moral action as something beneficial, either to the individual or to society. Smith makes the case that moral action is indeed beneficial, but it is not a matter of calculation. Rather, human beings have a natural empathy with each other, and we quickly learn what others will tolerate and what they will not.

Passions such as pain, hunger or love are very specific to the individual. But there are social passions (such as fellow-feeling) and unsocial passions (such as hatred) too, and these are where sympathy has a key role.

We are also more disposed to sympathise with a person's joy than with their sorrow. This explains why poor people conceal their poverty and rich people parade their wealth. Money does not really buy happiness, but we suppose that it does; and all our attention, sympathy and admiration is worth far more to the rich than the baubles and minor conveniences that money actually delivers.

Reward, punishment and society

Rewards are important for encouraging the social passions, and punishments for discouraging the unsocial. Hence it is the intention, more than the outcome, which excites our approval or disapproval. Only when a helpful action stems from a positive motive do we believe it merits reward; and only when a harmful action stems from a negative motive do we believe it merits punishment.

Indeed, as social creatures, our very existence requires that unmerited and unprovoked malice should be restrained through punishment, and nature has given us strong instincts to guide us in this (though we may conceitedly put it down to our own reason). We cannot look into people's hearts, of course, so rather than punish everyone we suspect of having bad motives, we punish people only when their actions are intended to cause harm. Even robbers and murderers can live peacefully together, provided they restrain their urges to rob and murder each other. The rules we have to prevent people harming others, we call justice. Without justice, society could not possibly survive – which is why our instinct to preserve it is so strong.

Conscience

But nature has given us something far more effective for this purpose than our laws and punishments, namely conscience. We judge other people's actions, but we also judge our own too. That internal judge is a harsh critic. Never mind if others praise us: we need to feel worthy of that praise.

Conscience has a powerful social function. It stops us from becoming too absorbed in ourselves and too forgetful of others. The loss of a little finger may be more immediate to us than an earthquake that consumes the whole of China. But conscience would never let us permit the loss of so many distant lives, if by sacrificing our little finger we knew we would prevent it. To nature, all people are important, and conscience gives us some of that perspective. It makes us unwilling to harm others merely for our personal gain.

Another useful instinct is our disposition to make and follow rules. We see how our actions affect others and how theirs affect us, and gradually we develop ideas of what sorts or actions are appropriate or inappropriate. These moral rules give us a quick indication of how to behave, without having to think out each situation afresh.

Different societies may have slightly different norms, but if each system did not promote social welfare, it would soon cease to exist. Even though we observe the rules only to spare ourselves a guilty conscience, we end up helping to promote the well-being of society.

To Smith, morality is a matter of social psychology. Certain rules of action generate a well-functioning society. When they are followed, society prospers, and when they are not, it is destroyed. Smith was writing a century before Darwin, but he is trying to express an evolutionary view: nature has endowed us with conscience and morality because it helps us to survive.

Morality and money

The rich, too, benefit the rest of us without meaning to. They give employment to all those people who make the luxuries and status symbols they demand; it is a great equalizer. The supposed benefits of wealth may be a delusion, but the pursuit of riches drives people to enormous exertions, which improve not just manufactures, but science, the arts and intellectual life along the way. [The rich] are led by an invisible hand to make nearly the same distribution of the necessaries of life, which would have been made, had the earth been divided into equal portions among its inhabitants.

Virtue and the good society

A truly virtuous person has prudence, justice and beneficence. Prudence helps moderate the individual's excesses and therefore benefits society. The rules of justice prevent us harming others. Beneficence promotes the happiness of others, so helps society too. Self-command over our violent passions can be virtuous too: but it can be double-sided, turning into the cold steel of the zealot.

Normally we are most concerned for ourselves, then our family, and only then for others. But since humanity is more important than the individual, self-sacrifice is sometimes needed. Nature does give some individuals the self-command to make such sacrifices, which we admire – insofar it is used for beneficial purposes rather than destructive ones.

Affection for our country implies respect for its institutions, and is not the same as sympathy for other people. In times of turmoil, the institutions of a country can collide against the happiness of its citizens. Politicians then start proposing to overthrow existing institutions and replace them with 'rational' alternatives. But we should remember that old institutions may deliver real benefits that are not obvious to reformers, and that all individuals have motivations of their own that may submit so easily to the politicians' great plans. Freedom and human nature are a surer guide to the creation of a harmonious, functioning society than the supposed reason of visionaries, or fanatics.

The man of system... seems to imagine that he can arrange the different members of a great society with as much ease as the hand arranges the different pieces upon a chess-board. He does not consider that in the great chess-board of human society, every single piece has a principle of motion of its own, altogether different from that which the legislature might choose to impress upon it.

Smith's ethical analysis here is much like his economic analysis. Morality and the market are both functional systems. They work on instinctive principles, and left to themselves, they work reasonably well to promote human welfare. If we had other, destructive instincts, we would not be here to discuss the matter. We should therefore be cautious of trying to re-shape these systems in ways that might appear sensible to us but could in fact destabilize the whole mechanism.